The New Middle Class in India and Brazil

Published by
ACADEMIC FOUNDATION
in association with

HEINRICH
BÖLL
STIFTUNG

The New Middle Class in India and Brazil

Green Perspectives?

Editors

Dawid Danilo Bartelt

Axel Harneit-Sievers

ACADEMIC FOUNDATION

NEW DELHI

www.academicfoundation.org

First published in 2017
by

ACADEMIC FOUNDATION
4772-73 / 23 Bharat Ram Road, (23 Ansari Road),
Darya Ganj, New Delhi - 110 002 (India).
Phones : 23245001 / 02 / 03 / 04.
Fax : +91-11-23245005.
E-mail : booksaf@gmail.com
www.academicfoundation.org

Cataloging in Publication Data--DK
Courtesy: D.K. Agencies (P) Ltd. <docinfo@dkagencies.com>

The new middle class in India and Brazil : green perspectives?
/editors, Dawid Danilo Bartelt, Axel Harneit-Sievers.
pages cm
"... workshop held in Delhi on 13-14 April 2015, co-organised by the Brazil and India offices of the HBF and the Development Alternatives"--Introduction.
ISBN 9789332704145

1. Middle class--India--Congresses. 2. Middle class--Brazil--Congresses. 3. Middle class--Political activity--India--Congresses. 4. Middle class--Political activity--Brazil--Congresses. I. Bartelt, Dawid Danilo, editor. II. Harneit-Sievers, Axel, 1957- editor. III. Heinrich Böll Foundation-India, organizer. IV. Heinrich Böll Foundation (Brazil), organizer. V. Development Alternatives (New Delhi, India), organizer.

LCC HT690.I4N49 2017 | DDC 305.550954 23

Typeset, printed and bound by The Book Mint, New Delhi.
www.thebookmint.in

CONTENTS

New Middle Class Politics

New Middle Class Consumption and Green Politics

About the Editors/Contributors

Editors:

Dawid Danilo Bartelt studied History and Social Sciences in Bochum, Hamburg, Berlin (Germany) and Recife (Brazil). As a historian, he specialised on Brazilian and Latin American history, completing his PhD in 2001. He worked as a journalist and as senior press officer for NGOs, including the German Section of Amnesty International since 2002 until 2010 when he joined the Heinrich Böll Foundation to head the Foundation's office in Rio de Janeiro, Brazil. Since 2017, he is the head of the Mexico and Caribe office of Heinrich Böll Foundation in Mexico City. His publications include numerous articles and radio programmes, and several books as author and editor.

Axel Harneit-Sievers, by professional background, is a historian specialiaing on Africa. He completed his PhD at Hannover University in Germany in 1990 and worked for many years at the Centre for Modern Oriental Studies in Berlin, and other research institutions and universities in Germany, with numerous publications on the history and politics of the continent. In 2002 he moved to Lagos, to take over the new Heinrich Böll Foundation's country office in Nigeria, and later to Nairobi, Kenya, as director of the Foundation's East & Horn of Africa office. Since 2011, he is heading the Heinrich Böll Foundation's India office in New Delhi.

Contributors:

Carla Barros is Professor at the Department of Media and Cultural Studies and Graduate Program in Communication of the Federal Fluminense University (UFF), Rio de Janeiro, Brazil. She is PhD in Business Administration and Post-Graduate in Antropology at Federal University of Rio de Janeiro (UFRJ), Brazil. Her main research interest is in anthropology of consumption, with a particular focus on working class groups.

Candido Grzybowski is a philosopher, sociologist. Director of IBASE (Brazilian Institute of Social and Economic Analyses) for 27 years and currently he is senior advisor in the same institution. He holds a PhD from the Paris University I Pantheon-Sorbonne (FR) and a Post-Doctoral at the University College London (UK). He was world-renowned for his active membership at the Organizing Committee of the World Social Forum between 2001 and 2010. Earlier he was Sociology of Development lecturer at FGV-RJ (Getúlio Vargas Foundation).

Surinder S. Jodhka is Professor of Sociology at the Jawaharlal Nehru University, New Delhi (India). His research interests include the dynamics of rural society and agrarian change; social inequalities and their reproduction; caste and the varied modes of its articulation in contemporary India; and the political sociology community identities. His research publications include *The Indian Middle* (with Aseem Prakash, OUP 2016); *Caste in Contemporary India* (Routledge 2015) and *Caste* (OUP 2012). He is recipient of the ICSSR-Amartya Sen Award for Distinguished Social Scientists, for the year 2012.

Devesh Kapur is Madan Lal Sobti Professor for the Study of Contemporary India and Director, Center for Advanced Study of India at the University of Pennsylvania. He has a BTech and MS in chemical engineering and a PhD in Public Policy from Princeton University. His books include: *The World Bank: Its First Half Century*; *Rethinking Public Institutions in India*; *Diaspora, Democracy and Development*; *The Other One Percent: Indians in America*; and *Navigating the Labyrinth: Perspectives on India's Higher Education*.

Govind Kelkar has PhD in Political Economy of China and is the Senior Adviser, Landesa/Rural Development Institute, New Delhi, India; and Regional Council Member of Asia-Pacific Forum on Women, Law and Development, Chiang Mai, Thailand. She has extensively worked on gender and energy transition in rural Asia. She has contributed numerous articles to scholarly journals and published 14 books with a focus on gender relations in Asia and has been in close touch with women's movements in the region.

Celia de Andrade Lessa Kerstenetzky is PhD (with honors) in Political and Social Sciences by the European University Institute (1998), PhD in Political Science by the Instituto Universitário de Pesquisas do Rio de Janeiro, IUPERJ (1997), Master in Economics by UFRJ (1989), bachelor degree in Economics by Universidade Federal Fluminense (UFF, 1980). She was a visiting researcher at Columbia University, MIT, University of Illinois and at Pompeu Fabra University in Barcelona, and visiting teacher at the University of Siena in Italy and INAG in Cape Verde. She is currently teacher at the Institute of Economics at UFRJ and is coordinator of the Center for Studies on Inequality and Development (CEDE). Her current research interests include the analysis of socioeconomic inequalities, development processes and purposes, and contemporary welfare states.

Ashish Kothari, Founder-member of Indian environmental group Kalpavriksh, has taught at the Indian Institute of Public Administration, coordinated India's National Biodiversity Strategy and Action Plan process, served on Greenpeace International and India Boards, helped initiate the global ICCA Consortium, and chaired an IUCN network dealing with protected areas and communities. He has (co)authored or (co)edited over 30 books (including *Birds in Our Lives* and *Churning the Earth*). Currently, he helps coordinate the Vikalp Sangam process in search of alternative well-being pathways to globalised development, and a global project Academic-Activist Co-produced Knowledge for Environmental Justice (ACKnowl-EJ).

Ashok K. Lahiri, currently the Chairman of Bandhan Bank, retired as Executive Director, Asian Development Bank (ADB), Manila in 2013. Before ADB, he served as Chief Economic Adviser, Government of India; Director, National Institute of Public Finance and Policy; Senior Economist, International Monetary Fund; and Reader, Delhi School of Economics. A graduate in economics from Presidency College, Kolkata, he did his MA and PhD from the Delhi School of Economics. Dr Lahiri has served as a member or chairman of various Committees appointed by the Government of India, including as a member on Fiscal Responsibility Legislation (2000). He has served on boards of various organisations, including Securities and Exchange Board of India (SEBI). He was the Dean of the ADB Board during 2012-13. Election analysis is his hobby, and he has published several books and articles on electoral behaviour in India.

Marilene de Paula is the program coordinator for the Heinrich Böll Foundation in Brazil in the area of Human Rights. She has a degree in

History from Rio de Janeiro State University and a master's degree in Culture and Social Projects from the Getúlio Vargas Foundation (FGV). Together with civil society institutions, she has organised campaigns against and debates about police brutality and in defence of human rights.

Nita Mathur is Professor of Sociology at the Indira Gandhi National Open University, New Delhi. She has been visiting scholar at Fondation Maison des Sciences de l'Homme, Paris, and Visiting Faculty at the School of Planning and Architecture, New Delhi and School of Environmental Studies, University of Delhi. Her research interests range from lifestyle choices to modernity and fashion. Her books, *Consumer Culture, Modernity and Identity* (ed.), *Cultural Rhythms in Emotions, Narratives and Dance, and Santhal Worldview* (ed.), deal with the central issue of social construction of identity. Some of her critical publications in national and international journals are in the area of consumer culture, shopping enclaves, brand choices, and the middle class.

Nelson do Valle Silva, Retired Researcher at Laboratório Nacional de Computação Científica, Ministério de Ciência e Tecnologia, former teacher at Instituto Universitário de Pesquisa do Rio de Janeiro (IUPERJ), is currently Senior Visiting Researcher at the Institute of Social and Political Studies at Universidade do Estado do Rio de Janeiro. He works in the field of Population and Social Stratification Studies.

Neelanjan Sircar is a senior fellow at Centre for Policy Research, New Delhi. His recent work has focused on understanding electoral behavior in India through both data work and ethnographic methods. He is also a Non-Resident Fellow at the Center for the Advanced Study of India at the University of Pennsylvania. He received a bachelor's degree in applied mathematics and economics from UC Berkeley in 2003 and a PhD in political science from Columbia University in 2014.

Richa Singh is a political scientist and bridges the world of academics and activism. She has served Centre for Democracy and Social Action as its Executive Director, and *Wada Na Todo Abhiyan* (Don't Break Your Promises Campaign) as Co-convener. Her research interest include: gender conflict and peace building, and state-society interactions in South Asia and West Asia. She has worked with women's groups, national and international organisations that include Hienrich Boell

Foundation, Amnesty International, Aman Trust, Global Call to Action Against Poverty. She has been a Shastri Fellow at the Department of Political Science, McGill University; DAAD Fellows in Gender Studies at the University of Hanover. Her PhD is on Gender and the Israeli-Palestinian conflict.

Paranjoy Guha Thakurta is (or has been) a visiting faculty member at reputed educational institutions including the Indian Institutes of Management at Ahmedabad, Kolkata and Shillong, University of Delhi, Jawaharlal Nehru University, Jamia Millia Islamia, Lal Bahadur Shastri National Academy of Administration and Visva Bharati University, among other educational institutions. He served as the Editor of the *Economic and Political Weekly* from 4 April 2016 to 18 July 2017. His work experience, spanning over 40 years, cuts across different media: print, radio, television and documentary cinema. He is a writer, speaker, anchor, interviewer, teacher and commentator in three languages: English, Bangla and Hindi. His main areas of interest are the working of the political economy and the media in India and the world, on which he has authored/co-authored books and directed/produced documentary films.

Christiane Uchôa is PhD in Economics by Universidade Federal Fluminense. Presently she is doing post-doctorate research in the Energy Planning Program at COPPE/UFRJ, and is part of the technical team of the Energy Balance and Energy Matrix of the State of Rio de Janeiro. She also collaborates with the ECOPA project, carried out through a partnership between Brazil (COPPE/UFRJ) and France (ANR). Her areas of interest include: middle class, lifestyle, sustainable development and growth, electric power, poverty, consumption patterns and energy.

Milan Vaishnav is a senior fellow in the South Asia Program at the Carnegie Endowment for International Peace. His primary research focus is the political economy of India. He is the author of *When Crime Pays: Money and Muscle in Indian Politics* (Yale University Press and HarperCollins India, 2017) and co-editor (with Pratap Bhanu Mehta and Devesh Kapur) of *Rethinking Public Institutions in India* (Oxford University Press, 2017). He holds a PhD in political science from Columbia University.

Acknowledgements

This volume emerged from discussions within the international structures of the Heinrich Böll Foundation (HBF), the Green Political Foundation from Germany. We wish to thank especially our colleagues Layla al-Zubaidi, Christina Sadeler and Heike Löschmann for their interest in driving forward intellectual exchange and project cooperation within the BRICS group of countries.

The idea for starting a comparative discussion on the 'greenness' of the new middle class in the emerging economies of the BRICS countries took off from a publication by HBF's office in Brazil. Noticing major variations in what has often been simplistically seen as the 'rise of the new global middle class', and realising manifest differences in the respective national discourses, the editors decided to convene a debate with contributions from both India and Brazil. The conference titled "Green Perspectives of the New Middle Class: A New Reality and an Opportunity for Social and Environmental Just Development in India and Brazil?" took place in New Delhi during 13-14 April 2015. In order to make this happen, a major tribute goes to the respective programme coordinators at the HBF India and Rio de Janeiro offices, Shalini Yog Shah and Marilene de Paula.

We wish to express our gratitude to Development Alternatives (DA) who did not only host our conference in their remarkable conference facility located at their headquarters in Qutub Institutional Area in Delhi. DA leaders and staff also provided inputs and support in so many different ways. Our special thanks in this regard go to Ashok Khosla, Zeenat Niazi, Kavneet Kaur, Prerna Vinod, Rambha Tripathy and Abhishek Dubey.

We also wish to thank, for their contributions to the conference, a number of people who participated but have, for one reason or another, been unable to contribute to this volume, especially Sonia Fleury, Niranjan Khatri, Ashraf Patel, Dev Nathan and Aarti Mohan. Finally, our thanks go to Sanu Kapila and the staff of Academic Foundation in Delhi for making this volume a reality.

DAWID DANILO BARTELT and
AXEL HARNEIT-SIEVERS

Introduction

Since the turn of the millennium, the rise of the 'new global middle class' has been one of the most remarkable aspects of the rapid growth of the emerging economies. The trend continues, despite the financial crisis of 2008 and various tendencies of economic downturns since then. Some emerging economies have growth issues—most remarkably notably since 2015—but growth optimism remains strong in many places, and certainly so in India.

Debates about the rise of the NMC (new middle class) and its character have been going on since years—in the public, the business community, in the academic world, among government strategists, and in civil society. Much has been written about this, predominantly from the perspective of economics, i.e., looking at middle class growth as a case of growing markets and rising numbers of consumers (and the ramifications of the latter trend has interested a good number of anthropologists). Their political impact—do middle classes really promote democracy?—has also been noted frequently.

Among the 33 offices that the Heinrich Böll Foundation (HBF) is operating around the world, several are located in emerging economies. The question of NMCs has been intriguing office staff and partners for a while. After all, the impact of the rise of the NMCs on politics, society and ecology, its opportunities and risks, are particularly challenging from a 'green perspective' as we understand it, i.e. a political agenda that is promoting ecological sustainability, democratic participation, and social and gender justice.

Background to this Volume

A debate among Brazilian academics and political activists—a debate about the very validity of the concept of the 'NMC' and the politics around it—formed the starting point of the process that led to this volume. In India, the perception of the NMC appeared to be very different from the Brazilian situation. We wanted to find out more about how the idea of a seemingly homogenous 'global' NMC in the emerging economies played out in two rather different socio-political contexts—and to identify what this means for green politics.

During the government of the Workers' Party under President Luiz Inácio Lula da Silva (2003-2010), official Brazil 'discovered' the NMC and argued that, with systematic support by government policies, the majority of the population in Brazil had overcome poverty to become a 'NMC'. Supported by a government-backed academic apparatus, this assumption established as a strong discourse. Not everybody agreed, especially so not on the Brazilian left, and on this background, the HBF's Brazil office decided to take a more critical look. There was an obvious discrepancy between, on the one hand, the way how Brazil is perceived by the international community—as a socially-oriented, economically successful state sensitive to environmental and climate issues—and, on the other hand, the view that many groups and individuals within the Brazilian civil society hold of the state and the politics associated with it. The Brazilian office of HBF brought together a group of analysts from academics and civil society who looked at this social stratum called NMC both 'as a concept and as a political project', as the title says. The book argued that using the concept of middle class here was misleading, since most of the assumptions and features related to the traditional Brazilian middle class did not apply here. Nevertheless, there was a political purpose related to the poverty reduction programme and the modernisation of society to use the term for what would rather be a better-off part of the working class that still has low formal education level, little assets and savings, relies on credit, is rather fragile, and half of it or so still working in the informal economy.[1]

On the surface, the situation and the discourse around the NMC in India look quite different. There, the middle class has grown strongly, but clearly continues to constitute a minority of the population; in fact, many Indians aspire to being middle class, rather than being it in the material sense. The co-editors of this volume found these differences intriguing and engaged in discussions comparing the experiences of both the countries. In the end, this conversation led to a workshop held in Delhi on 13-14 April 2015, co-organised by the Brazil and India offices of the HBF and the Development Alternatives, a leading Indian research and action organisation dedicated to sustainable development, with more than 20 participants from both countries. This volume documents some of the presentations and discussions of this workshop following the objective to contribute to the debate on a complex issue which is still narrowed down, in many contributions, to an economic perspective of income.

While definitions used to describe and define the 'NMC' vary considerably, most of them focus on household income. Depending on the range, estimates about its size differ accordingly. But with several hundred million people in emerging economies having moved beyond an income threshold of 10 PPP (purchasing power parity)-USD per capita per day, and many hundreds of millions more expected to reach there after having grown out of absolute poverty levels, expectations about the future development of the global NMC continue to be high, and debates remains intense. Many observers question whether it makes sense to characterise the middle class as those groups who have more or less just managed to step out of absolute poverty. Academics and social activists look

1. See Bartelt (2013). Chief economist Marcelo Neri from the biggest and prestigious thinktank Getúlio Vargas Foundation was crucial for popularising the concept of the 'NMC' in Brazil. He carried out studies since 2008 and published a widely-discussed book, see Neri (2011). In the same year, he was appointed director of the government-run Institute for Applied Economic Studies, and the year later, Minister for Strategic Affairs in the Federal Government. In both institutions, he continued to focus on poverty reduction and the NMC.

into the concepts and methodology as well as the projects set up by governments with regard to these emerging new social strata. One also has to ask about the social and economic sustainability or resilience of this social rise: Are the educational, social and economic structures really in place that might prevent these classes to fall back into poverty in times of economic crisis?

Business, on the other hand, hopes for the rise of the NMC and focuses on its huge consumer potential, which is expected to further and rapidly expand commercial opportunities worldwide. Liberal political commentary hopes for the middle classes' increasing demand for governmental accountability and transparency. For politicians, these new classes—and only for the numbers—are key to their electoral aspirations.

From a 'green', i.e., socio-environmental and human rights perspective, however, the rise of the NMC appears in an ambivalent way. There are positive and negative elements in the global narratives about the rise of the NMCs in emerging economies. It is the purpose of this volume to have a closer look at these narratives, focusing especially on India and Brazil. In a nutshell, however, the fundamental lines of argument could perhaps be sketched as follows, in an optimistic perspective.

- The rise of the NMC can be seen as proof that socioeconomic development is actually possible—after all, the hope for such fast development had nearly vanished by the late 1990s, and the boom of the 2000s came rather unexpectedly.
- The rise of the NMC may be seen to constitute human progress in broad sense, bringing about material well-being and a great increase in individual freedom alongside advances in health, education, science, and even the arts.
- The NMC is expected to increasingly make its voice heard in politics for democracy (where is does not yet exist), for transparency and against corruption, and for an increased quality of life that includes core green values and objectives such as a clean environment, healthy food, and even 'post-materialist' orientations.

However, a green perspective on the NMC may also include decidedly more sceptical views:

- While some segments of the NMC have indeed acquired some degree of wealth and independence, major parts of those groups that governments call 'middle class' today, in fact constitute a—'new' working class; for the lower strata of them, it is too early to not consider them 'poor', especially since they lack crisis resilience.
- The NMC is widely regarded as 'consumerist' in orientation, interested primarily in its own material well-being, prone to incorporate manipulation by advertising media.
- While providing high GDP (gross domestic product) growth, the NMC' consumption patterns further rapidly increase the already severe global human footprint, worsening environmental devastation and climate change.
- The NMC is also often criticised for either being apolitical, individualistic and conservative, not interested in joint political organisation structures, and without concern for, or even acting against what in India may be called the 'pro-poor, pro-community' political agenda.
- Not only in Brazil, the state is openly calling upon the NMC to purchase basic social services like quality education and adequate healthcare in the private market (private schools, private health insurances), while continuously failing to provide these services as basic obligations to guarantee the rights of its citizens.

Comparing India and Brazil

Emerging economies are a diverse lot, and among them, the BRICS (Brazil, Russia, India, China and South Africa) countries are perhaps most extremely diverse. Within the group, however, while there are still many obvious differences between India and Brazil (for a comparison of fundamental indicators see Table 1.0), both countries make for a number of interesting similarities and parallels as well, making them accessible to some comparative analysis.

Table 1.0

General Comparative Indicators: India and Brazil

Indicator	*India*	*Brazil*	*Source*
Land area (sq km)	2,973,190	8,358,140	*http://data.worldbank.org/indicator/AG.LND.TOTL.K2?end=2015&start=2012*
Population (2015)	1,311,050,530	207,847,530	*http://data.worldbank.org/indicator/SP.POP.TOTL?end=2015&start=2012*
Population density (person per sq km land area, 2015)	441	25	*http://data.worldbank.org/indicator/EN.POP.DNST?end=2015&start=2012*
GDP (million USD at market prices, 2015)	2,073,543	1,774,725	*http://data.worldbank.org/indicator/NY.GDP.MKTP.CD?end=2015&start=2012*
GDP PPP (million current international USD, 2015)	7,982,528	3,192,398	*http://data.worldbank.org/indicator/NY.GDP.MKTP.PP.CD?end=2015&start=2012*
GDP per capita (million current USD, 2015)	1,582	8,539	*http://data.worldbank.org/indicator/NY.GDP.PCAP.CD?end=2015&start=2012*
GDP per capita PPP (million current international USD, 2015)	6.089	15,359	*http://data.worldbank.org/indicator/NY.GDP.PCAP.PP.CD?end=2015&start=2012*
Income Gini Coefficient (2013)	33.9	54.7	*http://hdr.undp.org/en/content/income-gini-coefficient*
Human Development Index (2014)	0.609	0.755	*http://hdr.undp.org/en/data*
Life expectancy at birth (2012)	67	74	*http://data.worldbank.org/indicator/SP.DYN.LE00.IN?end=2015&start=2012*
Infant mortality rate (per 1,000 live births, 2015)	38	15	*http://data.worldbank.org/indicator/SP.DYN.IMRT.IN*
Total fertility rate (births per woman, 2014)	2.4	1.8	*http://data.worldbank.org/indicator/SP.DYN.TFRT.IN*
Adult literacy (% of population, 2008-2012)	62.8	90.4	*https://www.unicef.org/infobycountry/india_statistics.html, and.../brazil_statistics.html*

Urban Population (% of total, 2015)	33	86	*http://data.worldbank.org/indicator/SP.URB.TOTL.IN.ZS*
Tax-to-GDP ratio (%) (Economic Survey, Government of India)	16.6	35.6	*http://www.thehindu.com/business/Economy/only-55-who-earn-are-tax-payers-economic-survey/article8286548.ece*
Tax revenue (% of GDP, 2014) (World Bank)	10.8	14.1	*http://data.worldbank.org/indicator/GC.TAX.TOTL.GD.ZS*

Note: All accessed on 30 December 2016.

First of all, politically, both India and Brazil are functioning democracies, providing substantial space for political participation by its citizens. This is especially true—in principle at least—for the middle class. Of course, the political history of both countries is rather different, but democratic elections and competitive party politics are well-established enough to allow for a study of NMCs within a democratic setting (including the question as to whether the middle class may have tendencies to allow for a strong and perhaps authoritarian state, if 'development' is at stake).

Secondly, economically, different from China and Russia, both countries have never been socialist, but they carry a long tradition of 'statism', i.e., state control over the economy or state-led economic development strategies. Elements of this tradition continue to be important in the economics and politics in both countries until today. In Brazil, the decision of the government against initial corporate protest to substantially raise the minimum wage, connected to the commodity prices boom in the first decade of the millennium, was primary responsible for the fact that millions of Brazilians crossed the poverty line in order to join the 'NMC', as the government claimed. In India, the tradition of statism is strong as well, but in the end it was liberalisation and the opening of the internal market ending the protectionist, import-substituting regime which led to rapid growth and the emergence of a broader NMC.

Thirdly, ecologically, both countries comprise vast geographic areas and are highly diverse with regard to geo-climatic zones and biodiversity. While population densities and the resulting pressure on land and forest resources differ considerably, recent large-scale economic development encroaches upon high biodiversity zones in both countries (the Amazonian rainforest in Brazil; the mineral-rich forest areas in the tribal areas of eastern peninsular India), resulting in ecological threats and intense, sometimes violent social struggles.

Concept of the Middle Class: Homogenous or Diverse?

Many references to the 'NMC' in the emerging economies use the term as a generic concept with—fundamentally—global applicability. From an analytical perspective that prioritises income, purchasing power, and 'global lifestyle', the middle classes exhibit the same or very similar characteristics throughout the world. In this perspective, the category is homogenous, economically forward, politically opinionated and consumerist; thus, the middle class is those people who are the front runners of economic growth in their own countries and the world, and they are fundamentally alike everywhere.

However, any closer look reveals otherwise. Sociologists and especially anthropologists have often stressed the differences and the relevance of local conditions; and the differences played out strongly in the discussions of this dialogue. The historical development of middle classes in both countries has been somewhat different: While in Brazil, much of the 'old' middle class is linked to public service, but also includes liberal professionals, military and white collar employees in the corporate sector since industrialisation began in the 1930s, middle class development in India historically is strongly linked to the bureaucratic class created by the colonial and post-colonial state, and to the politics of reservation for disadvantaged groups operated in the country since independence. But the balance between state support and what may be called middle class belief in its capacity to help itself (rather than to rely on the government) has changed. Much of the NMC in India is a child of the policies of economic liberalisation since the 1990s; it tends to feel that it and its progress owes most to its own efforts, and little to government policies—beyond the state's role in creating the liberal framework within which the middle may prosper, of course. In India, social policy over the last two decades has remained primarily about uplifting the poor, and supporting those who turn out to be unable to socially rise in a society that is increasingly well-off, but also increasingly unequal.

In Brazil, however, the role of government social policy, especially under the Workers' Party (Partido dos Trabalhadores, PT) since 2003, has been much more direct in creating the conditions and systems to reduce poverty and social inequality, the latter being traditionally extremely high in Brazil. In the PT's own official rhetoric, the creation of the middle class has been a major political project, and the government pursued it with what may be called a social democratic agenda. President Dilma Rousseff explicitly referred to the demands of the NMC by stating that the main objective of the Brazilian nation is to 'transform Brazil into a huge middle class society'. The mass protests of new and old middle classes that took place in Brazil in 2013 during the Confederation Cup paradoxically proved the success of establishing this agenda, as people related the costs of what would be the most expensive 'Soccer World Cup' ever to the continuing inability of the government to improve basic public services of acceptable quality in education, health, and transport. As Rousseff herself put it, for people who have climbed the social ladder, it would be natural to be more demanding regarding the quality of public services. Even while not naming them explicitly, the protests were about civic and social rights, bringing about, as Cândido Grzybowski inputs it in his essay (in this volume), an 'explosion of citizenship'.

Dynamics of Middle Class Development

As the growth of the middle class in India and Brazil has followed somewhat different trajectories, certain differences resulted in its character and outlook.

The NMC in Brazil is indeed in the middle of the social pyramid/ structure ('class C' in the income stratification scheme that divides Brazilians into five classes, A to E)—and it has consequently been criticised of being basically only the working class in a new disguise. At least, as Celia Kerstenetzky, Christiane Uchôa and Nelson do Valle Silva put it in their contribution to this volume, "it is not enough to have escaped poverty in order to enter the threshold of the 'Middle Class'". In fact, the majority of scholars working on the subject in

Brazil today do not accept the term. 'Class C' has few assets, and spends considerable parts of its income to purchase, from private providers, educational and health services that were once provided by the state. A good part of its income derives from loans and intensive use of credit cards for consumptive purposes, implying risks especially in times of economic crisis. The economic and political crises in Brazil since 2015 have seriously endangered this social democratic project. Given that members of class C have low levels of formal education, lack savings but rather live on credit, and do not have the social relationships among the 'real' middle class which would help them to find job alternatives, the crisis resilience of the Brazilian NMC is low, if not non-existing. Eight million members of this class had to stop travelling by plane, which had been perhaps the most marked symbol of consumerist achievements for this class. Worse, many of them lost their formal job and fell back into the informal economy, where even in better days roughly half of Brazil's NMC still worked. Today, the overarching feeling in this social stratum is that of insecurity, of disappointment, and loss of trust in the system.

By contrast, the new and still growing middle class in India appears far more self-confident, even though its income levels are lower than those of their Brazilian counterparts. But the general attitude for India's middle class continues to be one of optimism about the future. As Devesh Kapur, Neelanjan Sircar and Milan Vaishnav show in this volume, middle class aspirations appear to fuel the imagination of people even in social groups who, if measured merely by their income levels, would hardly qualify as members of a middle class. In India, the idea of the middle class appears to be far more widespread than its reality.

Of course, this general optimism among the Indian middle class, be it really justified or merely aspirationally hopeful, continues to be driven by the continuous overall rapid growth of the Indian economy. By 2015-16, government and media in India did not tire to call the country 'the world's fastest growing major economy', and middle class self-perceptions very much bank on this perception.

Social Position of the Middle Class

The NMC in Brazil—however problematic and fragile this concept may be—grew considerably since the turn of the millennium. By 2014, according to government figures, it had become the majority of population in Brazilian society, even though it has shrunk to some extent during the current crisis.

The situation is decidedly different in India where the middle class—despite rapid growth and its considerable size in absolute numbers—remains a minority (and a rather small minority, by most accounts) in India's vast, and still rather poor population. This means that (social) policies in the Indian context are still to a great extent driven by poverty alleviation strategies, i.e., they are directed at the poor. A broad middle class project would have a long way to go, and Indians do not necessarily expect much direct political or social support for it by the government. Many members of the Indian middle class take it for granted that quality educational and health services need to be paid for privately; they may rather resent what they perceive as the use of their money to fund social services for the poor, and they certainly resent corruption by government officials (even though of course many of them themselves are ready to pay bribes to get licences and applications moving). At the same time, there is distance between the middle class and the state: In India, only a small minority of the population—5.5 per cent of income earners, mostly in the formal sector—actually pays income tax.[2] This forms quite a contrast to Brazil, where the tax-to-GDP is more than twice as high as in India (see Table 1.0). The relationship between the NMC and the state remains a complex one.

Social divisions in both countries evolve not only around class, and consequently, the middle classes does not necessarily represent any societal average in terms of race or identity group. In Brazil, social valuation and discrimination operate along lines of skin colour,

2. "Only 5.5 per cent of those who earn are tax payer: Economic Survey", *The Hindu*, 27 February 2016, *http://www.thehindu.com/business/Economy/only-55-who-earn-are-tax-payers-economic-survey/article8286548.ece*. The survey, undertaken by the Indian government, "estimated that just four per cent [of] India's voters are taxpayers, though it should be closer to 23 per cent, and 85 per cent of the net national income fall outside the tax net".

and, as Carla Barros shows in this volume, the culture industry promotes a predominantly white middle class imagery. In India, the same applies, as can be easily seen in Bollywood and advertisements; but there is even more to it. As Surinder Jodhka argues in his essay, caste continues to be a strong determinant of social status, including middle class position. While reservation policies have achieved to create a (numerically rather small) Dalit middle class, and a good number of lower caste rural populations have become successful farmers, India's dynamic modern private sector—the epitome of middle class existence—continues to be dominated strongly by traditionally upper caste groups. While urbanisation helps, to an extent, to break down caste, numerous other factors in India's modernity continue to uphold these barriers.

On a different front, the NMC appears to allow for an increasing degree of gender equality resulting from greater work opportunities for women. This is certainly true for India where a patriarchal ideal of the 'homemaker' housewife dominated the older middle class since the colonial period. The rise of the IT (information technology) sector—the epitome of India's post-liberalisation growth story—has opened many new opportunities for women. As Govind Kelkar shows in this volume, according to a study undertaken in 2011-12, more than half of the employees in the sector were women for whom employment has led to increased individual capacity and agency and, to an extent, mobility. There is a decided shift from human resources careers seen as 'soft' into technology fields. This finding, of course, does indicate a gradual increase of gender equality, at best: employment in the IT sector remains relatively small (compared to the overall economic relevance of the sector), and middle class women working here continue to experience similar forms of wage discrimination and double-burden due to domestic duties as their counterparts, in many other parts of the world. The double-burden has been a traditional problem for working class women, and continues to be in the 'NMC'.

Feminists in Brazil have criticised the government to underrate the multidimensionality of poverty by focusing its policies on income only. Female heads of households constitute a common feature in the working and NMC whose lower strata is unable able to afford domestic employees. Having employees that take care of household duties and child care has been a classic tool for the 'emancipation' of traditional middle class women in Brazil, providing them with time to spend on higher education and on pursuing a professional career. Gender-related studies on the Brazilian NMC are still a desideratum.

Gender could also be but not necessarily is an important element of distinction when it comes to the religious bias of the new strata. Brazil has undergone major changes in the last decades, as Marilene de Paula shows in her essay. What used to be the largest catholic country has a rapidly rising share of evangelical, mostly neopentecostal denominations, while Catholicism is facing a sharp decline. It is estimated that by 2050, catholics will not be the majority anymore. Among those who manage to step out of poverty, the share of evangelical believers is overwhelming. The 'prosperity theology', proclaiming and strengthening the individual struggle for a Better Life and material improvements as a divine reward, seems to be tailored-fit for this class. The share among the traditional middle classes is much smaller.

Middle Class Political Attitudes

Different from other major BRICS countries, both India and Brazil are democracies. Despite differences in the way democracy operates in the two countries, a democratic system provides a particular political space to an emerging middle class which is clearly different from, say, China.

Major political parties in both countries strive towards developing an expanded NMC and catering its demands and expectation, whether it is President Dilma Rousseff's PT Workers' Party government in Brazil or the Bharatiya Janata Party (BJP)—and earlier the Congress Party—in India. However, they have done so in rather different ways.

In Brazil, as we have seen and the authors in this volume argue as well, the NMC has been a 'political project' of the governing PT. It has focused on bringing about new consumers rather than citizens with enhanced social and economic rights, but since it has had a strong focus on reducing poverty and inequality, it has consequently brought about an enhanced materialisation of rights. In 2016, the PT government was overruled by a questionable impeachment process organised by the conservative majority in both houses of the Brazilian parliament. But political parties of all colours are increasingly addressing the large social group in the middle. Regardless of whether it is an homogenous group or not, whoever gains its support wins elections. The new mayor of Rio de Janeiro, a former bishop of the neopentecostal Universal Church of the Reign of Christ, won the elections quite easily because the poor and ex-poor voted for him overwhelmingly.

It is too early to say what the political aspirations of this group are. By their very nature as 'strugglers', they tend to be individualistic and socially conservative, which is underpinned by the over representation of (conservative) evangelical believers. Many of the former poor, especially in the poorer parts of the country like the Northeast (the same region that former President Lula da Silva left as a small child with his family fleeing poverty), voted in the PT but abandoned it when economic crisis and corruption scandals shattered the PT government (see for this Cândido Grzybowski's essay). The PT's social and political origins are to be found with organised labour, in the unions of the industries of São Paulo; with progressive intellectuals; and with more leftist sectors of the traditional middle class, while the poor historically have voted in clientelistic parties. The former poor in the 'NMC' tend to vote for more conservative candidates; even though they are deprived of social justice, they would rather not go for parties or organisations that strongly advocate it.

Middle class politics in India has a decidedly different flavour. It oscillated in recent years between political disinterest, new forms of issue-based popular mobilisation, and affirmation of what is seen as a 'development-oriented' political leadership (i.e. Prime Minister Narendra Modi and his BJP). Since the 1980s, as Paranjoy Guha Thakurta argues in this volume, parts of the Indian middle class showed an affiliation to Hindu nationalist ('Hindutva') politics which combined the ideology of Indian greatness (past and future) with an enmity towards affirmative action favouring religious, ethnic and caste minorities. However, concrete political affiliations remained fluid; much of the middle class voted for the Congress Party as long as it promised to continue growth-oriented economic policies. Different from other democracies, poor Indians tend to strongly participate in electoral politics, as certain forms of redistribution provided by government (especially the food distribution system) continue to be of high relevance to the survival of the poor. All this tended to limit the relevance of the middle class vote in the overall outcome.

By 2011, new forms of political mobilisation and protest emerged in India, especially in Delhi and other big cities. They were issue-based, arising from outrage over widespread corruption and crony capitalist practices and over a prominent case of rape and murder of a young middle class woman in Delhi. Richa Singh shows in this volume how these new forms of campaigning and mobilisation—carried forward by middle class and urban youth—operated and, at least for some time, became powerful enough to challenge the usual ways of doing politics in India. But non-traditional, non-parliamentary protest politics of this type had only a limited lifespan. It led to the rise of the Aam Aadmi Party (AAP) that continues to fuel the imagination of the lower middle classes in the capital, but in the 2014 national elections, the BJP recorded a massive victory (with an absolute majority of seats in the Lower House); and one major reason for this happening was, as Tharkurta explains, the turn of the middle class towards the 'developmental' agenda (spiced with Hindutva ideology) of the BJP under Modi. However, it remains to be seen whether this winning combination—and the important role that the middle class played in it—was more than a singular event and could shape Indian politics in the years to come.

Middle Class Culture and Consumption

Brazil has its telenovelas, India has Bollywood. Both are extremely popular products of the culture industry of their respective countries, and they both present and reflect changes in social structures and values, sometimes early in the process, anticipating new trends, views and values, sometimes just documenting change that is already happening on a large scale. Telenovelas and Bollywood alike strongly present (old) middle class ideals of life and style. Carla Barros, in her essay in this volume, shows how, in some prominent telenovelas, formerly rigid boundaries between the traditional settled middle class on the one hand, and workers, domestic staff and others who are rising into the NMC on the other, have become more permeable. Or perhaps one should say they have become breakable, as the heroes of these stories are depicted sometimes as 'warriors', aspiring and succeeding to rise based on merit, and challenging established privilege, if necessary. The NMCs or new working classes are certainly of darker skin colour than the old, traditionally white middle classes. Race and colour, and subsequent racism, is one of the most defining and at the same time most down played, even hidden, factors of Brazilian society until today. Being a class of mixed colour, among them many people considered black, this part of the society that forms the majority, yet remained invisible for long, has gained visibility in commercials and in the telenovelas. In the two-fold sense, they have not only become a target audience but have also acquired a status as protagonists, as subjects of their own action and pursuance of happiness.

One of the defining features of middle class existence is a certain level of income and consumption. Perhaps the most visible aspect of middle class growth throughout the emerging economies over the last two decades has been the rise of brands, advertising and brand consciousness, and the emergence of shopping mall complexes, the new palaces of conspicuous consumption not only in the major cities, but virtually everywhere. For economists and business consultants, the rise of the middle class, its growing incomes and expanding consumption constitute just different aspects of the same process.

From a green political perspective, rising consumption is perhaps the most single problematic aspect of the growth of NMC, as it goes along with rapidly increasing use of natural resources and similarly rapidly increasing production of waste, driving climate change and environmental destruction. Liberals and social democrats traditionally saw increased consumption of large population groups in the middle of the society as a case of applied social justice, and certainly as a great social leveller. Considerable parts of the left today, however, do not share any more that optimism and look for sustainability beyond the profit logic of capitalism. Another concern is that—at least in Brazil—a good part of the consumption of the NMC is financed by consumer credit (made easy through the widespread use of credit cards), thus posing questions not merely to the ecological, but even the economic sustainability of their position and practice, especially in situations of economic fragility.

But is (new) middle class really about mindless consumption, as claimed by its critics from the green-left political spectrum? Ashish Kothari, in this volume, clearly sees 'consumerism' at work and thus contemplates the concept of a 'sustainable consumption line' that may have to be applied or imposed; more on this below. However, Nita Mathur, in her essay in this volume, draws a somewhat different picture for India, especially for India's urban youth. Surely, young India consumes, and the Indian middle class creates its own world of consumption and lifestyle. But based on a qualitative study, Mathur shows many ambiguities of a middle class youth turning towards 'modern', brand-oriented consumption, but also being careful and insecure in the process. Mathur shows how more traditional ideals about frugality and lean lifestyle still have an impact on middle class thinking and behaviour. Such ideals are rooted to some extent in Hindu religion; they also derive from a strand of Gandhian thinking that was (and still is) officially promoted (though of course not necessarily implemented) by the Indian state since after independence, and that has surely influenced middle class lifestyles in the pre-liberalisation period. Thus, it appears that India, and especially India's youth, is in a transitory position; while India is surely moving towards a consumer culture, this is far from a straightforward process. This could provide openings for mental and behavioural changes necessary to move towards a more sustainable economy and society. Interestingly, Carla Barros also observes a 'timid increase of environmental awareness' among the youth of the emerging consumer segments of society, even though their predominant feeling might be 'now it is our time to consume', especially as consumption, for poorer Brazilians, serves as a mode of social inclusion. To a certain extent, ecological issues have become a discourse that cannot longer be ignored, and young people grow into it in the same way as they grow up learning to be a brand-aware consumer.

How Green is the New Middle Class?

Then, how much 'green' political potential is there in the NMC of India and Brazil? This question can be asked against the background of the experience of green politics in Western Europe, such as Germany and France, the Netherlands and the Scandinavian countries. There, green socio-political movements and, in some cases, successful green political parties have emerged since the 1970s-1980s. While their appeal had always been strongest among relatively young, well-educated parts of the population, at the beginning they very much defined themselves as an alternative to the established party political system. This changed over time, as green political issues gained wider acceptance in society. They even became mainstream, being picked up by established political parties, while green political parties successfully established themselves in the middle of the political system. Today, in Germany, among the electorate of all major political parties represented in parliaments, the electorate of the Green Party has among the highest levels of education and income. The green electorate constitutes perhaps the epitome of a middle class that is well-established in socioeconomic terms, but is at times concerned and self-critical about the future of a socioeconomic system that threatens to destroy the very natural foundations of its own existence. The gap between having arrived 'in the middle of society' on the one hand, and the wish to stand for an alternative approach and do things differently on the other, is constantly being played out in Western European green politics.

This, of course, cannot be simply compared to the Indian or Brazilian experiences. The rise of a NMC in the emerging economies does by no means necessarily lead to 'green' politics. The new, broadened middle class in India has made its voice relevant in politics and appears to have contributed decisively to the 2014 electoral victory of Narendra Modi who campaigned on a 'development' agenda which is widely regarded as pushing environmental safeguards and restraints on a backseat. This surely supports the observation made by Ashok Lahiri in his contribution to this volume, that the mind of the Indian middle class, as a whole and very generally speaking, is still very much within a growth-oriented mindset that views economic growth as an unreservedly positive objective and treats environmental concerns and consequences as a luxury item of secondary relevance, if at all. In fact, the NMC may even be seen as structurally antagonistic to the 'environmentalism of the poor' that has characterised various social and ecological movements in India, and that tries to defend local livelihoods from damage or destruction by developmental strategies of the state, corporations and urbanisation processes—all of which, of course, are dear to the heart of the Indian middle class.

In Brazil, a Green Party does exist, but while it finds its electorate mainly among the traditional middle class (and certainly not among the 'NMC'), it has never managed to establish itself as a major political force and has been deteriorating to the extent of vanishing among the large group of 'dwarf parties' that fill the Brazilian parliament.

Under these circumstances, an environmentalism of the middle class and the development of a Green Party, seems merely a distant possibility, while any political strategy that explicitly aims at limiting growth (or 'transcending the growth paradigm', to make it more palatable) is unlikely to go far among the vast majority of Indians. To be fair, this is a complex task since the way economies and markets are organised today around the world, growth is a necessary precondition for socially more inclusive policies (although of course it does not guarantee these at all), whereas the lack of growth leads to recession and subsequent unemployment, increasing poverty. There is very much debate about whether there is, or can be, such thing as an environmentally and socially sustainable, i.e. truly 'green' growth.

This may appear to be a bleak picture—and perhaps an expectedly bleak one, for that matter. But if one takes a closer look, there is far more ambiguity, diversity and hope in social and political reality.

As regards politics, as both Ashok Lahiri and Ashish Kothari (in this volume) show for India, certain green themes and environmental concerns—especially local ones—have and do become objects of middle class political activism, from local greening initiatives to the protection of reserves etc. Much of this takes place in urban settings. No doubt, at times there is a manifest tension between this type of activism and social concerns of the poor in the society (whom some middle class actors regard merely as disturbance, if not cause of environmental problems). But political movements that take the interest of both the poor and the environment into account are possible. This is especially true for youth-based organisations that often include a marked tendency to think in terms of both social and ecological responsibility transcending individual or group interests, even though this may be dismissed as 'idealistic' by the mainstream.

When it comes to individual and group behaviour, issues of lifestyle and consumption are of course of major relevance to green politics. No doubt, the NMC in India and Brazil has a strong feeling that it needs 'to catch up', and that it has every right to do so. But even here, there are national traditions in India that put qualifications on such a view, allowing and encouraging restrictions and self-restrictions on consumption as a moral value. Ashish Kothari creatively connects to such traditions (specifically the concept of 'below poverty line' for allocation of public services that is well-known in and operating since decades in India) when he proposes the idea of creating a 'sustainable consumption line' as a marker to let people know where unsustainable consumption begins, and discourage consumption beyond that point. In Brazil, any traditions of that kind do not exist; the traditional middle and upper classes rather see excessive consumption as a legitimate confirmation of their social status. The idea of self-restrictions is being debated in environmentally sensitive sectors of civil society and academia, but this debate does not transcend these small circles so far.

This volume is best understood as a starting-point contribution to what is about to become—and should become—a global debate. As stated in the outset of this introduction, the global NMC is an issue still very much incarcerated in a debate marked by simplistic economic perceptions and categories, in which per capita income is the overwhelming and almost self-explaining category. This volume has made very clear that this is not the actual case. It has also made it very clear that middle class must be analysed thoroughly in the national context, in a broad sense, i.e. historically, culturally, politically, sociologically, and also, of course, economically. Only through this analysis, it will be possible to identify the common features which help us to understand the phenomenon globally, and nationally.

References

Bartelt, Dawid Danilo (ed.) (2013). *A Nova Classe Média como Conceito e Projeto Político*. Rio de Janeiro.

Neri, Marcelo (2011). *A Nova Classe Média. O Lado Brilhante da Base da Pirâmide* (*The NMC: The Brilliant Side of the Pyramid*, Editora Saraiva). Rio de Janeiro.

The New Middle Class

Data and Perceptions

1

DEVESH KAPUR, NEELANJAN SIRCAR
and MILAN VAISHNAV

The Importance of Being Middle Class in India[1]

Introduction

Whether you follow developments in India closely or not, you have likely heard about the emergence of the 'Indian middle class.' The private sector, especially large multinational corporations, view the emergence of a large pool of Indians with increasing disposable income as the most vital consumer market of the future. The McKinsey Global Institute (2007) refers to India's expanding consumer market as the country's "bird of gold", a phrase merchants used thousands of years ago to describe its vast economic potential. The growth of a middle class is expected to play a transformative role in modernising the Indian economy, create new pressure points on the government to tackle the vestiges of the License Raj, and enable a more propitious environment for private entrepreneurship and job creation (Fernandes 2006). And those who are frustrated with the corruption and cronyism that has characterised Indian politics for decades view the rise of the middle class as a force for positive change, a palliative to the twin vices of identity and patronage politics (Das 2012).

1. The authors are grateful for comments received on a preliminary version of this chapter presented at the "Green Perspectives on the New Middle Classes" conference hosted by Heinrich Böll Foundation (HBF) and the 2015 American Political Science Association meetings. We would like to acknowledge the assistance of Megan Reed in carrying out the research on which this chapter is based and Saksham Khosla and Aidan Milliff for research assistance. All errors are our own.

Despite these tall claims, the research on the middle class globally is quite divided on its social and political impact. On the one hand, one strand of the literature argues that middle class can be a dynamic force for change (Lash and Urry 1987) while on the other hand, some scholars have argued that they can often a powerful votary of the status quo and traditional social and economic structures (Erikson and Goldthorpe 1992). For instance, while the middle class might desire a reduced role of the state in the economy and a corresponding greater role for the private sector, it also wants better safety and environmental standards across a diverse array of sectors which, ironically, bring the state back in—this time in its regulatory capacity. This is one reason why—as far as India is concerned—the 'Inspector Raj' has replaced the 'License Raj' (Chandra 2015).

But leaving this debate aside, there is an even more fundamental problem with making statements about, or on behalf of, the middle class; there is no commonly accepted definition of what it means to be 'middle class.' To the contrary, there is a wide-ranging debate among analysts and scholars over various conceptualisations of the middle class (Kapur 2010). Some prefer an income or wealth-based measure that may either be relative or absolute, while others prefer to focus on aspects of human development, while still others argue in favour of behavioural measures.

In this chapter, we argue in favour of a distinct measurement strategy: self-identification. Given the inconclusive debate over the use (and abuse) of objective measures of class belonging, we argue that there are pay-offs to resorting to more subjective measures. After all, if what we care about from a political economy standpoint is class consciousness, self-identification presents a useful metric. For the working classes (as Georg Lukács famously argued a century ago), class-consciousness was not inherent—it was achieved through constant struggle against the owners of capital. In the 21st century, do media and consumption habits shape middle class consciousness, as some have argued (Marsh and Li 2015)?

In a national survey carried out in 2014, we asked a sample of Indians from across the country whether or not they would classify themselves as 'middle class.' We draw on this data to examine how self-identification maps onto objective measures based on income or education. We then test whether individuals who self-identify as middle class hold distinct views when it comes to economic and social mobility in India. Regardless of how one interprets its broader impacts, we argue that the notion of 'middle class' can be understood as a cognitive identity with some degree of class-consciousness or feeling of belongingness. In turn, this cognition should result in certain distinct views about the world, compared to other social classes. For instance, if the middle class is supposed to be 'aspirational', then being middle class should result in greater optimism about the future.

To preview our findings, we find that almost half of all respondents we surveyed across India identified themselves as part of the middle class. While there is substantial variation across states, which is not altogether surprising, identification is stronger in urban areas when compared to rural ones. However, middle class identification is broad-based, spanning all income groups and educational strata. While there is an almost linear correspondence between income/education and middle class affinity, what is striking is not necessarily the difference between groups but the consistency across them. When it comes to social aspiration and economic optimism, there is a distinct middle class positivity on both counts. Statistical analyses suggest that middle class self-identification accounts for a good deal of the variation in economic optimism and social aspiration that is not attributable to either income or education.

The rest of this chapter proceeds as follows. We first briefly discuss the debate on measuring the middle class in India. Next, we describe the methodology behind our new, subjective measure of middle class identity. Following this, we present descriptive data on middle class self-identification. We then look at the association between subjective middle class identity and aspirational views on the economy and social mobility—first with descriptive data and then in a simple, regression-based framework. The final section outlines some likely implications of the impact of the growing middle class on Indian politics.

Defining the Indian Middle Class

Given the attention the emergence of the Indian middle class has received, it is perhaps not surprising that there is much debate over how to measure membership in this category. Table 1.1 presents a list of metrics that have been offered in recent years. The list is not exhaustive, but it does amply illustrate the traditional reliance on subjective indicators. It also demonstrates that small differences in definition can lead to wildly divergent estimates about the overall size of the middle class.

Table 1.1

Various Definitions of the 'Indian Middle Class'

Source	*Size*	*Year*	*Definition*
Beinhocker et al. (2007)	50 million	2005	Households with disposable income between ₹200,000-₹1,000,000 per year (approx. \$11-\$55/day and \$4,200-\$21,000/year)
McKinsey Global Institute (2010)	32 million (households)	2008	Households with disposable income between ₹200,000 - ₹1,000,000 per year
Singh (2005)	113 million 250 million	1992-93 1998-99	Broadest middle class: household income greater than ₹35,000 per year (in 1998-9 rupees)
Sridharan (2004)	55-248 million	1998-99	By household income - Elite: > ₹140,000/yr. - Expanded: > ₹105,001/yr. - Broadest: > ₹70,001/yr.
Desai (2007)	7 per cent of all households 11 per cent of all households	1983 1999-2000	Proportion of households with consumption expenditure above ₹60,000 (in 1999 rupees)
Government of India (2016)	28.7 million	2011-12	Number of people filing tax returns.
Shukla (2010)	4.5 million households 10.7 million households 28.4 million households	1995-96 2001-02 2009-10	Income between ₹0.2-₹1.0 million

Asian Development Bank (2010)	224 million (lower middle class)	2005	$2-$4 (PPP)
	45 million (middle-middle class)		$4-$10 (PPP)
	5 million (upper middle class)		$10-$20 (PPP)
Kharas (2010)	5-10 per cent of all households	2010	$10-$100
Birdsall and Meyer (2012)	70 million	2012	Income between $10-$50
India Human Development Survey (IHDS), 2011-12 Round (*https://ihds.umd.edu/*)	40 per cent of all households	2014	Income between ₹55,000-₹88,000
Birdsall (2015)	2.6 per cent of all households	2015	Income between $10-$50
Pew Research Center (2015)	3 per cent of all households	2015	Income between $10.01-$20 (2011 PPP)

Overall, we can classify existing measures into three categories. The most popular approach relies on income-based thresholds.[2] For instance, Birdsall (2015) argues in favour of $10 or above (PPP or purchasing power parity, 2005) as the threshold for what she describes as an 'income-secure' middle class. Some studies, like one conducted by the Asian Development Bank (2010), present different 'bands' or 'strata' of the middle class. For instance, individuals with an income of between $2-4 (PPP) per day are classified as lower-middle class, while those making between $4-10 (PPP) and $10-20 (PPP) are classified as middle middle-class and upper middle-class, respectively. Birdsall's rejoinder to such a definition is that individuals making below the $10 cut-off are vulnerable to economic shocks, especially in an increasingly globalised world. It is for this reason that she terms people belonging to the $4-10 category as 'strugglers', or those who are upwardly mobile but susceptible to falling back below the poverty

2. Some scholars prefer a relative, rather than absolute, definition of well-being that is built around the income distribution. A cross-national analysis by Easterly (2001), for instance, defined the middle class as those individuals who were living between the 20th and 80th percentiles on the consumption distribution. The problem with this approach stems from the variation in relative income and income inequality across countries (Wietzke and Sumner 2014). To the best of our knowledge, scholars in the Indian context have not focused on measures based on overall income distribution, primarily because of the absence of good household income data.

line. Similarly, a measure developed by the McKinsey Global Institute (2007) defines middle class as households with a disposable income between ₹200,000-1,000,000 per annum. Research by scholars behind the IHDS has proposed a definition that encompasses households making between ₹55,000 and ₹88,000 (Rukmini 2014). Although this approach focuses on 'income', it more often than not relies on consumption measures, which are more readily available in the Indian context (typically, large sample surveys do not capture reliable information about income). Moreover, absolute numbers should be tethered to the year of the survey since, given India's relatively high inflation, the real value of these numbers falls rapidly with time.

Some scholars believe income-based measures are too restrictive because they do not fully capture non-monetary dimensions of well-being, and prefer a definition that incorporates broader measures.

For instance, Kapur (2010) proposes two alternative definitions that do not use income (consumption) as the principal building block. The first is the number of income tax payers in India. This reflects the number of individuals who earn a salaried income in the formal sector and who also demonstrate a willingness to pay taxes. The most recent government data, covering the financial year 2011-12, shows that 28.7 million Indians (2.3% of the population) filed income tax but 16.2 million were exempt from making tax payments. This means that the effective number of taxpayers was around 12.5 million. Assuming there are approximately 1.1 taxpayers per taxpaying household and roughly 200 million households in India, the total number of taxpaying households in India were about 5-6 per cent at the time.[3]

The second measure proposed by Kapur is the share of Indians who have a college degree, which he estimates to be approximately 50 million in 2010. Obviously, education is highly correlated with, but not a perfect substitute for income. The choice of higher education, as Kapur notes, is more reflective of the notion that middle class

3. Given that more than a quarter of India's population is below the age of 20, we should not expect this segment to be paying taxes in any case. Therefore, the number of households is a better denominator.

individuals share a common value orientation—one likely facilitated by a certain degree of formal schooling.

A third category, espoused by scholars such as Fernandes (2006), consists of behavioural measures that take into account the role of social, cultural, and economic forces in the construction of class identity.

A fourth category is the nature of employment. Historically, in countries with large public sectors, government employees dominated the ranks of the middle class. The hallmarks of such employment were lifetime job security, steady albeit modest growth in incomes, and post-retirement pensions and healthcare safety nets. Today's middle class has a much larger share of private sector workers, and many are self-employed with incomes that are higher (albeit more volatile) and safety nets that are largely self-constructed. The economic interests of these two middle-classes are rooted in distinctive economic models.

As the preceding paragraphs reveal, it can be difficult to measure middle class by relying on the conventional metrics. Our strategy is to shift from an objective to a subjective measure of middle class. Objective measures rely on some form of the statement that 'X person is in the middle class,' where X's inclusion is based on meeting some arbitrarily determined threshold. Subjective measures rely on personal statements such as: 'I am in the middle class.' This form of self-identification is a distinctive way to define an amorphous group where there is little agreement on objective measures.

Methodology

Between January and May 2014, the Lok Foundation sponsored a survey of the social attitudes of a broad cross-section of Indians. The survey piggybacked on a standing quarterly panel consumer survey of more than 150,000 households conducted by the Centre for Monitoring Indian Economy (CMIE).[4] Working with the Lok Foundation and CMIE, a research team consisting of the authors designed the survey instrument and analysed the data.

---

4. A brief description of the CMIE Consumer Pyramids Survey can be found here: *http://www.cmie.com/kommon/bin/sr.php?kall=wcontact&page=consumer_pyramids*.

The total sample size of this survey was 68,516 respondents across 24 states and union territories in India. Although respondents were randomly selected within each locality, the sampling frame itself is not statistically representative of India due to the goals of the aforementioned consumer survey. The sample includes data from each city that had at least 200,000 inhabitants as of the 2001 Census of India as well as a smaller rural sample. As such, the data are skewed towards larger cities in India and the data are biased towards urban respondents. India is 32 per cent urban and 68 per cent rural according to the 2011 Indian Census; using the same classifications, the Lok sample is 62 per cent urban and 38 per cent rural.[5] To address this mismatch, urban and rural estimates are population-weighted by size of city/local rural population within state and adjusted by rural/urban percentage at the state level for all-India estimates.

The sample was drawn as a cluster random sample in the following way. The 24 states and union territories under study were broken into 98 'homogeneous regions'. A homogeneous region is a set of contiguous districts (the largest administrative unit inside a state) that possess similar agro-climatic conditions. Within each homogeneous region, at least 1 city (and often multiple cities) and a set of villages was selected. To select households in villages, CMIE chose a random position in each village and selected every nth household in a randomly chosen direction. Cities, in contrast, were broken into wards, which were further subdivided into CEBs (census enumeration blocks). The wards in the city were stratified by average asset wealth (as determined by the 2001 Indian Census) and selected randomly. CEBs (which are of roughly equal population) were selected randomly from each selected ward. Within each CEB, CMIE selected households starting from a randomly selected position and selecting every n^{th} household from a randomly selected direction. Within each household, it randomly selected an individual over the age of 18 to interview.

5. As an aside, it is worth pointing out that the actual urban population of India is much larger than what the official statistics report, due to the idiosyncrasies of Census definitions. For instance, if the Census defined urban according to standard population thresholds, as much as 50 per cent of India would be classified as urban (Jana et al. 2014).

Middle Class Self-Identification

To measure middle class identification, the survey asked respondents: 'Do you consider your family to be a middle class family' (in Hindi: *Kya aap ke vichar se apka parivaar ek madhyam varga parivaar hai*)? The survey results reveal that nearly one in two respondents (49%) answered in the affirmative (Figure 1.1). As befits a country as diverse as India's federation, there was a significant degree of variation across states. Whereas 68 per cent, or more than two-thirds of respondents in the southern state of Karnataka believed they belonged to the middle class, just 29 per cent of respondents in the Hindi heartland state of Madhya Pradesh (MP) did so. The states with the highest proportion of self-identified 'middle class' respondents are not far out of line with what one would expect. In addition to Karnataka, the urban city-state of Delhi and Gujarat are placed on the upper end of the spectrum. On the opposite end, following MP, sit Odisha and Maharashtra.

Figure 1.1

Middle Class Self-Identification, by State

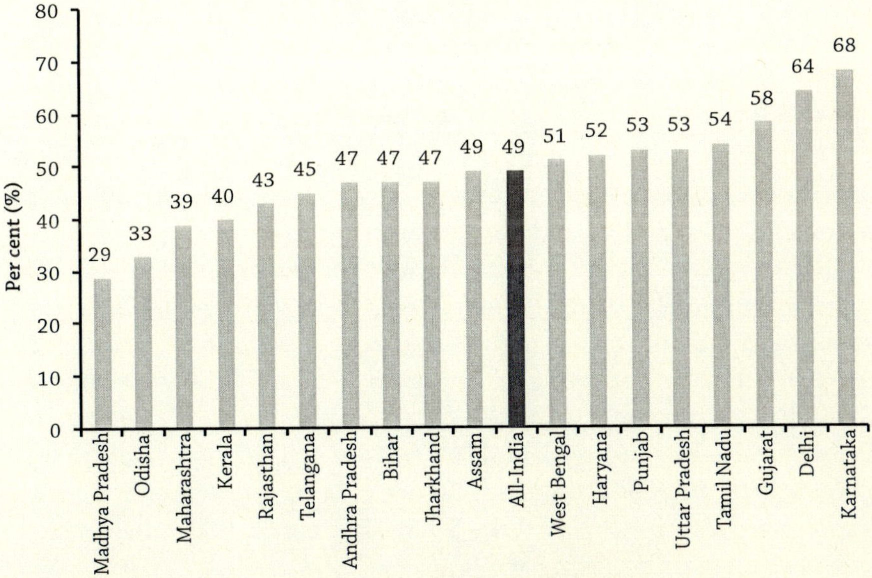

Note: Authors' analysis based on data collected by the Lok Foundation.

Most conventional descriptions of the middle class focus on urban dwellers. Our results reveal a 10 percentage point difference between urban and rural residents (56% versus 46%, respectively) when it comes to middle class identification (Figure 1.2). While this is not an insignificant difference, the proportion of residents in both places claiming middle class status is still quite large.

Figure 1.2

Middle Class Self-Identification, by Rural/Urban Status

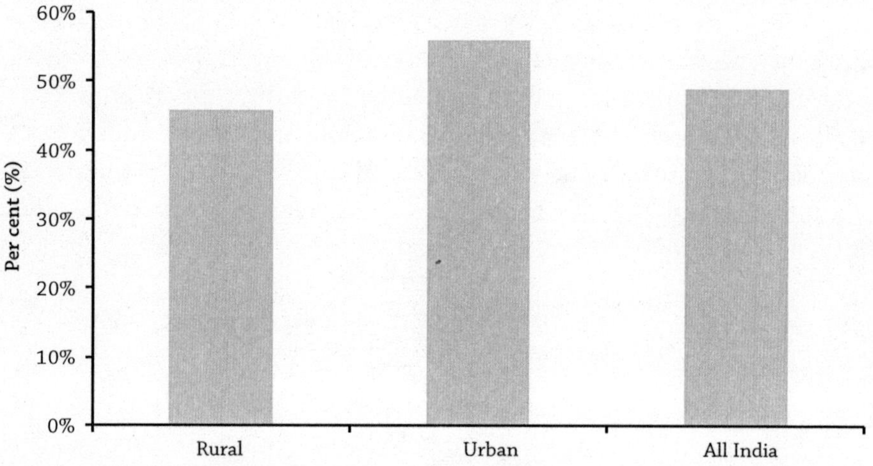

Note: Authors' analysis based on data collected by the Lok Foundation.

Where this is brought into starker relief is when one contrasts self-identification with objective income and education-based criteria. We divided up our sample into 5 income categories, based on self-reported annual income data collected by CMIE, as well as by geography (urban/rural). The contrast between respondents' self-perception and objective reality is marked. As one would expect, there is a near-monotonic relationship between subjective middle class identification and annual income. Forty-seven (47) per cent of lower middle-income respondents self-identified as 'middle class', while half of middle income and 54 per cent of upper middle-income respondents did so (Figure 1.3). Somewhat expectedly, this declined to 48 per cent for those in the highest income bracket.

Figure 1.3

Middle Class Self-Identification, by Income and Education

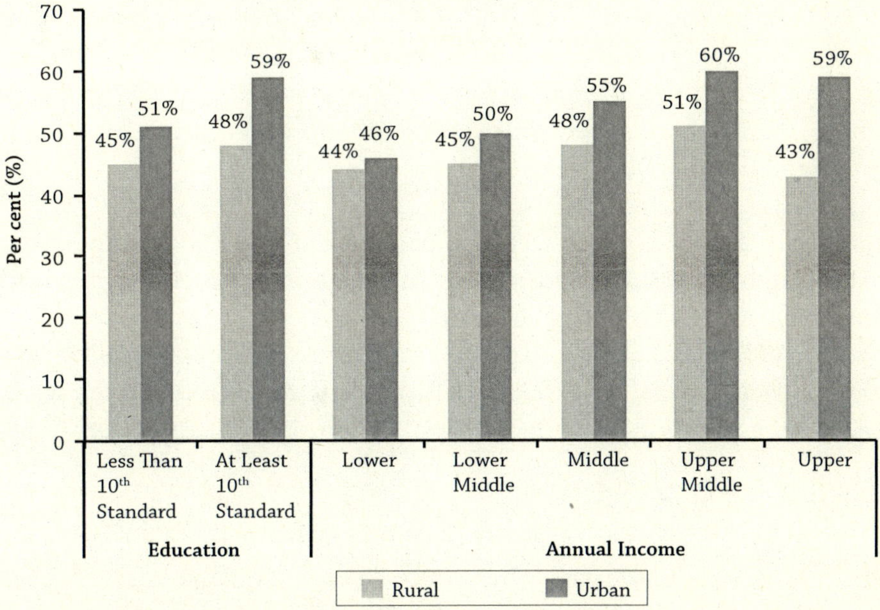

Note: Authors' analysis based on data collected by the Lok Foundation.

A second takeaway is the difference between urban and rural respondents, even within income categories. For every category of income, the share of urban respondents who self-identify as middle class is noticeably larger when compared to their rural counterparts. The lone exception is the poorest category (lower) where the differences are very small. Furthermore, even among respondents in the lowest income bracket, 45 per cent self-identify as middle class—just 3 per cent less than the richest income group. The fact that nearly half of respondents belonging to the lowest income group self-identified as middle class, not to mention the modest difference between them and upper middle-income respondents (only 9%), raises several questions. Is 'middle class,' a status marker that the poor aspire to in a status-conscious society? Or, is middle class affinity about an emerging sense of agency as age-old social hierarchies begin to fray? Or, perhaps, is the validity of the measure itself an issue since respondents across language groups might have interpreted the question in different ways?

As we described in Kapur and Vaishnav (2014), there are several potential explanations for this. First, the income data we employ compares nominal incomes and not real incomes, which does not factor in the higher cost of living in urban areas. Second, and this is debatable, it is quite possible that ethnic (especially caste-based) identities are more salient in rural relative to urban India (Chhibber and Varshney 2013).

Turning to education, we find that middle class identification tends to increase with educational attainment. We use a simple, but rather blunt, dividing line to categorise respondents: whether or not they have a 10th standard education. On balance, those who clear this minimum threshold are more likely to believe they are middle class, especially in urban areas. However, 47 per cent of individuals with less than a 10th standard education still claim such an affiliation.

Aspiration and Optimism

The large share of respondents who identify as middle class begs the question as to whether these 'middle class' Indians hold distinct world views. Do they have coherent views on the state of the country and the direction in which it is travelling? Are they more aspirational and optimistic about the future or fearful and pessimistic? Members of a first generation middle class, whose parents were poor but whose income has been buoyed by a rapidly growing economy, are likely to be optimistic about the future. But a second (or later) generation middle class whose income has stagnated or declined because of structural changes in labour markets and an anaemic economy is likely to be more pessimistic and fearful about the future. The middle classes in emerging markets are of recent vintage and the product of upward mobility stemming from rapid economic growth (as in China or India), while those in advanced industrialised economies such as the United States (US) have experienced downward mobility. Consequently, it is not middle class identification per se, but the direction of socioeconomic mobility (upward or downward), that is likely to determine their views of the future.

To answer these queries, the Lok survey posed five questions regarding respondents' social attitudes. These questions concerned children's social mobility, the improvement in family social status, the country's progress overall, India's economic situation, and respondents' household economic situation.

Across each of these measures, those who self-identify as middle class are more optimistic—both about the status of their lives today as well as the outlook for the future (Figure 1.4). When compared to those who believe they are not middle class, larger proportions of so-called middle class respondents believed that their children will have a higher standard of living than they currently enjoy, that their family's social status has improved in a generation, and that India is progressing. When it comes to assessments of the economy, both in terms of the overall macro picture (what political scientists refer to as a sociotropic evaluation) as well as the situation of their household (egotropic or pocketbook evaluation), self-proclaimed middle class respondents are similarly bullish.

Figure 1.4

Social Attitudes, by Middle Class Self-Identification

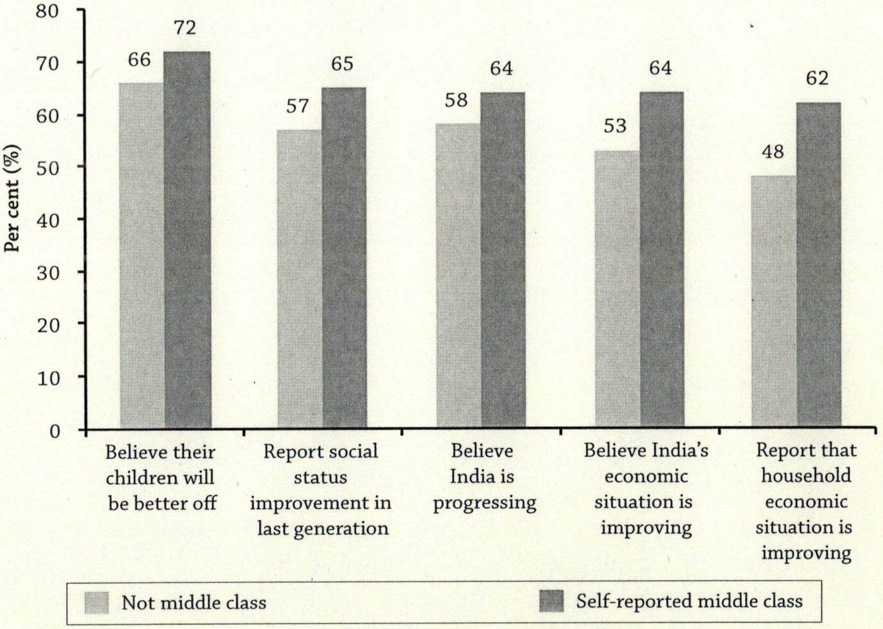

Note: Authors' analysis based on data collected by the Lok Foundation.

The numbers break on similar lines when we add a rural/urban location filter (Figure 1.5). Three things are worth noting. We saw above that middle class respondents are uniformly more optimistic in their evaluations about their current state of affairs as well as their future outlook. When we disaggregate responses by location, this remains the case among both rural and urban sub-populations. Second, urban middle class respondents are the most optimistic in their responses. However, rural self-identified middle class respondents, though they are less positive than their urban middle class peers, are marginally more optimistic than urban residents who do not believe they belong to the middle class.

Figure 1.5

Social Attitudes, by Urban/Rural Status and Middle Class Self-Identification

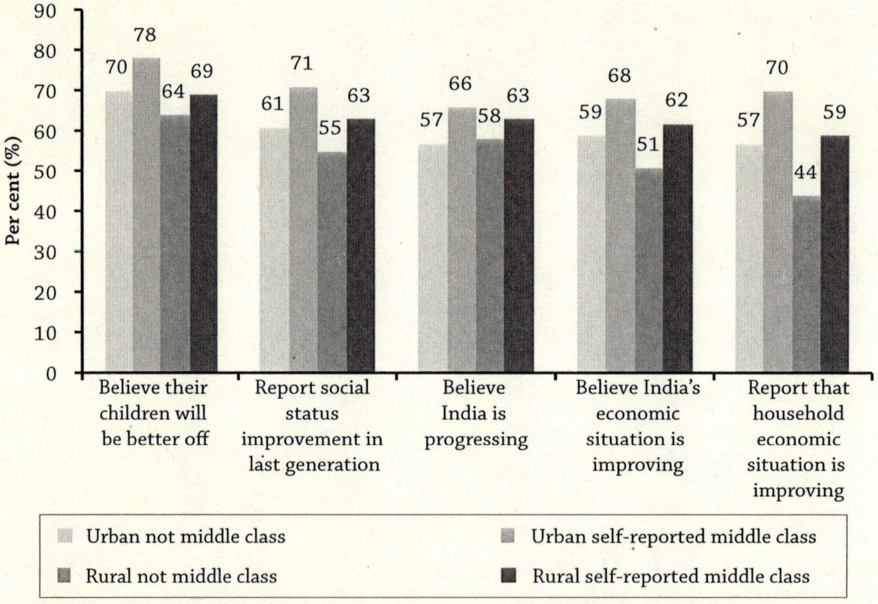

Note: Authors' analysis based on data collected by the Lok Foundation.

Finally, given the urbanising nature of Indian society, we decided to further unpack our 'urban' category into three groups: those living in megacities, larger cities, and smaller cities. We find that, in each sub-category, middle class respondents are more optimistic. Those that reside in megacities are slightly more bullish than residents living in other urban locales (Figure 1.6).

Figure 1.6

Middle Class Self-Identification and Economic Optimism

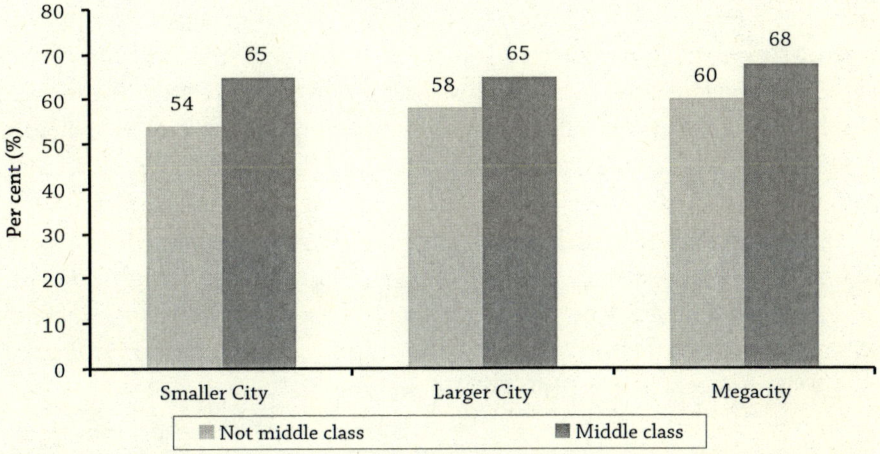

Note: Authors' analysis based on data collected by the Lok Foundation.

Statistical Analysis

The previous section supports the contention that middle class self-identification is a good predictor of aspirational and optimistic views about the future. To assess this association more systematically, we set up a simple regression looking at two, distinct outcomes: beliefs about children's well-being and the condition of the Indian economy. The former is a commentary on social aspiration, while the latter relates to economic optimism.

As predictors, we consider four variables: whether an individual is in the middle 60 per cent of the income distribution; whether he or she is 'rich,' defined by being in the top 20 per cent of the distribution; education, as denoted by passing 10th standard; and our measure of middle class self-identification. The baseline respondent, against which we are making comparisons, is a poor individual (located in the bottom 20%) who has not passed 10th standard, and does not identify as middle class. We run the model separately for urban and rural residents and include state fixed effects—which captures any unobserved variation across Indian states that is relatively time invariant, or 'fixed'.

The results of both models are broadly similar. Beginning with the question of children's well-being, middle class status—in both urban and rural areas—significantly corresponds to a more optimistic evaluation (Figure 1.7). Urban, middle class respondents are nearly seven per cent more likely to believe their children will be better off in the future than the respondents are today. The effect is slightly smaller for rural respondents. The effects of education are positive and significant, though at a reduced level. Respondents who are classified objectively as 'rich' are, on balance, more positive in their assessment, although the magnitudes are smaller. There is no statistically meaningful effect of belonging to the objectively determined 'middle wealth' category. In other words, the effect of subjective self-identification with the middle class is more impactful than belonging to the middle of the income distribution.

Figure 1.7

Impact of Middle Class Self-Identification on Social Aspiration and Economic Optimism

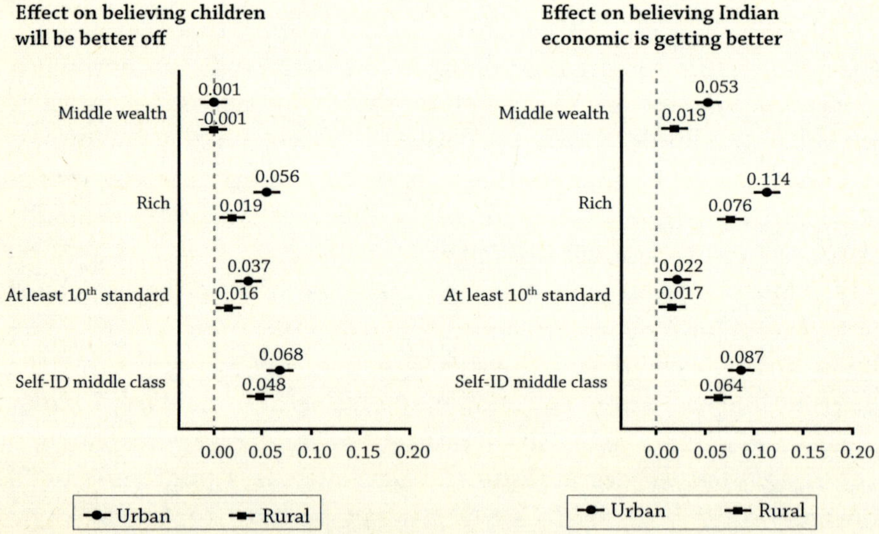

Note: Authors' analysis based on data collected by the Lok Foundation.

These findings more or less remain when one considers the second outcome of interest: whether the Indian economy is getting better. As with our measure of social aspiration, middle class self-identification is a strong predictor of economic optimism. Middle class respondents are more likely, in both urban and rural areas (though more so in the former), to have a favourable assessment of the Indian economy. Education plays a modest role while 'middle income' is significant and positive, but does not eliminate the independent impact of self-identification. Interestingly, those who belong to the 'rich' category are much more optimistic about the country's economic future. While this is not entirely surprising, we note the much larger effect on economic optimism as opposed to social aspiration. Again, given the deeply stratified nature of Indian society, economic change is relatively easier to achieve than social change. Since the American Civil War a century and half ago, incomes in the US have increased dramatically, but changes in race relations have lagged. We might similarly expect more rapid improvements in incomes in India, while social change related to caste, gender, religion, and region are likely to evolve much more gradually.

There are three principal takeaways from this brief analysis. First, middle class self-identification accounts for a lot of the variation in economic optimism and social aspiration that is not picked up by either wealth or human capital. Second, the association between middle class affinity and aspiration are comparatively larger in urban (than rural) parts of India. Finally, while income is positively linked with economic optimism, its impact is smaller on social aspiration.

Conclusion

The novel contribution of this chapter is to offer a new way of framing 'middle class' identity that relies not on income, distributional, or human capital measures, but on an individual's subjective beliefs. Drawing on findings from a large survey of Indians across two dozen states, we find that middle class identification is large—between 40 and 60 per cent—for virtually all demographic groups in the country. It seems likely based on this initial evidence that India's aspirational middle class may be less ideologically driven and instead more focused on gaining social and economic status in a country where there is a tremendous amount of churn taking place. As urbanisation picks up pace and human capital levels continue to rise, we can expect the size of the aspirational middle class to continue to expand.

While this chapter has emphasised the importance of beliefs in the construction of a middle class identity, it does not provide answers on how these beliefs have been constructed. For the working classes, class struggle and unions played critical roles in developing such an identity. For the upper classes, these identities were constructed by attending specific schools and universities (as in the United Kingdom). Media, especially the electronic media, and the construction of a consumer society are factors that appear to be playing an important role in shaping middle class identities. But how and with what consequences remain open questions.

In India's 2014 general election, research has found that the middle class (measured in more conventional terms) supported the opposition Bharatiya Janata Party (BJP) and its leader, current Prime Minister Narendra Modi, in large numbers (Sridharan 2014). However, the government would be well advised not to take the support of the middle class for granted, as partisan identification could change rapidly if the aspirations of the middle class are thwarted. Indeed, some research has shown that the middle class also backed the previous Congress-led government, which had presided over the fastest economic growth rates in Indian history (Jaffrelot and Verniers 2009). Once economic conditions began to deteriorate, particularly toward the final stage of their second term in office, the support of the middle class also began to falter. In other words, it seems logical that the ideological tether of the middle class to political parties will likely remain weak for the foreseeable future—not least because middle class identification cuts across most social groupings. However, while social bases will continue to matter for politics, as the importance of the aspirational middle class grows, one can expect a concomitant growth in economic voting—although it is as yet unclear whether this voting will take place on retrospective or prospective lines.

References

Asian Development Bank (2010). "Part I—Special Chapter: The Rise of Asia's Middle Class", in *Key Indicators for Asia and the Pacific 2010.* Manila.

Beinhocker, Eric D., Diana Farrell and Adil S. Zainulbhai (2007). "Tracking the Growth of India's Middle Class", *The McKinsey Quarterly* 3: 51–61.

Birdsall, Nancy (2015) "Does the Rise of the Middle Class Lock in Good Government in the Developing World?", *European Journal of Development Research* 27(2): 217-29 (April).

Birdsall, Nancy and Christian Meyer (2012). "Is India's Middle Class Big Enough For...?", *Center for Global Development (blog).* 26 November. *http://www.cgdev.org/blog/india%E2%80%99s-middle-class-big-enough*

Chandra, Kanchan (2015). "The New Indian State: The Relocation of Patronage in the Post-Liberalisation Economy", *Economic and Political Weekly* 50(41): 46-58 (October).

Chhibber, Pradeep and Ashutosh Varshney (2013). "Citizens of Tomorrow", *Indian Express*, October 31, 2013.

Das, Gurchuran (2012). *India Grows At Night: A Liberal Case for A Strong State.* London: Penguin.

Desai, Sonalde (2007). "Indian Middle Class", in Kaushik Basu (ed.), *Oxford Companion to Economics.* New Delhi: Oxford University Press.

Easterly, William (2001). "The Middle Class Consensus and Economic Development", *Journal of Economic Growth* 6(4): 317-35 (December).

Erikson, Robert and John H. Goldthorpe (1992). *The Constant Flux: A Study of Class Mobility in Industrial Societies.* Oxford: Clarendon Press.

Fernandes, Leela (2006). *India's New Middle Class: Democratic Politics in an Era of Economic Reform.* Minneapolis: University of Minnesota Press.

Government of India (2016). *Income Tax Department: Time Series Data, Financial Year 2000-01 to 2014-15.* Available at: *http://www.incometaxindia.gov.in/Documents/Time-Series-Data-Final.pdf*

Indian Express (2016). "Keep Inspectors Away", *Indian Express*, 26 May.

Jaffrelot, Christophe and Gilles Verniers (2009). "India's 2009 Elections: The Resilience of Regionalism and Ethnicity", *South Asia Multidisciplinary Academic Journal* (online). 23 December. *http://samaj.revues.org/2787*

Jana, Arindam, Neha Sami, and Jessica Seddon (2014). *How 'Urban' is India?.* Presentation prepared for the International Growth Centre, *http://www.theigc.org/wp-content/uploads/2014/08/Arindam-Jana.pdf*

Kapur, Devesh (2010). "The Middle Class in India: A Social Formation or Political Actor?" in Julian Go (ed.), *Political Power and Social Theory.* Vol. 21. Bingley, UK: Emerald Group Publishing Limited. pp.143-69.

Kapur, Devesh and Milan Vaishnav (2014). "Being Middle Class in India", *Hindu*, 9 December.

Kharas, Homi (2010). "The Emerging Middle Class in Developing Countries", *OECD Working Paper* 285, January.

Lash, Scott and John Urry (1987). *The End of Organized Capitalism.* Madison: University of Wisconsin Press.

Marsh, Leslie L. and Hongmei Li (eds.) (2015). *The Middle Class in Emerging Societies: Consumers, Lifestyles and Markets.* Abingdon, UK: Routledge.

McKinsey Global Institute (2007). *The 'Bird of Gold': The Rise of India's Consumer Market.* San Francisco.

———. (2010). *India's Urban Awakening: Building Inclusive Cities, Sustaining Economic Growth.* London.

Pew Research Center (2015). *A Global Middle Class Is More Promise than Reality.* Washington, D.C.

Rukmini S. (2014). "Middle Class Better Off, but Not Well Off", *Hindu*, 5 April.

Saxena, Rachna (2010). "The Middle Class in India: Issues and Opportunities", *Deutsche Bank Research Note*, 15 February.

Shukla, Rajesh (2010). *How India Earns, Spends and Saves: Unmasking the Real India.* New Delhi: Institute for Human Development.

Singh, Nirvikar (2005). "The Idea of South Asia and the Role of the Middle Class", *Working Paper.* Department of Economics, University of California-Santa Cruz. 29 April.

Sridharan, E. (2004). "The Growth and Sectoral Composition of India's Middle Class: Its Impact on the Politics of Economic Liberalization", *India Review* 3(4): 405-28.

———. (2014). "Class Voting in the 2014 Lok Sabha Elections: The Growing Size and Importance of the Middle Classes", *Economic and Political Weekly* 49(39): 72-76 (27 September).

Wietzke, Frank-Borge and Andy Sumner (2014), "What are the Political and Social Implications of the 'New Middle Classes' in Developing Countries?", *Working Paper*. London: King's International Development Institute, King's College. 27 November.

2

CELIA LESSA KERSTENETZKY, CHRISTIANE UCHÔA and NELSON DO VALLE SILVA

The Elusive New Middle Class in Brazil

A characteristic that strongly marked the world economy in the last 20 years—at least before the full unfolding of the consequences of the 'Great Recession' that started in 2008—was the intense growth experienced by practically all countries, the developing ones in particular, in the wake of the process of market globalisation and the rise of China. In social terms, the main consequence of this phase of growth of developing countries was the dramatic reduction of poverty in the world population, and today one may even envisage its virtual disappearance, at least in its more extreme form.[1]

This process has been accompanied by the growth of intermediate layers between the poor and the rich, which, by having access to new levels of mass consumption, some analysts prefer to consider people who have access to additional resources (nearly a third of the total) after the satisfaction of basic needs like food and housing, as members of a presumed 'NMC' (new middle class). It is estimated that, in emerging markets as a whole, the so-called middle class increased from nearly a third of the population in 1990 to more than half today.[2]

A point to be considered is that these analyses admit that it is not enough to have escaped poverty in order to enter the threshold of the 'middle class'. For this, it would be required to have enough additional monetary resources to allow the discretionary spending in material and cultural consumption. The hypothesis seems to be that there is

---

1. See, for instance, the cover feature of *The Economist*, 01-07 June 2013, under the symptomatic title "Towards the End of Poverty".
2. See the special report of Parker (2009).

an intermediate stratum between the poor and the middle class, a stratum whose position is still precarious and unstable, without full access to the consumption market and constantly besieged by the ghost of social decadence.

A recent study by the World Bank on the emergence of the middle class in Latin America (Ferreira et al. 2012) explicitly considers these criteria. The study defines the middle class in terms of economic security, i.e., of a low probability of falling down (for many, falling back) into income poverty. As may be guessed, their results show that the 'vulnerable', who do not make enough to enjoy economic security, is the largest group of Latin American population, including that of Brazil. Following the lead of this study, Birdsall et al. (2014) look into the prospects of this group, which they call 'the strugglers', and predict that they may well end up marginalised in the not-too-distant future.

Figure 2.1

Number of Households with Per Capita Income Below and Above the Poverty Line, Brazil, 2003-2011

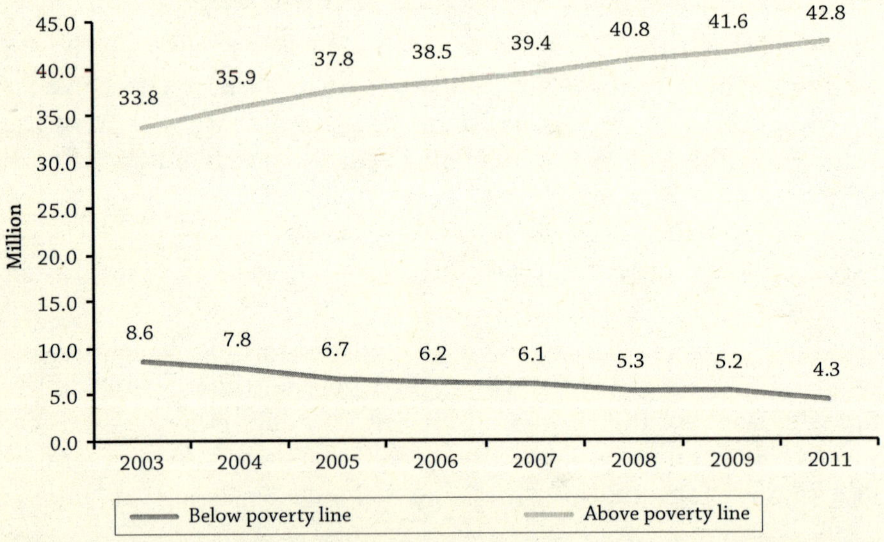

Source: PNADs 2003 to 2011/IBGE, 2012. Poverty line = R$143.41; adjusted to January 2013 values. That line was established considering Hoffmann's (2007: 98-99) work.

Still, the Latin American case awakens interest inasmuch as the reduction of poverty was accompanied by a sustained contraction of inequality; in any case, a rarity in the history of the region (Cornia 2014).[3] Lustig et al. (2013) estimate, using a US$ 4 dollar PPP per day poverty line, that the decline in inequality contributed about 40 per cent to the total reduction of poverty (the rest is explained by growth). In Brazil, between 2003 and 2011, nearly 9 million households (more than 30 million people) crossed upwards the poverty line roughly equivalent to a fourth of the minimum wage (Figure 2.1).

The decline in inequality as the income of the poorer increased in a proportion larger than that of the richer seems to be an established fact (see Table 2.1)—and its contribution to the reduction in poverty is only somewhat lesser than the regional average (Lustig et al. 2013).

Table 2.1

Evolution of the Income Share of Income Deciles, 2002 to 2012

	Growth Rate 2012/2002 (%)	*Income Share IR 2012 (%)*	*Income Share IR 2002 (%)*
1% richest	-6.0	12.6	13.4
10% richest	-4.9	44.7	47.0
9º.decile	-3.7	15.5	16.1
8º.decile	3.8	10.9	10.5
7º.decile	10.5	8.4	7.6
6º.decile	18.9	6.9	5.8
5º.decile	22.2	5.5	4.5
4º.decile	26.5	4.3	3.4
3º.decile	32.0	3.3	2.5
2º.decile	35.3	2.3	1.7
1º.decile	30.8	1.02	0.78

Source: Kerstenetzky (2015) from the Ipeadata data source, Income: household per capita income from the PNADs/IBGE.

Some works empirically relate such changes with stable democracies and centre-left coalition governments in the region (e.g.

3. See especially chapters 1-2, pp.3-69.

Cornia 2010, 2014, Huber et al. 2008). In fact, in Brazil, if currency stabilization with the Real Plan was crucial to cutting poverty levels from their 1980's 30 per cent peak level down to 20 per cent in 1995. While poverty levels had been pretty much pro-cyclical before that, after 2002 and up to 2011 poverty halved (see Figure 2.2), also on account of policy-induced inequality reduction.

Figure 2.2

Proportion of People in Poverty and Extreme Poverty, 1970-2011

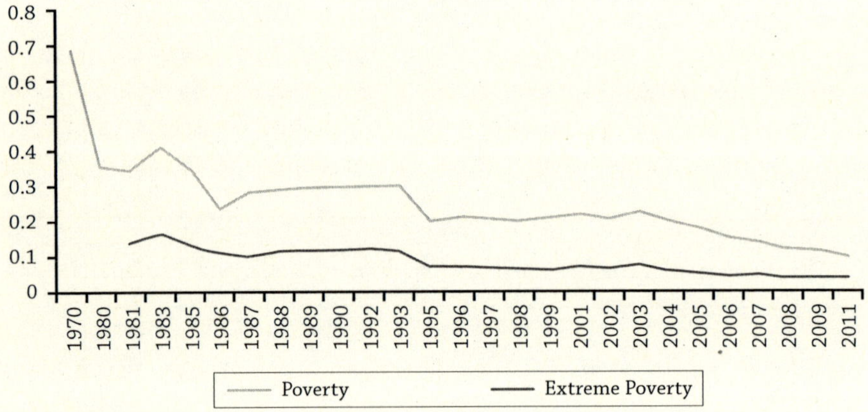

Source: Rocha (2013).

It is generally acknowledged that public policies were important in this period (Huber et al. 2008, Huber and Bogliaccini 2010, López-Calva and Lustig 2010, Lustig et al. 2013, Soares 2011). Among them are the expansion of educational attainment, labour market policies, such as minimum wage valorisation, cash transfers to the poor and non-contributory pensions to rural workers.

However, the jury is out as to whether this large group of socially better-positioned people migrated to the middle class, as has been repeatedly suggested. The question is not simple. Beyond the issue of class formation, there are different definitions and ways to measure social positions but, in any case, there is a wide consensus that family income is far from being a sufficient criterion for class belonging and that other sociological criteria are to be adopted. This assumption also underscores the work of Ferreira et al. (2012) on Latin American countries, where the chances for social demotion were the point of departure for the definition of a stratum of 'vulnerable' people, distinct from both the poor and the middle class. At the very least, we would need to evaluate the stability of the new positions attained, in view of the material and symbolic legacies, as well as the obvious risks, such as the situation of the head of household in the labour market or adverse economic conjunctures that might cancel fragile gains.

The Brazilian debate to a large extent centres on the reception of economist Marcelo Neri's research on this issue. His seminal analyses (Neri 2008, 2010, 2011) support the positive view that the income gains have qualified a significant stratum of the former Brazilian poor to the middle class club, 'the NMC', and were met with relative sympathy by the empirical work of the sociologist Bolívar Lamounier and political scientist Amaury de Souza (2010). Recent studies have questioned the 'class' interpretation, though. Most of them criticize the exclusive focus on income and lack of reference to social structure, especially the occupational structure (Pochmann 2012, Quadros 2010, Scalon and Salata 2012, Sobrinho 2011). According to the age-old social stratification tradition, occupational traits and labour market insertion, secondary aspects in Neri's study, are essential markers of class positions.[4] Other analysts take issue with Neri's analysis but also with critical efforts directed to it (Souza 2010), since these pay too much heed to the economic dimension of stratification and neglect essential cultural dimensions such as class culture (e.g. lifestyles, tastes) and the symbolic production of social distinctions in processes of class formation and reproduction. Otherwise diverging in their starting points, all of these authors converge to the conclusion that the shortening of social distances we have been witnessing is mostly the emergence of a 'new working class', or 'struggling class' (Souza 2010), still deprived of the social and economic security that distinguishes the full-fledged middle class (Ferreira et al. 2012).

4. Our own calculations on the basis of the POF questionnaire on occupations, in fact, show that most of the heads of households in the 'NMC' are (mainly) manual or rural workers, confirming the results of the literature just mentioned. See Table 6, in the on-line appendix. Available at: *http://www.bpsr.org.br/index.php/bpsr/article/view/250*

This paper aims at dialoguing with that small but growing literature by attempting to introduce the perspective of 'lifestyle'[5] in the debate, a marker privileged in the field of sociology of consumption studies.[6] This is actually done through the gauging of the standards of living of the households that, by the income criterion proposed by Neri (2008, 2010, 2011), have been identified as members of a 'NMC', in order to examine the adequacy of such a classification.

We are aware that the translation of some sociological concepts into statistical indicators is risky, and this is not exactly what we intend to do. We are rather interested in the idea of class differentiation occurring at the level of combinations of capitals and resources (economic, social, cultural), but are obviously limited by the available statistical information. Indirect evidence of differential access or possession of resources is given by indicators of standards of living and, in particular, of consumption patterns.

In contrast to the work of Ferreira et al. (2012) and Birdsall et al. (2014), which exclude from the middle class those non-poor people with a high probability of falling into poverty, we do not depart from a previous poverty line definition and income range. To check the adequacy of Neri's classification, we rather start out from a standard of living that characterises a middle-class lifestyle, according to common perception. Also we do not establish an objective cutoff, but rather search for similarity among economic strata. But the mentioned authors' intuition is similar to common perceptions in Brazil, that economic security is central to the middle-class identity.

To this end, we examined the data of the Survey on Family Budgets (Pesquisa de Orçamentos Familiares–POF, conducted by the Instituto Brasileiro de Geografia e Estatística–IBGE) from 2008-09, a database not yet explored (probably because of its

5. Admittedly, this criterion is also adopted by Souza (2010), but his qualitative analysis is based on interviews.

6. For a recent review of the literature dealing with consumption, status and class distinctions, including an evaluation of the contributions of classical and contemporary authors, such as Weber, Veblen and Bourdieu, as well as of their critics, see Stillerman (2015), especially chapter 4, pp.83-108. See also Savage (2012).

complexity) in the debate on the NMC, but rich in information on the socioeconomic profile of Brazilian households and their individual members. In comparison to previous papers (Kerstenetzky and UCHÔA 2013, UCHÔA and Kerstenetzky 2012), where we already began the exploration of that base, pointing out the fragility of the educational performance of the small children and youngsters of the 'new middle class' families, which would help predict their precarious life perspectives (Kerstenetzky and Uchôa 2013), in this paper we present a wider palette of elements that imply the ideas of consumption patterns as proxies to lifestyle. Along with the critical literature, our observations from the new angle do not support the optimistic diagnosis that the former income poor migrated en masse to the 'NMC'. Most of them seem to have ended up quite vulnerable or even (standard of living) poor.

To avoid misunderstandings, a couple of disclaimers are in order. In this paper, we do not intend to develop an alternative classification of the middle class but instead check the strength of the classification that has been proposed on the basis of the income criterion against consumption patterns criteria. Our hypothesis is that a considerable proportion of the people that on the median/average income criterion have been classified under the NMC label are more like a vulnerable social stratum than a well-established middle-class stratum when consumption patterns are considered. Secondly, the approach is essentially descriptive and does not intend to advance any kind of normative analysis on inequalities and forms of reparation thereof.

In the remainder of this paper, we present the rationale for the choice of markers in section 1, the adopted methodology in section 2, and the results for the analysis of the so-called 'NMC' in section 3. In the last section, we briefly mention some of the implications.

How to Identify Middle Class?

In his recent study on what he calls the new Brazilian middle class, Neri (2011) states that this stratum is the one that "gets on average the average (sic) income of society, i.e., constitutes the middle class in statistical terms" (Neri 2011: 83).[7] The total household income of this 'new Brazilian middle class' goes from R$1,200 to 5,174 per month (Neri 2011: 27), being thus located above the poorer 50 per cent and below the richer 10 per cent.

However, in spite of being amenable to statistical categorisation, the middle class as a social stratum is difficult to categorise in sociological terms. This difficulty appears in different theoretical efforts in social stratification, drawing, e.g. on asset possession, knowledge or unique credentials/skills, authority positions in organisations, distinctive labour contracts and among other forms of identification. In any case, the option of treating it as a class of mean or median income is far from convincing: for one, given the still highly-concentrated income distribution in Brazil, a very large proportion of the population might simultaneously have an income level around the median income and still be economically/socially insecure, not to say plainly poor, given the low values demarcating the median interval and deficient public provision of various needed services. More generally, this simplistic criterion does not accommodate many of our intuitive judgments about what characterises a bona fide middle class, economic security, one among them.

But instead of normatively establishing what a middle-class standard of living should look like, in this paper, we adopt an inductive approach. On the basis of studies about shared perceptions on what is supposed to distinguish the middle class, we identify some of the characteristic markers of this stratum and their incidence in the mean income group as identified in Neri's (2011) study. Our intent is to verify the equivalence between socially-shared perceptions and the statistical classification based on income. To this end, we combine the markers with the information available in

7. Neri is not the only reference in this discussion. Economist Ricardo Paes de Barros, working at the Secretaria de Assuntos Estratégicos da Presidência da República during the Rousseff administration, has also been very vocal for the new middle class as a new economic and social actor (Secretaria de Assuntos Estratégicos 2012). However, the published work of Neri (2011) remains the more important reference for this view in the academic discussion in Brazil.

the POF database. Given that this database provides information on family budgets, we concentrate on consumption patterns.

It turns out that our path to the analysis of the socioeconomic profile of that income bracket finds a rationalisation in many sociological approaches, including some of Bourdieu's seminal analyses (2008, 2012). According to these theoretical perspectives, social strata are constructed by the marking of their relative positions, as well as by a general perception and recognition of these positions, and not solely as a function of the property of some specific resource. The element of perceived differential consumption or distinction plays a central role. People's perceptions on the middle class seem to confirm this, as we explain below.

Souza and Lamounier's study (2010), on which we draw, indicates the saliency of a certain set of markers, which are socially acknowledged as distinctive of the middle class.[8] Among these, some markers figure a stable standard of living, house ownership, high income, university education, and a prestigious profession, access to leisure and amusement, and access to good schools for the children.[9] The qualifications 'stable', 'ownership', 'high', 'university', 'prestigious', 'good', besides access to things not considered as primary needs, like leisure and amusement, indicate differentiation relative to the consumption of lower strata (the poor and median strata), from which the middle class wishes to be kept apart. To this list, we added access to 'modern' means of communication and information, we qualified the owned house in terms of 'good' housing conditions, and we also added free time to the item access to leisure and amusement. It is worth noting that, in contrast to the study authors, who do not call into question the proposition that the families situated in the income bracket defined by Neri (2011) are

8. This study is based on the 2008 Middle Class Survey, a representative sample of interviews with 2,002 voters aged 16 years or older in 141 Brazilian municipalities that took place between 8 and 12 December 2008.

9. The percentage varied from 77 per cent (good schools) to 93 per cent (stable standard of living) of positive answers across the board, pointing to these markers as distinctive of the middle class.

members of the middle class, we utilised the markers they identified precisely to examine the proposition's adequacy.

Our variable selection, explained in the next section, resulted from the combination of the markers and information available in the database. Our distinction criteria, restricted to information in the database, were limited to possession and access to specific resources (goods and services).

Methodology

The focus of analysis, following Neri (2011), is the total household income and the database, as already mentioned, is the Survey on Family Budgets, 2008-09, or POF, for short.

Table 2.2

Criteria, Variable and Proxies Used in the Analysis

Criteria	*Variables*	*Proxies*
Stable standard of living	Savings account, private pension plan, health insurance plan	Has a passbook savings account
		Has a self-funded private pension plan
		Has a health insurance plan from employer or no own account
	Car	Owns a car
	Credit card*	Has a credit card
	Checking account with overdraft*	Has a checking account with overdraft coverage
Home ownership and dwelling conditions	Own home	Condition of occupation of dwelling
	No crowding**	Number or residents per bedroom
	Indoor bathroom	Number of indoor bathrooms per dwelling
	Adequate material***	Predominant material of walls, floor and roof
	Public services***	Has public services available
University education	University education*	Highest educational level of head of household
	Leisure and sports services	Has service in evaluation of dwelling conditions
	Subscription TV	Has a subscription TV plan or package

Access to leisure diversion and spare time	Theater	Has expenses to attend plays
	Cinema	Has cinema expenses
	Colour	Owns a colour TV
	DVD player	Owns a DVD player
	Washing machine	Owns a washing machine
	Vacuum cleaner	Owns a vacuum cleaner
	Maid	Has a maid/clearing person
Access to good schools	Children attend private school	Has children enrolled in a private school
Access to information and communication	Internet in home	Has internet access
	Computer	Owns computer
	Mobile phone	Owns a mobile phone

Note: * refer to the head of household. All the other variables refer to the dwelling; **: up to 2 people per bedroom; ***: Adequate material = adequate construction material of walls + floor+ roof; Adequate wall material: masonry and/or wood; Adequate floor material; carpet, ceramic tiles, wood over cement slab; Adequate roof material; wood shingles, corrugated steel sheets or cement slab; ***: Services: water, trash collection, street lighting, storm drains, electricity, rapid transit, education, health, street cleaning and maintenance, sewerage.

Source: Prepared by the authors based on Neri (2001), Souza and Lamounier (2010), O'Dougherty (1998). POF 2008-09 and living condition and social indicators—IBGE (2013).

The POF is a national household survey that is conducted during a whole year every five years by the Brazilian Institute of Geography and Statistics, the IBGE. The sample is representative at both individual and household levels. The basic unit of investigation is the so-called 'consumption unit'. Data collection includes 7 different questionnaires that allow a detailed reconstitution of households' physical characteristics, individual and household expenditures, income, net worth and other socioeconomic traits. Thus, the POF gives an in-depth picture of the standard of living of Brazilian households, being for this reason especially suitable for the kind of research we undertake here. Among the 16 files that make up the whole database, we selected the following: living conditions, 90-day expenses, individual expenditures, car expenses, household, inventory of goods, resident, "other income" (rental income, interest from financial investments, etc.), and domestic help.

As already mentioned, we examined households in the income bracket from R$1,052.00 to R$4,537.00, to which was attributed the status of 'NMC' (from now on NMC stratum or segment).[10] Besides, having in view a more detailed analysis of the differentiation within the NMC, we further divided this large segment into 3 equal-length sub-segments, as shown below in section 3. Once we determined the households to be studied, we examined the many aspects of such units and the heads of households' attributes in such a way as to answer whether these households may plausibly be considered as typically middle class ones. This way, we associated the markers or selected criteria (cf. section 1) to variables and for each of these, we identified 1 question in POF, according to Table 2.2.

The equivalence between criteria and variables is to some extent self-explanatory, but it is worth reflecting on the decisions here taken. First, the identification of variables that correspond to markers was limited by two parameters: on the one hand, by the belief that there is not a necessary relation between marker and variable and that other variables could equally well indicate the occurrence of these criteria. Besides, variables could be classified in a different way than that presented here. In this sense, our sole claim is plausibility. On the other, we are limited to the information available in the database. As a consequence, and additionally, we want to make explicit our reasons to classify variables the way we did.

Beginning by the 'stable standard of living' criterion, we focused on the access to forms of private pension and sources of resources (such as wealth, credit and investment income) that reduce uncertainty in the middle and long run, stabilising the standard of living while making it less dependent on monthly income. This correlates directly with the Souza-Lamounier (2010) survey in which most people explicitly cited a stable standard of living as a characteristic of the middle class. Economic security, a trait suggested in the Ferreira et al. (2012) study, is also captured here.[11]

10. This corresponds to Neri's 2011 income bracket, in 2009 values. For value actualisation, we used the generalised National Index of Prices for Consumers (IPCA, from the Portuguese), estimated by IBGE.

11. The idea here is not so much that these people have access to basic goods but that they enjoy a more permanent sense of economic security, given by their 'economic capital' in the terminology of Bourdieu (2008). In this sense, economic security distinguishes them from vulnerable or outright poorer strata.

The 'home ownership with good housing conditions' criterion refers to housing conditions in general and, by not concentrating solely on the property of the dwelling and also taking into account its habitability, especially the access to public services, directs attention to the effective quality of housing. This criterion—home ownership—also appeared with distinction in the Souza-Lamounier (2010) survey.

In the 'services' indicator, we decided to consider all 10 selected ones, for they are all considered essential. Our interest in this case was to observe the existence of the services as a way of qualifying the housing situation.

The criteria 'university education of the household's head' and 'access to good schools', which also appeared prominently in the LS (2010) survey, may give us an approximate notion of the level of cultural capital made possible by different income strata, especially its intergenerational transmission.

In the criterion 'access to leisure, diversion and spare time', another element cited in the LS (2010) survey, we decided to include both leisure inside and outside the house and availability of free time—elements that conform to a distinctive consumption pattern, not included in what are commonly considered basic needs. The variables that allowed us to identify the availability of free time, to which we associate a decent living standard, were ownership of washing machine and vacuum cleaner, and spending on domestic help, a peculiarity of the Brazilian middle class.

Finally, the criterion 'access to information and communication technology' was included to give some sense of possession of social capital or social connections.

Having selected the variables and defined the proxies in the database (as shown in Table 2.2), we register the numbers, absolute and relative of households that answered 'yes' to the questions. We break the income distribution into six income brackets and proceed to analyse the similarity among them, as we explain in the next section.

A warning applies here. We decided to include expenditures on health insurance plans (in the stable living standard criterion) and private schools (in the access to good schools criterion) as markers of middle class consumption patterns, in spite of the high market stratification of these services, because, as a matter of fact, they seem to constitute distinctive middle class traits in Brazil. If what new consumers are getting is real quality, which is doubtful, is a different matter and something we are not able to assess with the data at our disposal. In concrete terms, this means that we may be overestimating the amount of middle class households, which runs counter to our own hypothesis.

Results

A first approximation to the data shows that the households in the income bracket that correspond to the so-called 'NMC' amounted, in 2009, to 31.6 million, or 55 per cent of the Brazilian households. The sheer width of the income bracket that has been identified as the NMC is very large, and this suggests that different situations may have been considered uniformly when we look at the income bracket as a whole.

In fact, a preliminary analysis indicates that this segment is characterised by a strong inequality within it, and the predominance is of dwellings in the lower NMC income segment, where apparently the largest growth occurred in recent years, be it in absolute terms or in percentage points. This lower NMC sub-segment alone accounts for almost one-third of all households in Brazil and about 60 per cent of all NMC households

So, in view of these observations, we broke the NMC group into three subgroups of equal income range, and, to keep our results comparable with Neri's (2011), we decomposed the household income distribution as a whole into six strata: the first stratum corresponds to Neri's class E, where the poor households are located; the second one corresponds to Neri's class D, of vulnerable people; the third, fourth and fifth ones are Neri's class C or the NMC; and the sixth one stands for Neri's classes A and B (see Table 2.3).

Table 2.4 shows the observed profile of Brazilian households by income brackets (as a proportion of the households in each income bracket), considering the selected criteria and variables taken as reasonable approximations for middle class identification.

Table 2.3

Dwellings by Income Range, 2008-09*

*Monthly Income Ranges (R$)****	*Amount***	*Per cent*
Up to 658.59	8.5	14.7
658.60 to 1,052.34	9.4	16.3
1,052.35 to 2,214.02	18.9	32.8
2,214.03 to 3,375.70	8.4	14.6
3,375.71 to 4,537.37	4.2	7.3
More than 4,537.37	8.2	14.3
Total	57.7	100.0

Note: * amounts updated by the Consumer Price Index—IPCA/IBGE, January 2009; **: million; ***: Brazil's currency is the Real (R$). Over the study period of this paper, the exchange rate with the dollar fluctuated in an interval between approximately R$1.65 to R$3.10/US$, with a rough average of R$2.20/US$.

Source: POF 2008-2009/IBGE.

A preliminary general observation is that there are some relatively 'universalised' things: various housing conditions, as well as possession of colour TV sets, are present in most households in all income brackets examined (the same happened with refrigerators, not included in Table 2.3). These items do not seem to differentiate much along the income groups, at least on the basis of the data at our disposal. However, an interesting second finding in regard to our exploration of the NMC segment was to see that the second poorest stratum (class D) and the first income stratum of the NMC group (class C1) seem indeed to show substantial affinities: most of the households in strata D and C1 do not possess 17 and 16 items, respectively, of a total of 23, the shortest distance considering all pairs of adjacent strata on this criterion. To be sure, only the richest stratum (Neri's [2011] classes A and B) enjoys the situation of most of the households holding most of the items, but, again, the absolute distance is somewhat larger among any other adjacent strata than it is between D and C1. Poor households (class E) stood alone only in the minority of those who possessed DVD equipment.

In addition, in variables like private healthcare, checking accounts with overdraft, private school, internet in home and domestic help, poor and not poor, from the 1st to the 5th income stratum including the NMC group as a whole, share a similar situation: most of their households simply do not have access to these resources. Henceforth, the 6th stratum is distinctive in its exclusive access to them. Segments 5 and 6 are together with exclusivity only in credit card, computer and car ownership; symmetrically, not having access to them negatively marks out groups 1, 2 and 3. Thus, even the affinity of the highest income stratum within the NMC group and the adjoining richer stratum seems weak. Segments 4, 5 and 6 are together exclusively as to access to services and mobile phone ownership. The NMC group appears to be united (to the exclusion of the poorer classes D and E) only in 2 variables: DVD ownership and leisure and sports services.

The relations between income and every item listed in Table 2.4 were statistically significant. Our initial visual impression of a non-robust NMC group was double-checked with the use of a common technique of multivariate analysis that aims at grouping objects on the basis of their profiles.

Table 2.4

Percentage of Households that Possess the Item by Income Range, 2008-09*

Criteria	*Variable*	*Up to 658.59*	*658.60 to 1,052.34*	*1,052.35 to 2,214.02*	*2,214.03 to 3,375.70*	*3,375.71 to 4,537.37*	*More than 4,537.37*
Stable standard of living	Saving account	3.8	6.7	14.3	24.7	28.9	41.0
	Private pension plan	0.1	0.1	0.5	1.9	3.4	11.8
	Health insurance plan	2.3	4.9	14.3	33.7	48.2	67.7
	Car	4.4	9.3	23.7	48.3	63.0	81.5
	Credit card	8.6	16.3	26.7	42.8	53.3	69.0
	Checking account with overdraft	1.9	3.7	9.3	24.4	35.9	62.8

Home ownership and housing conditions	Own home	64.5	67.7	72.4	76.6	79.0	80.6
	No crowding	26.7	23.8	19.4	14.3	11.6	5.8
	Indoor	86.5	94.6	98.2	99.5	99.9	99.9
	Bathroom adequate	85.5	93.6	95.8	97.3	97.7	96.1
	Public service	23.9	34.2	44.1	56.2	60.3	69.3
University education	University education	0.8	0.9	2.9	9.2	16.5	40.5
Access to good schools	Children who attend private school	3.3	5.6	9.9	19.2	29.8	60.7
Access to leisure, diversion and spare time	Leisure and sports services	45.3	48.8	56.0	62.1	67.5	74.4
	Subscription TV	0.4	0.7	1.7	5.2	9.7	26.1
	Colour TV	92.6	95.0	96.6	97.7	98.0	98.8
	DVD player	44.9	53.0	64.4	75.1	79.8	85.9
	Washing machine	13.7	23.2	41.0	62.8	73.3	83.4
	Vacuum cleaner	0.9	1.7	5.8	15.0	24.6	42.1
	Maid	4.0	6.5	11.8	21.6	32.3	60.6
Access to information and communication technology	Internet in home	0.8	2.1	6.5	17.5	30.2	52.1
	Computer	2.7	6.6	17.9	40.2	57.1	75.8
	Mobile phone	22.9	34.1	46.5	58.5	64.1	71.9

Note: Amount updated by the Consumer Price Index—IPCA/IBGE, January 2009.

Source: POF 2008-09/IBGE.

As a way of summarising the profile similarities delineated above, we furthermore submitted the data in Table 2.4 to a hierarchical cluster analysis, using the SPSS software. In its first step, the clustering algorithm aggregated the two poorer income strata; after that, the two upper NMC strata were clustered, clearly differentiating them from the lower NMC stratum; and in its third step, this lower

NMC stratum is clustered with the first group produced, those with lowest incomes.[12]

Therefore, stopping the analysis at this point, we would end up with three strata clusters:

- a 'poor' group, those earning up to R$2,214.00, composed of the 3 poorer strata (i.e. including the first NMC segment) and comprising 63.8 per cent of Brazilian households (according to POF 2008-09 data represented in Table 2.3);
- a "middle" group with the two upper NMC strata, those earning more than R$2,214.00 but less than R$4,537.00 (21.9% of households); and, finally,
- a "high" income group, those earning more than R$4,537.00 (14.3% of households).

It should be noted that the first segment of the NMC, which is clustered with the poorer strata in the 'poor group', is where the median income (R$1,586.63) is located.

Final Comments

There are many problems with the positive identification of a 'NMC' in Brazil, but various attempts support the suspicion that it is not correct to classify the people that just emerged from poverty in that social stratum characterised by economic safety and by distinctive consumption patterns and lifestyles. Taking these elements as a reference, our study showed the heterogeneity of the NMC group, the similarities between the lower layer of this group (accounting for more than 60% of the households) and the poorer income classes, as well as the weak similitude between the moneyed sectors of the NMC and the families with higher income.

In our search for the NMC, we found a group of relatively well-off families still far away from a stable standard of living and other desired and distinctive attributes. This group, the first stratum of the NMC and the more populous one, thus looks much more like a vulnerable, 'non-capitalised' social segment than an economically

---

12. For more detail on methodology and data see an earlier version of this article published in the *Brazilian Political Science Review* 2015, *http://dx.doi.org/10.1590/1981-38212015000300018*

secure one, distinctively middle-class according to ordinary opinion and sociological canon.

In the wake of the global crisis and in the face of deflated expectations of economic and social stability of this group following economic stagnation and the cooling of the labour market, it seems more than a matter of semantic precision to unveil the condition of this chunk of households. Classificatory mis-specification, signalling the false premise that poverty and vulnerability might have been overcome, may have harmful consequences in terms of policy priorities and decisions.

Thus, in contrast to what has been assumed on the basis of average income criteria, the NMC social stratum is markedly heterogeneous. In terms of its consumption patterns, most of it is similar to the economically vulnerable or outright poor strata. So, we conclude that, from a sociological perspective that demands additional conditions besides income levels to identify social classes, it is a category mistake to call this entire social stratum a NMC. We conjecture that this may be consequential in terms of policy priorities and choices.

References

Birdsall, Nancy, Nora Lustig and Christian Meyer (2014). "The Strugglers: The New Poor in Latin America?", *World Development* 60: 132-46.

Bourdieu, Pierre (2012). *O Poder Simbólico*. Rio De Janeiro: Bertrand Brasil. p.322.

———. (2008). *A Distinção: Crítica Social Do Julgamento*. São Paulo: Edusp and Porto Alegre: Zouk. p.560.

Cornia, Giovanni Andrea (2014). *Falling Inequality in Latin America: Policy Changes and Lessons*. Oxford: Oxford University Press. p.400.

———. (2010). "Income Distribution Under Latin America's New Left Regimes", *Journal of Human Development and Capabilities* 11(1): 85-114.

Ferreira, Francisco H.G. et al. (2012). *Economic Mobility and the Rise on the Latin American Middle Class*. Washington: World Bank.

Hoffmann, Rodolfo (2007). "*Queda da Desigualdade da Distribuição de Renda no Brasil, de 1995 a 2005, E Delimitação dos Eelativamente Ricos em 2005*", in Ricardo Paes de Barros et al. (ed.), *Desigualdade de renda no Brasil: Uma Análise da Queda Recente*. Volume 1. Brasília: IPEA. Available in: *http://www.ipea.gov.br* (accessed in December 2011).

Huber, Evelyne, Thomas Mustillo and John D. Stephens (2008). "Politics and Social Spending in Latin America", *The Journal of Politics* 70(2): 420-36.

Huber, Evelyne and Juan Bogliaccini (2010). "Latin America", in F.G. Castles, S. Leibfried, J. Lewis, H. Obinger and C. Pierson (eds.), *The Oxford Handbook of the Welfare State*. Oxford: Oxford University Press. pp. 644-55.

IBGE (Instituto Brasileiro De Geografia E Estatística) (2010). *Pesquisa de Orçamentos Familiares* (POF), 2008, 2009 (Microdata). Available a: *http://www.ibge.gov.br*>

———. (2013). *Living Condition and Social Indicators*. Available in: *http://www.ibge.gov.br*

Kerstenetzky, Celia Lessa (Forthcoming). *Consumo Social E Crescimento Redistributivo: Notas Para Se Pensar Um Modelo De Crescimento Para O Brasil*. Revista De Economia Política.

Kerstenetzky, Celia Lessa and Christiane Uchôa (2013). "Moradia Inadequada, Escolaridade Insuficiente, Crédito Limitado: Em Busca Da Nova Classe Média", *Texto Para Discussão* N.076. Cede/Uff. May.

López-Calva, Luis Felipe and Nora Lustig (eds.) (2010). *Declining Inequality in Latin America: A Decade of Progress?* Washington D.c.: Brookings Institution Press. p.253.

Lustig, Nora, Luis Lopez-Calva and Eduardo Ortiz-Juarez (2013). "Deconstructing the Decline in Inequality in Latin America", in R. Devlin, J.L. Machinea and O. Echeverria (eds.), *Latin American Development in an Age of Globalization: Essays in Honor of Enrique V. Iglesias*.

Neri, Marcelo Côrtes (2008). *A Nova Classe Média*. Rio De Janeiro: Fundação Getúlio Vargas/IBRE/CPS. p.70.

———. (ed.) (2010). *A Nova Classe Média: O Lado Brilhante dos Pobres*. Rio De Janeiro: FGV/IBRE/CPS. *http://www.fgv.com.br*. Accessed in December.

———. (ed.) (2011). *A Nova Classe Média: O Lado Brilhante da Base da Pirâmide*. São Paulo: Saraiva. p.149.

O'Dougherty, Maureen (1998). "Auto-retratos da Classe Média: Hierarquias de "Cultura" e Consumo em São Paulo", *Dados. Rio de Janeiro* 41(2): 411-44. Available in; *http://www.scielo.br* (accessed in August 2010).

Parker, J. (2009). "Burgeoning Bourgeoisie" (Special report: The new middle class in emerging markets), *The Economist*. 14 February. Available in: *http://www.economist.com/node/13063298*

Pochmannn, Marcio (2012). *Nova Classe Média*? São Paulo: Boitempo. p.128.

Quadros, Waldir José De (2010). "Estrutura Sócio-Ocupacional No Brasil", *Revista Economia Contemporânea* 14(3): 443-68. Rio De Janeiro.

Rocha, Sonia (2013). "Pobreza No Brasil: A Evolução De Longo Prazo (1970-2011)", in J.P.R. Velloso (ed.), *Transformando Crise em Oportunidade*. Rio De Janeiro: Inae. pp. 428-29.

Savage, Mike (2012). "Status, Lifestyle and Taste", in Frank Trentmann (ed.), *The Oxford Handbook of The History Of Consumption*. Oxford: Oxford University Press. Pp. 551-567.

Scalon, Celi and André Salata (2012). "Uma Nova Classe Média No Brasil Da Última Década?", *O Debate a Partir Da Perspectiva Sociológica* 27(2): 387-407, May/August. Revista Sociedade E Estado.

Secretaria De Assuntos Estratégicos (2012). *Relatório de Definição sa Classe Média no Brasil*. Available at *www.sae.gov.br*. Accessed in July 2014.

Soares, Sergei (2011). "A Desigualdade De Renda De 1995 A 2009 E Tendências Recentes", *Texto Para Discussão N.051*. Cede/Uff. Available at: *http://www.proac.uff.br/Cede/Sites/Default/Files/Td51.Pdf*. Accessed in March 2015.

Sobrinho, G.G.F.X. (2011). "Classe C" e Sua Alardeada Ascensão: Nova? Classe? Média?", *Indicador Econômico Fee* 38(4): 67-80. Porto Alegre.

Souza, Amaury and Bolívar Lamounier (2010). *A Classe Média Brasileira: Ambições, Valores E Projetos De Sociedade*. Rio De Janeiro: Elsevier and Brasília: Confederação Nacional Da Indústria. p.175.

Souza, Jessé (2010). *Os Batalhadores Brasileiros: Nova Classe Média ou Nova Classe Trabalhadora?* Belo Horizonte: Ufmg. p.354.

Stillerman, Joel (2015). *The Sociology of Consumption: A Global Approach.* Cambridge: Polity Press. p.224.

The Economist (2013). "Towards the End of Poverty", *The Economist,* 01-07 June. Available at *http:// Www.economist.com/News/Leaders/21578665-Nearly-1-Billion-People-Have-Been-Taken-Out-Extreme-Poverty-20-Years-World-Should-Aim*. Accessed in November 2014.

Uchôa, Christiane and Celia Lessa Kerstenetzky (2012). "É a "nova classe média" classe média?", *Texto para Discussão n. 066*, CEDE/UFF. Niterói. p.10.

Elements of Social and Cultural Life of the New Middle Class

3

CARLA BARROS

The New Middle Class in Brazilian Telenovelas

Cultural and Symbolical Aspects

The purpose of this essay is to address issues related to changes in Brazilian society in the context of the so-called 'NMC' (new middle class) social strata, focusing on cultural and symbolic aspects. An analysis will be made in the field of media and consumption—specifically in the universe of Brazilian telenovelas—trying to identify indications of ongoing disputes and the diversity of daily practices.

In 2012, two fictional productions from TV Globo—Brazil's largest broadcasting media—the telenovelas *Avenida Brasil (*Brazil Avenue*)* and *Cheias de Charme (*Full of Charm*)*, were considered icons of the rise of the NMC, for having these strata as protagonists and target audience. The discussion from such media products allows a reflection on the character of the changes and the meanings of social representations concerning the so-called 'emerging classes'. The debate on culture, media and consumption can reveal the way in which the class hierarchies in current Brazilian society are reorganised.

Before going into the issue of the Brazilian telenovelas, I want to present some important aspects for the understanding of the mechanisms of social reproduction of that society.

In Brazil, people grow up being aware of two dimensions—the law as it is written to be universally applied to every individual, and the network of social relationships by which one can actually get one's needs met and get the things done that are necessary to survive (DaMatta 1991, Holanda 2012). The individual, as a social creation, and its main attributes—freedom and equality—are very frequently competing with the person and its relational world view. Modernity attributes intrinsic value to all elements of a system, despite their relations to each other. However, the attribution of intrinsic value to all individuals, independently of their social relations (as would be the case within a strictly modern framework), is very difficult in Brazil. Here, performance tends to be bypassed or combined with a person's 'social capital'. When we analyse it more closely, we perceive the existence of a series of informal institutions that accommodate the tension among the social actors. Therefore, ways around the state law can be eventually obtained through a range of factors related to conditions of wealth, social status and ties of family and friendship (DaMatta 1991).

Thus, individuals perceive their relations with others in a complementary and not antagonistic manner and social differences tend to be naturalised. In this hierarchical system, social changes are not accepted very easily, because the place that each one occupies in the social system implies rights that are seen as immutable. The hierarchical face that exists in Brazilian society implies a certain difficulty in assuming a confrontation or open conflict between the parties (DaMatta 1991, Kant 1999). Crisis is seen as a type of 'catastrophe' that should be quickly resolved to return harmony to the universe.

In this social system where 'each one has his place', a difficulty is perceived in dealing with egalitarian situations in which everyone is understood to have the same rights and responsibilities. Two examples are presented below to illustrate this need to create distinction. In the buildings of Brazil, there are two types of elevators: the 'social' and the 'service elevator'. It is expected that a maid, whether in uniform or not, will always take the service elevator, and there is considerable discomfort if she does not. Another example is found in the prison system: there are special prisons for those with university education (an 'oasis' within Brazil's chaotic penitentiary system), a privilege existing during the period in which these 'super-individuals' await judgement. This difficulty in dealing with egalitarian situations can be summarised in a phrase of anthropologist DaMatta (1991): "In Brazil, when two people are together, one is a boss." From the perspective of the lower classes, there is a sense of exclusion, of 'invisibility' and of social disqualification–which does not involve an a priori attribution made by a researcher, but of the way by which these groups perceive themselves in relation to broader society (Vaitsman 1997).

Thus Brazilian society likes to see itself as an inclusionary nation, in which differences coexist harmonically, as in the myth of the 'triangle of the three races', that shows Blacks, Whites and Indians to be symbolically complementary (DaMatta 1983). In other words, a view based on the idea of an 'harmonious encounter' among the three races, ignoring the long-standing slavery in Brazil and the genocide of the Brazilian Indians.

New Middle Class: Social Mobility in Brazilian Society?

There has been considerable discussion in Brazil about the emergence of a NMC (Neri 2008, Souza 2010, Pochmann 2012, Bartelt 2013), especially since 2008 when the middle classes were said to have reached half the country's population. Before this, a new interest in the lower and working classes had already been observed, triggered by the increased income of a substantial portion of this population after the implementation of the Plano Real economic measures of the 1990s.

An often-recurring theme in the analyses of the Brazilian situation has been the recognition of the centrality of the phenomenon of consumption as a mode of social inclusion–both in the interpretations of scholars as well as the perspective of individuals.

The 'new' individual-consumer from the emerging segments has been identified as a 'target audience' by marketing and advertising professionals. Since LIGs (low income groups) did not have the goods needed to include them fully in the consumer society, they were even not considered to be 'consumers'. So, in the universe of marketing, there was a previous context of 'invisibility' of the LIGs until the late 1980s, what later came to be called the NMC—or 'Class C', how the emerging segments are also called in Brazil—began to take shape.

It is worth remembering that the issue of emergence of a NMC came to be discussed not only in Brazil, but in various other poor and developing countries (Fernandes 2006, Pelle 2007, Kornegay and Bohler-Muller 2013, Nordenstreng and Thussu 2015). Since the year 2000 in particular, business magazines around the world began to publish articles aimed at understanding and discussing new ways to explore this 'new market'.

At the same time, even if more slowly, academics from the fields of sociology and anthropology, in particular, began to look at the issue little by little, exploring economical and sociological themes related to the emergence of this 'new class'.

The discussion that has created the greatest polarisation among scholars of the new Brazilian context is that which refers to the very idea of a NMC, a term coined by economist Neri (2008). Neri's research, based on a quantitative approach, showed in what way a large portion of the population improved their living conditions in terms of income, employment and consumption.

In this debate on the NMC, there is a central confrontation between economic analyses that emphasise the expressive economic rise of a portion of the population—in addition to other factors, such as increased formal employment—as a prerequisite of true social mobility, and sociological analyses (Souza 2010) that affirm that the concept of social class should consider other criteria beyond just income.

This essay agrees with Souza (2010) in its analysis of the rise of the NMC in Brazil, avoiding a merely 'economic' approach and adopting the view that in order to identify a group within a certain class, it is necessary to analyse factors such as its genesis, its world views, lifestyles, modes of consumption, language, habitus, cultural, social and symbolic capital.

A significant increase in the consumption power of some segments of LIGs has occurred (Kerstenetzky et al. 2015), showing new priorities in their budgets, like more spending on better child education and on women's beauty treatment.

Furthermore, the question of religious adherence is of great importance in the debate on social mobility. Brazil, a country with a Catholic tradition, has seen an enormous growth in the number of Evangelical Christians, especially among the poorest. The idea of restricted social mobility was always resolved very well within Catholic fatalism, which accepted with resignation the world 'as it is', as formed by rich and poor in a complementary relationship. By contrast, the protestant vision in the Brazilian context, especially the neo-pentecostal churches as Igreja Universal do Reino de Deus (IURD), emphasise the value of work and the constant search for 'improvement of life'.

Another aspect to be highlighted is that, from an ecological perspective, a timid increase of environmental awareness can be sensed among youths from the emerging consumer segments, due to the presence of ecological education in schools. In general, the most present sentiment among the emerging groups is that 'now it is our time to consume', and not to think about the negative consequences of consumption. It is thus important to observe the young generation, which seem to be growing up with references from two worlds—unchecked consumption and ecological awareness.

Telenovelas in Brazilian Culture

Here is adopted the term 'telenovela'—and not 'soap-opera'—because the characteristics of Brazilian telenovelas are quite different from American 'soap-operas'. Telenovelas are fictional programmes of enormous success on Brazilian TV—they are broadcast nightly for an average of seven months at Prime-Time (9 p.m.), and have the largest audiences and advertising revenues. People of all social classes watch telenovelas, although not everyone likes to admit that they watch, because they are considered to be of 'low artistic quality'. In addition, the telenovelas are a comment on the nation (Lopes 2003, Newcomb 2007): their characters and plots have historically portrayed the changes in the country. Thus, viewers can discuss the country and their lives based on what they see in the telenovelas–the economic and social changes, the decadence of the business elite and daily morality, for instance. The phenomenon of the 'second screen' is also very important in Brazil. This consists in using social media to comment on what is being watched in another media, such as TV. People—especially middle-class individuals—watch the telenovelas and use Twitter in particular to comment on the chapters, in general in a funny and critical manner.

One of the biggest successes of this kind of fictional product was *Caminho das Índias*, (India: A Love Story),[1] a contemporary story set in Brazil and India. *Caminho das Índias* was the winner of 2009 International Emmy Awards for Best Telenovela and showcases Indian mores in a story of forbidden love between a Dalit man and an upper-caste woman, exploring the clash between different cultures and traditions. It was produced by TV Globo in Brazil and proved to be an astounding success. This telenovela used various cultural props from Bollywood, including the musical score, and has been broadcasted in more than 100 countries, but curiously, not in India itself. Thinking in terms of global flows, Rai (2015), in an interesting article, articulates *Caminho das Indias* as a new form of south-south media flow and a viable alternate media space.

Telenovelas permitted, over the years, the consolidation of conventions of narrative that are broadly dominated by the audience, as there is certainty that at the end of the story, good will triumph over evil. At the same time, different interpretations are possible because everybody 'knows how' to watch telenovelas in Brazil. Here the idea of the shared repertory (Canclini 2001, Hamburger 2014) comes in, through which people from different social classes comment and discuss the content of several programmes, in particular, of telenovelas, where the most important is one's own feeling of sharing, in a hierarchical society like the Brazilian one. In a country with strong oral tradition and intense sociability (DaMatta 1991) such as Brazil, just as important as watching the telenovela is the opportunity to talk about it. The concept of shared repertory does not imply in a consensus of sense; on the contrary, attracts attention to the field of negotiations of significations that can be understood when the focus of analyses falls on the reception.

Through the telenovela, as Almeida (2003) stressed in an ethnographic study, is possible that determined social segments

1. See *Caminho das Indias* international trailer: *http://www.youtube.com/watch?v=BG3DT1Y5Kzo)* and scenes from *Caminho das Indias*: *https://www.youtube.com/watch?v=_D-KgAJMwVk; https://www.youtube.com/watch?v=qKTEPH43xjc* (accessed 9 January 2014)

take knowledge of the lifestyle of other groups, what they would not have access in any other way. This sharing allows, through the conversation about the telenovela, the knowledge of the way how the relations among the social actors are established. Giving an example, in a previous ethnographic study (Barros 2007) about the world view of a group of maids, one of the women researched, Maria José (fictitious name), told me that her daughter has asked after viewing a scene of the telenovela Celebridade (Celebrity, aired by TV Globo in 2003), where the character Beatriz treats her maid in a rude way at the time of asking for a drink: "Mam, there at work." Mrs. Regina [Maria José's mistress] speaks: "Maid, bring me a glass of water!! Do you have to put everything in her hand?" So, Maria José answered: "No, no ... she calls me by my name, like this: Maria José, could you please bring some juice?; and I don't put everything in her hand; she goes to the kitchen to get the things alone, water, juice..."

Another important aspect to be highlighted refers to the understanding of how the viewing of telenovelas allows an intense learning towards immersion into consumer society (Almeida 2003, Barros 2007). One learns in the first place to realise how the goods are 'adequate' to express social distinctions–products appear inside determined social contexts, being consumed by specific people. Products are presented too and they are desired exactly for belonging to the universe of other segments. This 'learning' can be related to the discussion of aesthetic standards transported in some programmes, and serve as a discussion and exchange of information between individuals from different social classes.

Changes in Representation of Low-income Groups in Recent Telenovelas

In the telenovela *Babilônia*, screened in TV Globo's prime-time in 2015, the villain of the story states, after a confrontation with a 'favelada' (a pejorative term used to denominate favela residents), the heroine Regina: "The worst type of poor person that exists is the proud poor." Meanwhile, an older Brazilian expression, warned: "You can leave the favela, but the favela will never leave you." To a certain point, these statements summarise part of the traditional perception of the dominant classes about LIGs.

In 2012, TV Globo aired two telenovelas, which enjoyed enormous audience successes: *Avenida Brasil (*Brazil Avenue*)* and *Cheias de Charme (*Full of Charm*)*. The latter follows the story of three maids that band together to form a successful music group. *Avenida Brasil*, in turn, was an extraordinary audience phenomenon (Antunes 2012) by focusing on low middle class characters that live in the poor suburbs of Rio de Janeiro, instead of focusing on affluent people`s lives. The 'real' Avenida Brasil has an important local significance, as it is the main thoroughfare linking Rio de Janeiro's rich city centre with the poor distant peripheral suburban neighbourhoods.

The plot of this telenovela revolves around the character Rita, who was abused in childhood by her former stepmother, Carminha. To get revenge, Rita adopts the name Nina to take a job as a cook in Carminha's house. She winds up feeling the pain of the maids working at the house, who were constantly being humiliated by their employer. In a previous study (Barros 2015), I showed how the telenovela allows a collective conversation: Watching the telenovela on their mobile phone heading home, a certain 'class feeling' arose among a group of maids, and the women criticised the authoritarian and arrogant attitude of Carminha's character. It became a time that they could also criticise their employers and their excessive arrogance towards the maids, as the conversation revolved around their real situations. Conversations about television programmes may prove to be a privileged type of dialogue, opportunities to exchange information, moral judgements, and knowledge of new lifestyles between the worlds of the maids and their employers (Barros 2007).

These two telenovelas were announced as if they were showing a vision of the changing lifestyles of the emerging groups—now as protagonists of the plot—and there was a conscious effort to present this kind of plot to reach those groups for the first time.

Nevertheless, this is not really true—TV Globo had previously presented various telenovelas in which the main characters came from LIGs, as Moura (2015) showed. If these two telenovelas were not unprecedented in terms of the roles of the protagonists, what had changed in the representations about LIGs on Brazilian telenovelas?

On telenovelas prior to the rise of the NMC, the opportunity for social ascension was remote—it could occur by chance (as in the telenovela *Pecado Capital* (Capital Sin, aired by TV Globo in a first version in 1975, about the character Carlão, who finds a fortune in cash in a suitcase left in a taxi), or through a relationship with an individual of the upper classes, as in the telenovela of the character Nice, Anjo Mau (Bad Angel, aired by TV Globo in a first version in 1976), the 'bad' nanny who has a plan to rise socially by marrying her boss.

In the series *A Diarista* (The Maid, aired by TV Globo 2004 in 2007), which spoke of the adventures and misfortunes of Marinete, a maid, every time that the main character consumed according to middle and upper class standards, the consequences were disastrous—humiliation and punishment for the 'reproachable' behaviour—and she wound up returning to her former class condition.

In more recent telenovelas, as the referred *Avenida Brasil* and *Cheias de Charme*, the representations of LIGs suffer notable changes. Some of them are highlighted next:

First, the characters who rose economically during the plot were proud of their origins, and did not want to change their lifestyles. Giving two examples of the telenovela *Avenida Brazil*: the characters Tufão (a successful soccer player) and Mona Lisa (a very successful businesswoman in the beauty salon sector) want to remain in the Divino neighbourhood, located in a not very 'noble' region of the city, because they are recognized there and have a happy life and a lifestyle that they are accustomed to.

Secondly, the characters from the NMC are 'warriors' who overcome the difficulties presented to them through effort, work and talent–that is, the improvement in their economic condition comes from a meritocratic form, and no longer by chance.

Thirdly, the characters who are protagonists of the rising popular classes at some moment have an open confrontation with their former dominators (the stories focus on feminine characters). There is space in these telenovelas for a depiction of personal and social revenge—the maids, who in the past were regularly humiliated, subvert their condition and come to occupy a place of power, so that their old bosses become their servants.

And lastly, consumption appears as an important indicator in the story, revealing the changes underway—the emergent members of the NMC now have access to goods and services that had been beyond their reach. The change in the representations of the LIGs points, among other aspects, to a new perception of these individuals, now as consumers. It is as if in a previous moment the formerly 'poor' did not have this status, because they only used their money to maintain their own physical survival—now with the changes underway, the emerging individuals are seen as 'able to make choices', a fundamental requirement for consumption in the modernity (Slater 1997).

Final Considerations

A social dilemma arises with the rise of the NMC, and with the emergence of new media representations of these groups as we seen in the case of telenovelas. Some groups from the upper and middle classes strongly resent the presence of the broader social classes in their formerly exclusive spaces. The more privileged social groups feel the need to establish new borders of distinction. This is not new, but the question is: to what extent does this situation generate a degree of social discomfort for the rising classes, who may feel undesired in the new spaces where they move in?

One example of this new context of social dispute between classes can be found in the numerous complaints in discussion forums of cable TV operators, arguing that the massive arrival of NMC audience on pay TV would 'decrease the quality' of programming because of the increase of dubbed (synchronised into Portuguese) content. In Brazil, to watch dubbed content on pay TV is considered to some extent as an indication of lower social status. Thus, some internet users began to express themselves—often in a very prejudiced way—against the effects of the growing access by the lower classes to a upper pattern of consumption.[2]

In this sense, the field of consumption or of media consumption, specially, can be seen as an arena of distinction, power and symbolic disputes—as Bourdieu (1979) has indicated—where the more privileged classes seek to maintain their role of establishing borders and defining where and how the LIGs can consume in physical or media spaces. This example of manifestations from segments of middle and upper class against the access of emerging groups in the pay TV shows how those accusations are like a 'social weapon' (Bourdieu 1979) that distinguishes groups based on a process of social disqualification that appears to be extremely natural.

If on the one hand, it was highlighted the resistance of some groups to the economic rise of the poorest, on the other we can consider that something important is at stake in Brazil today, with the much discussed rise of the NMC. As seen in this article, a look at the recent media, in particular the telenovelas, shows how the scripts present commentaries about the country and its transformation, and reveal new representations of the emerging groups: 'consumers', 'warriors' or 'entrepreneurs', who assume the conflict when necessary, as they simultaneously preserve their identity and traditional way of life. If the telenovelas are, in a way, a 'comment' on the nation (Lopes 2003), it is important to monitor the social dynamics of everyday life

---

2. The following discourse found in an online forum is an example of this kind of extremely prejudiced attitude against the access of emerging groups to pay TV: People who like dubbed content are stupid!! It's obvious that the more that class C adheres to the taste for cable TV, the worse will be the level of content and quality of programming. It's already getting worse. The signs are there. Look at FX and other channels, [they are] dubbing everything and even advertising this as if it was something good, 'programming in your language'. I have nothing against it, as long as they respect the more intelligent people, and place a dual option for audio and captions so that no one will miss out. I hate dubbed content. More intelligent people perceive the blatant difference in quality of the audio and sounds with the original content, than the shitty dubbed version. Shout out: down with dubbing! If you don't like it watch open TV! Only idiots and lazy people like dubbed shows...I don't like the idea of class C migrating to cable TV because it will only get worse, because these people's taste is unfortunately dubious... (Rafael T. [fictitious identification], SKY TV forum, 09-08-2011). Available: *http://forum.outerspace.com.br/index.php?threads/revista-%C3%89poca-afirma-que-%E2%80%9Ca-dublagem-venceu-as-legendas%E2%80%9D.286049/page-4* (accessed 12 June 2014).

that point to the possibility of change of historical inequalities and of believing that the social world is not immutable.

References

Almeida, H.B. (2003). *Telenovela, consumo e gênero*. Bauru, SP: EDUSC.

Antunes, A. (2012). "Brazilian Telenovela 'Avenida Brasil' Makes Billions by Mirroring its Viewers' Lives", *http://www.forbes.com/sites/andersonantunes/2012/10/19/brazilian-telenovela-makes-billions-by-mirroring-its-viewers-lives/#3590cc1612ba* (accessed 28 May 2014)

Barros, C. (2007). *Trocas, Hierarquia e Mediação: Dimensões Culturais do Consumo em um Grupo de Empregadas Somésticas*. Tese de Doutorado. Rio de Janeiro: COPPEAD/UFRJ.

_________. (2015). "From Production to Consumption: Cultural Diversity in the Collective Uses of Technology among Low Income Groups", *Comunicação, Mídia e Consumo* 12(35): 129-48.

Bartelt, D. (Org.) (2013). *A 'Nova Classe Media' no Brasil como conceito e projeto politico*. Rio de Janeiro: Fundação Heinrich Boll.

Bourdieu, P. (1979). *La Distinction* . Paris: Minuit.

Canclini, N.G. (2001). *Consumers and Citizens: Globalization and Multicultural Conflicts*. Minneapolis: University of Minnesota Press.

DaMatta, R. (1983). *Relativizando: Uma introdução à Antropologia Social*. Petrópolis, RJ: Vozes.

__________. (1991). *Carnivals, Rogues and Heroes: An Interpretation of the Brazilian Dilemma*. Notre Dame: University of Notre Dame Press.

Fernandes, L. (2006). *India's New Middle Class: Democratic Politics in an Era of Economic Reform*. Minneapolis: University of Minnesota Press.

Hamburger, E. (2014). "Telenovelas, Gender, and Genre", in C. Carter, L. Steiner and L. McLaughin (eds.), *The Routledge Companion of Media & Gender*. New York: Routledge.

Holanda, S.B. (2012). *Roots of Brazil*. Notre Dame: University of Notre Dame Press.

Kant, R. (1999). "Polícia, Justiça e Sociedade no Brasil: Uma Abordagem Comparative dos Modelos de Administração de Conflitos no Espaço Público", *Revista de Sociologia e Política* 13: 23-38.

Kerstenetzky, C., C. Uchôa and N. Silva (2015). "The Elusive New Middle Class in Brazil", *Brazilian Political Science Review* 9(3): 21-41.

Kornegay, F. and N. Bohler-Muller (2013). *Laying the BRICS of a New Global Order: From Yekaterinburg 2009 to Ethekwini 2013*. Pretoria: Africa Institute of South Africa.

Lopes, M.I.V. (2003). "A Telenovela Brasileira: Uma Narrativa Sobre a Nação", *Revista Comunicação & Educação* 25: 17-34.

Moura, I.G. (2015). *Mulheres com Classe: Mídia e Classe Social num Brasil em Ascensão. Dissertação de Mestrado*. Niterói, RJ: PPGCOM/UFF.

Neri, M. (coord.) (2008). *A Nova Classe Média*. Rio de Janeiro: FGV/IBRE/CPS.

Newcomb, H. (2007). *Television: The Critical View*. 7th ed. New York: Oxford University Press.

Nordenstreng, K. and D.K. Thussu (Ed.) (2015). *Mapping BRICS Media*. New York: Routledge.

Pelle, S. (2007). *Understanding Emerging Markets: Building Business BRIC by Brick*. New Delhi: Response Books.

Pochmann, M. (2012). *Nova Classe Media? O Trabalho na Base da Pirâmide Social Brasileira*. São Paulo: Boitempo.

Rai, S. (2015). "Made in Bollywood: Indian Popular Culture in Brazil's Caminho das Indias", *Jump Cut: A Review of Contemporary Media* 56: 1-18.

Slater, D. (1997). *Consumer Culture & Modernity*. Cambridge: Polity Press.

Souza, J. (2010). *Os Batalhadores Brasileiro: Nova Classe Média ou Nova Classe Trabalhadora?* Belo Horizonte: Editora UFMG.

Vaitsman, J. (1997). "Pluralidade de Mundos Entre Mulheres de Baixa Renda", *Estudos Feministas* 2: 303-19.

4

SURINDER S. JODHKA

Caste and the Indian Middle Class

The 'middle class' as a category of social classification and analysis is not new to India. It was during the British colonial period, in the early decades of the 19th century, that the term began to be used for a newly emergent group of people in urban centres, mostly in Calcutta, Bombay and Madras, three cities founded by the colonial masters. Over time, this middle class spread its presence to other urban centres of the subcontinent as well. After Independence from colonial rule, the size of the Indian middle class grew manifold. This time again, it was largely through state action and expansion. The developmental state expanded its bureaucratic reach and invested massively in public sector enterprises and laid the infrastructure for social progress and economic growth. It opened many more schools, universities, hospitals and a range of other institutions required for building a modern nation-state.

Beginning with the 1990s, the story of the Indian middle class witnessed a major shift. The pace and patterns of its growth changed with the introduction of economic reforms. The new policies of liberalisation encouraged private capital to expand its spheres of investment. India's growing integration into the global economy and its cultural flows also enabled many more Indians to benefit through the opening of newer avenues of employment and mobility. By incentivising private capital and encouraging foreign capital to invest in India, the 'neo-liberal' economic reforms helped India accelerate the pace of its economic growth, from sluggish rate of around 2-3 per cent during the first four decades after independence to around 7 or 8 per cent per annum after the 1990s.

At another level, this acceleration of economic growth and expansion of the Indian middle-classes, both in numbers as well as in influence, has quite fundamentally transformed the structure of Indian society and its economy, from one characterised by 'a sharp contrast between a small elite and a large impoverished mass, to being one with substantial intermediate classes' (Sridharan 2008: 1). However, much of the popular discourse on the Indian middle class is focused around numbers and income categories.[1] Mostly framed in economic terms, this discourse tends to focus on the proportions of Indian population that could be described as middle class almost exclusively in terms of their earnings and expenditure levels, current and prospective. By implication, it tends to focus primarily on their consuming potentials in the emerging markets.

While incomes and consumption cultures are indeed important aspects of social and economic life, 'middle class' is not simply an economic category, but also a relational structure. The growth and expansion of the middle class also indicates a move towards the emergence of a new kind of society. As sociologists Landry and March (2011: 374) rightly argue, "the emergence of a middle class marks a decisive moment in a nation's history. It indicates an open rather than a closed opportunity structure, a society with the chance of upward mobility and achievement beyond subsistence".

This becomes particularly important in a society like India, which has been historically marked by rigid hierarchies of status and rank. The most important category in this context is indeed the institution of caste, which has not only moulded social and ritual life of the common people but has also shaped occupations, opportunities and rewards. Caste produces an environment of exclusions, segregations and avoidance, a culture marked by rigid status hierarchies and imperious structures of authority. Thus, the questions that become relevant in this context are: how does the emergence of a modern middle-class negotiate with the pre-existing realities of caste and cultures of rigid hierarchies, or in other words, has the rise of a middle class been accompanied by a social transformation as envisaged in the popular sociological theories of change and as promised by the Indian

1. Estimations of its proportion in the total population of India vary a lot, from a meagre 5 per cent to 25 or 30 per cent (see Jodhka and Prakash 2016: 104-39).

Constitution? What has been the nature of mobility into middle-class social locations across various caste groups and categories? How have the local cultures of hierarchy and difference influenced the emergent category of 'middle class' in contemporary India?

This essay attempts to look at the contemporary history of middle class formations in India and the dynamics of its relationship with caste. In the following sections, I provide a brief introduction to the caste system, followed by a broad overview of the patterns of its change over the past four or five decades. The next sections discuss the three phases in the history of Indian middle class followed by a concluding section that discusses the empiric of relationship between caste, and middle class, and manner in which the former has shaped formation of the latter.

Caste in India

The textbook view of caste has tended to see it in cultural terms, a uniquely Indian practice that fundamentally distinguished the traditional social organisation of India from the modern West. In this popular understanding, caste is an ancient institution of India, based on the ideas of *Varna, Karma* and *Dharma* pronounced in a classic Hindu text called the *Manusmriti*. These ideas translated into a hierarchical society, structured around the notions of purity and pollution. The *Varna* system divided the Hindus into four or five mutually exclusive and hierarchically ranked categories with the Brahmins at the top, followed by the Kshatriyas, the Vaishyas and the *Shudras*. Beyond the four *varnas* were the *achhoots* (the untouchables). Even though the hierarchy was inscribed in ritual terms, it also structured almost every aspect of social and economic life and had survived without much change for centuries.

While this popular view of caste still survives in many textbooks of sociology and Indian society, it has been very widely critiqued, conceptually as well as empirically, and has been abandoned by most serious students of the Indian society. Scholars working on India have convincingly shown that it was primarily Western writers, the Orientalists and colonial administrators, who constructed such a view in the 19th century. As these scholars argue, the colonial ideologues wanted to portray the region as having been eternally stuck in its cultural past and incapable of progressing on the path of history by itself (Cohn 1996, Dirks 2001, Guha 2013). Such a view, thus, provided a built-in justification for the colonial subjugation of India.

The empirical scholarship on the subject also questions the simplified religion-centric view of caste. Sociologists, social anthropologists and historians have extensively documented the fluid nature of hierarchies and the diverse modes of its formations. While hierarchies existed on ground, their structures and operations varied significantly across different regions of the subcontinent. Caste had also not been a static and closed cultural reality, which reproduced itself only through religious ritual and traditional beliefs. Being a part of social life, caste differences were structured and shaped also by economic processes, ecological possibilities and the nature of political regimes of a given region (see Srinivas 1955, 1962, Gupta 2000, Betielle 1986, Charsley and Karanth 1998, Jodhka 2012, 2015).

The popular Orientalist view of caste also shared its notion of social change with functionalist theories on the subject that predicted its demise through the process of modernisation. The colonial rulers had presumably unleashed such a process by introducing Western style secular education, industrial technology and modern frames of governance. Interestingly, many among the early Indian nationalists also took rather easily to this evolutionist view of caste and its possible modern futures. Independence from colonial rule, many of them believed would accelerate the process of modernisation of social life through economic growth and democratic politics, guided by a liberal-progressive Constitution and gradually end caste.

Changing Caste

India's independence from the colonial rule did accelerate the process of social and economic change, and these changes have also had a significant impact on the social order of caste. As I have argued elsewhere (Jodhka 2015, 2016), a variety of efforts and processes from 'below', from 'above' and from the 'side' have brought these changes about. Persistent and active mobilisations by those located lower down in the hierarchical order have gone a long way in delegitimising the ideology and cultural value of the traditions associated with caste. The values and aspirations for dignified life as citizens of a democratic country have successfully eroded the earlier notions of karma and despondency almost everywhere in the subcontinent. Since the early 1980s, such mobilisations from the margins of Indian society have only grown, and some have gone to the extent of describing them as a source of a 'silent revolution' (Jaffrelot 2003). Notwithstanding diversities and divergences, growing politicisation of the 'backwards' and increasing assertions by the Dalits, the ex-untouchables have fundamentally altered the grammar of Indian social and political life (Pai 2002).

After Independence, the democratic Indian state institutionalised a system of quotas or reservations, for the most deprived communities and listed them as SCs (scheduled castes). Similarly, some other social groups who were seen to be deprived because of their relative isolation from the mainland India were classified as STs (scheduled tribes). Under this system, seats approximating to their proportions in the Indian population were kept reserved for them in the state funded educational institutions, government jobs and legislative bodies, up to the highest level, the Indian Parliament. The constitutional provisions in form of reservation policy have not only enabled a process of social and economic mobility among the ex-untouchable castes but have also been instrumental in producing a modern leadership from within these communities.

India's quota system has expanded over the years. In addition to the quotas mandated by the national government, some provincial governments have had their own quota regimes. Following recommendations of various commissions set up by the Government of India to identify communities other than those listed as SCs, who remain 'backward' the Union government also decided to reserve jobs and seats in state funded educational institutions for the OBCs (other backward classes). Even though the Indian courts have fixed a ceiling of 50 per cent seats for quotas, the demand for quotas has continued to grow. Such state policies and other initiatives from 'above' have also changed caste.

Further, the larger processes and nature of social, economic and political transformations taking place in the country too have impacted caste relations in a variety of different ways. For example, the agrarian transformations ushered in by the success of the Green Revolution in some parts of the country, and the development of industry in urban centres have made many of the traditional caste occupations redundant. At the same time, they have also provided new opportunities for employment outside the older economic order. State investments in rural development and agricultural growth have provided a positive impetus to this process. The Indian agriculture gradually moved towards formalised and capitalist frames of production and social organisation. The traditional hierarchies and old structures of dependency, including the traditional hierarchies of caste gradually declined (Mendelsohn 1993, Srinivas 2003, Jodhka 2002, Charsley and Karanth 1998, Kapur et al. 2010).

Empirics of the Indian Middle Class

As discussed above, the historical context to the birth of Indian middle class was the need of the British colonial rulers' for a class of lower level native bureaucracy that would assist them rule over the vast regions of the subcontinent that they had come to occupy by the early 19th century. They were to be 'a class of persons Indian in blood and colour, but English in tastes, in opinions, in morals and in intellect.[2]'

As the popular narrative goes, thanks to these policies, such a class did emerge, which mediated between the colonial masters and local masses. These middle class individuals also became a vehicle for the spread of 'superior' Western culture and its message of modernity, including the ideas of democracy, which also became a source of conflict between the newly emerged middle class Indians and the colonial rulers, eventually unfolding into the movement for independence. According to this common sense, the Western educated middle-class of India continues to be a modernising social

---

2. "Macaulay's Minute on Education, 2 February 1835", Available at *http://home.iitk.ac.in/~hcverma/Article/Macaulay-Minutes.pdf*. Accessed 8 August 2014.

category, an important agent of positive social change in the Indian society, where the hold of tradition continues to be a critical source of its backwardness.

While the colonial context of its origin is indeed a fact, this celebratory representation of the Indian middle-class is a myth that, to a large extent, is produced by members of the Indian middle-classes themselves. It helps them perpetuate their position of privilege and power. The actual history of the Indian middle-class is far more complex and different.

The Indian middle-class did not just emerge as a modernising agent out of its traditional moorings. On the contrary there were many instances where it championed 'tradition'. Instead of being individualised and modern, its members actively represented and constructed local level 'sectarian' identities. The British did not always wish to change the pre-existing social realities. They often absorbed them into their policy frames and reinforced, or even strengthened, the pre-existing structures of social relations. In other words, they simultaneously transformed and reinforced the pre-existing structures of power relations. The Indian middle-classes actively participated in all these processes (see Jodhka and Prakash 2016).

The social base of recruitment of this class was also quite narrow. The British initiated a process of educating the 'natives' by opening schools and colleges in different parts of the subcontinent. These educational institutions first appeared in the new colonial cities like Calcutta, Bombay and Madras. Local communities, particularly those with resources and high social standing, responded enthusiastically and sent their children for 'modern' education. Unlike their Western counterparts, the social origins of this class did not lie in industry and trade, which remained under control of the British companies or local trading communities, such as the Marwaris, Khatris and Banias. While most of the educated modern professionals came from relatively privileged social backgrounds and had some connections with land, they generally occupied intermediary positions in the prevailing tenurial structure. In terms of their position in the traditional ritual hierarchies, they almost all came from relatively upper segments of the traditional caste system.

Some rich Indian families even sent their children abroad, mostly to England, for higher education in leading British universities, such as Oxford, Cambridge and London, with many returning home after securing degrees. These new native elite also brought with them modern ideas of 'liberalism' and 'democracy' that had become popular in the West after the French Revolution. Thus, they became carriers of not only British cultural values but also of modern ideas of freedom, equality and democracy. Those educated in local colleges were mostly absorbed in the colonial administrative structure. These jobs in the colonial government carried a 'high' social status and became a route to acquiring middle-class positions. Over the years, a new class emerged in India. Apart from those employed in the administrative jobs of the British government, it included independent professionals, such as, lawyers, medics and teachers. The size of this 'educated middle-class' thus continued to grow during the second half of the 19th century.

In some regions of the subcontinent, these newly educated individuals initiated a variety of social reform movements during the 19th and early 20th centuries. The middle-class leaders of these movements worked for negotiated adaptations of Western modernity. They underlined the need for retaining, what they saw as the core of the traditional religious belief and culture while simultaneously learning from Western and Christian cultures. The narrative was to selectively reinvent past tradition and glorify it in order to claim its superiority over Western Christianity. This reinvention and glorification of its ancient past also implied acceptance and advocacy of 'tradition', albeit in a reformed format, which included the hierarchical social order of *varna* and caste, presided over by the Brahmin. Unlike in the West, where the middle-classes were part of the processes of secularisation and individualisation, members of the Indian middle-classes invested in their community identities and many worked actively towards reinvention of their perceived traditions through 'reform' movements. Their quest for the so-called social reforms eventually produced 'new', and sometimes more rigid, cultural boundaries across and within the pre-existing communities (see Jodhka and Prakash 2016: 48-54).

As the middle-class expanded in size, its political aspirations also grew. It aspired to greater share in the state power. It is in this context that middle-class began to articulate the idea of India as an independent nation-state. However, they recognised the need of a cultural project, of producing a larger 'ethnic' and cultural community, beyond the simple agenda of social and religious reform of local level religious communities. Partha Chatterjee describes this as 'classicisation of tradition', which could become the foundational category of Indian nationalism (Chatterjee 1993). The Indian middle class thus campaigned and mobilised for a politics of citizenship by actively pursuing a sectarian agenda, even when it invoked ideas of democracy and modernity.

Independence and After

Independence from colonial rule in 1947 was an important turning point for the Indian middle class story. The new elite that inherited power from the colonial rulers largely represented the upper layers of Indian society, both in terms of caste as well as class. However, they were also confronted with the task of working with diversities and differences of Indian society, its poverty and disparities, the challenge of violence and communal harmony. The fault-lines were many and difficult to deal with. The framing of Indian constitution with B.R. Ambedkar, an untouchable by caste, as the Chair of its Drafting Committee had an important symbolic value for the new nation as it tried to signal that independent democratic India was to transcend caste. Membership of the Constituent Assembly also represented other forms of social diversities. Besides laying down a framework for a democratic governance system, the Indian constitution also recognised caste as a continued source of disparities and deprivations and put in place a set of measures that would work towards levelling the playing fields.

Even though India chose to follow the path of Western-style liberal democracy, it did so with a difference. Jawaharlal Nehru, the first Prime Minister of India, had also been inspired by the achievements of the then socialist-block countries. He initiated planning for development. Democracy and development were to together help India move on the path of modernisation with the Indian state playing an active role in creating an enabling environment for economic growth with social justice. It even initiated direct participation in setting-up modern industry. Besides investing directly in public sector industrial units, the state also spent a lot of resources on laying down institutional and material infrastructure required to extend its physical reach to diverse communities and regions of the subcontinent. To pursue these activities, the state required skilled human resources. The state sector thus emerged the biggest employer and the most important site for middle class expansion. The number of those employed in the state sector went up from 5.23 million in 1956 to 15.48 million in 1980. Even though employment in the private sector also expanded, it grew at a slower rate, from 5.05 million in 1960 to 7.24 million in 1980 (see Jodhka and Prakash 2016: 76).

As indicated above, the introduction of economic reforms in 1990s quite significantly changed the pace and pattern of economic growth in India with a clear shift towards the private sector. This is also reflected in the nature and patterns of employment. Though available data of organised sector employment reflects that the state sector still has more people on its rolls than the private sector, the trend had clearly changed. During 2010-11, total employment in state-supported sectors was 17.55 million, lower than what it was 20 years back in 1990-91 (19.14 million). In contrast, the organised private sector, though employing lesser numbers still (11.45 millions) in 2010-11, had grown significantly over the past 20 years (7.68 millions in 1990-91).

Caste and Middle Class Mobility

How do these dynamics of numbers and economic changes intersect with social processes? As is evident from the discussion above, the available historical research suggests that the rise of middle class in India during the British colonial period did not dent caste hierarchies. On the contrary, the middle class grew within the pre-existing ascriptive frames of communities and identities.

Over the past century and more, social and economic structures, including those of caste, have seen many changes. However, while change in relational and ideological sphere is apparent, the reality of caste does not seem to be going away. Inequalities across caste groups have persisted, and in some cases they have sharpened. Caste continues to matter beyond its conventional sphere of influence, the village, its ritual life and its agrarian economy. Even after moving out of the rural, into an urban job or a business, individuals often remain tied to their caste. Those from the upper stratum of caste hierarchy find caste to be a useful resource in the urban context and often feel comfortable in company of fellow caste men and women. Almost all of them marry within their caste kinship. They form caste associations and set-up caste-community based business cartels. Even when the growing anonymity of urban economy makes it difficult to sustain such monopolies, kinship networks continue to play a critical role in the reproduction of urban business (Iyer et al. 2013).

The modern corporate sector is also not free from caste. Even when they manifestly claim to be caste-blind, they care for the social and family backgrounds of their staff. They often screen out candidates from communities such as the SCs, the Muslims and those from 'rustic' rural backgrounds (Jodhka and Newman 2007). A recent study based on a sample of 1000 companies reported that as many as 92.6 per cent of the board members of the Indian Corporate houses are from the upper castes (44.6% Brahmins and 46% from various Vaishya castes). In contrast, the SCs and STs together made for only 3.5 per cent. Even the proportion of OBCs, who make for nearly half of India's total population, was quite negligible (3.8%) (Ajit et al. 2012). At the upper-end of the corporate management, 'caste diversity is non-existent'. The limited volume of empirical literature we have on social mobility in India reinforces the point that caste indeed works to block those located at the lower end of the caste hierarchy (Kumar et al. 2002, Thorat and Newman 2010, Vaid and Heath 2010).

The urban upper castes that are otherwise located in modern spaces work hard to preserve the privileges that come with caste, construct boundaries around the middle class locations. In a recently published book (Fuller and Narasimhan 2015) based on a prolonged fieldwork among the Brahmins of Tamil Nadu, exploring the changes brought about by their social mobility and migrations from rural settlements to urban centres over the past century and more, Fuller and Narasimhan, found that though they had all begun to see themselves as members of the middle class, they remained strongly tied to their caste identity. This identification of being Brahmin was so central to their identity as middle class persons that the two authors chose to describe the Brahmin case of mobility as, *The Making of a Middle-Class Caste* (sub-title of their book). As they write:

> All Tamil Brahmins today regard themselves as urbanites and members of the middle class, so that their caste and class status are intertwined and Tamil Brahminhood is congruent with middle classness (Fuller and Narasimhan 2015: 210).

Another study of the upper caste Brahmins in Bangalore found them forming their associations with clear purpose of countering politics of democratisation being articulated by the 'backwards'. They advocated the need of preserving traditional values, which by implication also implied protecting Brahmin caste privileges (Bairy 2009).

However, this is not to suggest that the caste system did not change at all. Despite these persisting inequalities and cultures of exclusion, India's middle class story and its interface with caste are far more complex than being a simple case of reproduction of caste in a new avatar, this time called the middle class. Over the years, the middle class space in India has become socially far more diverse. Even when the traditional upper castes continue to dominate, they are not the only ones who claim middle class identity or occupy such positions in the secular and professional economies of India. Nearly seven decades of affirmative action policies for the SCs have been able to open-up possibilities of mobility even for the most deprived, the ex-untouchables. However, the quality and extent of change has been limited.

It was during the British colonial period that caste began to be enumerated. It was during the later years of colonial rule that the idea of affirmative action began to be framed through classification of caste communities into categories like the 'depressed classes'. This classification became a source for identifying communities to be listed as SCs for the reservations policy. Further, the western-style secular education introduced by the British rulers was in principle open to all, including those from the 'untouchable' communities. The colonial government also employed individuals from these communities in their administrative system. Thanks to all these policies, a few members of the 'untouchable' communities and those from the other 'backward' classes could study and move to urban middle class spaces, which had so far been the monopoly of the Brahmins and other upper castes. Some of these individuals, such as Jyotiba Phule and B.R. Ambedkar in Maharashtra or E.V. Ramasamy in the south of India initiated a range of anti-Brahmin and anti-caste movements (Omvedt 1976, Pandian 1997). They were to become a source of inspiration for the later middle-classes that emerged from these communities in the post-independence period.

Perhaps the most visible effect of the quotas, particularly in case of the SCs, has been the emergence of a Dalit middle class. Even when their communities remain largely poor and marginalised, individuals from these communities have been able to move up, to senior positions in political institutions, the bureaucracy and academia. Their experience of being middle class has been a site of struggles and challenges.

Normally, in such processes of individual mobility, the upwardly mobile individual tends to moves out of his/her group of origin to another group compatible with his/her class location. This, however, has generally not been the experience of mobile Dalits. Available empirical literature tends to show that even when such individuals move to secular employment and middle class occupations, their identification with the communities of their origin tends to remain strong. Why does this happen? First and foremost, economic mobility does not always lead to disappearance of prejudice of the dominant groups against the upwardly mobile Dalits. They often resent the quota system and tend to see Dalits occupying middle class jobs as illegitimate, as if those jobs have been taken away from them, a violation of their privileged monopoly. In such environments of hostility, the social mobility that should accompany the individual's economic mobility becomes rather limited. Even when a Dalit occupies a high position of authority, his upper caste colleagues tend to identify him/her with first the caste of his/her origin and only later with his/her position of authority. Such a lack of collegial acceptance produces disorientation, and often anger and agitation (Jodhka 2015) among the upwardly mobile Dalits. Their responses to such situations vary. Some try to conceal their caste identity (Mallick 1997), some others turn back to their communities with the realisation that without a larger social change that gives dignity to the communities of their identity, their individual achievements remain of limited value. They become community activists. Thus, in either case, mobility to a middle class for many Dalits does not produce individualisation and secularisation of status (see Jodhka 2010, Prakash 2015).

Upwardly mobile SCs also find it difficult to realise their middle-class status because of their larger economic context. They are invariably the first members of their families to earn a middle-class salary. In many cases, their privileged position within the family also puts pressure on them monetarily. They are morally expected to look after their poor kin by sending home a portion of their income (Naudet 2014: 244). Even though mobility through education, followed by a job, is an individual achievement, the community tends to see educated members of their community as 'collectively shared' resource (Ciotti 2012). The imperative of 'paying back' to the community often has a strong moral appeal with such successful individuals, given that an SC individual invariably acquires education and a secure job using quotas, which are viewed as an outcome of their collective struggle for rights (Naudet 2014: 245, Jodhka 2015: 169-209).

However, notwithstanding this sense of identification with the larger caste identity and caste question, their upward mobility also inhibits their return. While they realise the need for change through political mobilisations and activism, they are no longer similar to those they have left behind and also feel a sense of alienation from their communities (Guru 2001). They tend to form their own caste-based enclaves where they feel comfortable by expanding the boundaries of their caste communities through categories such as 'Dalits'. This also gives them a sense of a new identity, a sense of being modern and dignified but their social life tends to be limited to fellow Dalits (Ram 1988). Their perception of state and economy is often shaped by the prism of caste and the associated hierarchies and discrimination experienced by members of their community, if not they themselves. Hence their image and understanding of India's modernity is generally at variance with that of the dominant section of the middle class. They still look up to the state, which alone, for many of them, could be above the caste-divided institutions of civil society and market economy. Recognition of the deficits of social and cultural capital in their communities also makes them suspect advocates of free market and meritocratic regimes. Even when they mobilise for their increased participation in the neo-liberal market economy, they seek quotas and state support.

Processes of middle class consolidation in countries of Western Europe during the 20th century were accompanied by institutionalisation of a new language of citizenship. Even when economic disparities persisted, middle-class identification brought about a sense of commonness and homogeneity. Middle-class expansion implied the dissolution of the traditional hierarchies of status/rank and an advent of new notions of citizenship based on ideas of equality, fraternity and fairness. Even when differences of ethnicity, race or gender did not go away, the growing identification with being middle-class also implied an acceptance of a democratic public where nearly everyone could participate as equal members of the national political community. The Indian experience has so far been quite different.

References

Ajit, D., Han Donker and Ravi Saxena (2012). "Corporate Boards in India: Blocked by Caste", *Economic and Political Weekly* 47(31): 39-43.

Bairy, Ramesh (2009). *Brahmins in the Modern World: Association as Enunciation Contributions to Indian Sociology* (n.s.) 43(1): 89–12.

Beteille, A. (1986). "The Concept of Tribe with Special Reference to India", *European Journal of Sociology* 27(02): 296-318.

Charsley, S.R. and G.K. Karanth (1998). *Dalits and State Action: The 'SCs' Challenging Untouchability: Dalit Initiative and Experience from Karnataka*. New Delhi: Sage Publications.

Chatterjee, Partha (1993). *The Nation and its Fragment: Colonial and Post Colonial Histories.* Princeton: Princeton University Press.

———. (1990). "The Nationalist Resolution of the Women's Question", in K. Sangari, and S. Vaid (eds.), *Recasting Women: Essays in Indian Colonial History.* New Brunswick. New Jersey: Rutgers University Press. pp.233-53.

Ciotti, Manuela (2012). *Retro-modern India: Forging the Low Caste Self.* New Delhi: Routledge.

Cohn, B. (1996). *Colonialism and its Forms of Knowledge: The British in India.* Princeton: Princeton University Press.

Dirks, N.B. (2001). *Castes of Mind: Colonialism and the Making of Modern India.* Princeton: Princeton University Press.

Fernadez, Leela (2006). *India's New Middle-class: Democratic Politics in an Era of Economic Reform.* Minneapolis: University of Minnesota Press.

Fernandes Leela and Patrick Heller (2006). "Hegemonic Aspirations: New Middle Class Politics and India's Democracy in Comparative Perspective", *Critical Asian Studies* 38(4): 495-522.

Fuller, C.J. and H. Narasimhan (2015). *Tamil Brahmans: The Making of a Middle-Class Caste.* New Delhi: Social Science Press.

Guha, Sumit (2013). *Beyond Caste Beyond Caste: Identity and Power in South Asia, Past and Present.* Leiden: Brill (Brill's Indological Library).

Gupta, D. (2000). *Interrogating Caste: Understanding Hierarchy and Difference in Indian Society.* New Delhi: Penguin Books India.

Guru, G. (2001). "Dalit Middle Class Hangs in the Air", in Imtiaz Ahmad and Helmut Reifeld (eds.) *Middle Class Values in India and Western Europe.* New Delhi: Social Science Press. pp.141-51.

Iyer, Lakshmi, Tarun Khanna and Ashutosh Varshney (2013). "Caste and Entrepreneurship in India", *Economic & Political Weekly* 48(6): 52–60.

Jaffrelot, C. (2003). *India's Silent Revolution: The Rise of Low Castes in North Indian Politics.* Delhi: Permanent Black.

Jodhka, S.S. and K. Newman (2007). "In the Name of Globalisation: Meritocracy, Productivity and the Hidden Language of Caste", *Economic and Political Weekly* 4125-32.

Jodhka, S.S. and Aseem Prakash (2016). *The Indian Middle Class.* New Delhi: Oxford University Press.

Jodhka, S.S. (2016). "Ascriptive Hierarchies: Caste and its Reproduction in Contemporary India", *Current Sociology* (Monograph 2016) 64(2): 228-43.

———. (2015). *Caste in Contemporary India.* New Delhi: Routledge.

———. (2012). *Caste Oxford India Short Introductions.* New Delhi: Oxford University Press.

———. (2010). "Dalits in Business: Self-employed Scheduled Castes in North-West India", *Economic and Political Weekly*: 41-48.

———. (2002). "Caste and Untouchability in Rural Punjab", *Economic and Political Weekly* 37(19): 1813-23.

Kapur, Devesh, Chandra Bhan Prasad, Lant Pritchett and D. Shyam Babu. (2010). "Rethinking Inequality: Dalits in Uttar Pradesh in the Market Reform Era", *Economic and Political Weekly* 45(35): 39-49.

Kumar, S., Anthony Heath and Oliver Heath (2002). Determinants of 'Social Mobility in India'. *Economic and Political Weekly* 37(29): 2983-87

Landry, B. and K. Marsh (2011). "The Evolution of the New Black Middle Class", *Annual Review of Sociology* 37: 373-94.

Mallick, R. (1997). 'Affirmative Action and Elite Formation: An Untouchable Family History', *Ethnohistory:* 345-74.

Mendelsohn, O. (1993). "The Transformation of Authority in Rural India", *Modern Asian Studies* 27 (04): 805-42.

Naudet, Jules (2014). "Finding One's Place among the Elite: How Dalits Experiencing Sharp Upward Social Mobility Adjust to Their New Social Status", in Clarinda Still (ed.), *Dalits in Neoliberal India: Mobility or Marganilization?* New Delhi: Routledge. pp.236-58.

Omvedt, G. (1976). *Cultural Revolt in a Colonial Society*. Scientific Socialist Education Trust.

Ram, N. (1988). *The Mobile Scheduled Castes: Rise of a New Middle Class*. New Delhi: Hindustan Publishing Corporation.

Pai, S. (2002). *Dalit Assertion and the Unfinished Democratic Revolution The Bahujan Samaj Party in Uttar Pradesh 2013*. New Delhi: Sage Publications.

Pandian, M.S.S. (1997). *Brahmin and Non-Brahmin: Genealogies of the Tamil Political Present*. Ranikhet: Permanent Black.

Prakash, Aseem (2015). *Dalit Capital: State, Markets and Civil Society in Urban India*. New Delhi: Routledge

Sridharan, E. 2008. *The Political Economy of the Middle Classes in Liberalising India*. Institute of South Asian Studies.

Srinivas, M.N. (1962). *Caste in Modern India and Other Essays*. Bombay: Media Promoter and Publishers.

———. (1955). "Village Studies and their Significance", *Eastern Anthropologist* 8: 215-58.

———. (2003). "An Obituary on Caste as a System", *Economic and Political Weekly* 38(5): 455-59 (Feb. 1-7).

Thorat, S. and K. Newman (2010). "Economic Discrimination, Concept, Consequences, and Remedies", in S. Thorat and K. Newman (ed.), *Blocked by Caste: Economic Discrimination in Modern India*. New Delhi: Oxford University Press.

Vaid, D. and A. Heath (2010). "Unequal Opportunities: Class, Caste and Social Mobility", *Proceedings of the British Academy* 159: 129-64.

5

GOVIND KELKAR

IT Industry in India

Testing the Limits of Change in Gendered Spaces

India is the world leader in offshore services market with a 58 per cent share of the global outsourcing industry. With its outsourcing services through IT (information technology), business process and knowledge process centres, the IT firms provide direct employment to three million and indirect employment to 9.5 million people (NASSCOM 2013). Reportedly, most IT and business process companies employ 25 to 45 per cent women. But, at the mid-senior management levels, their number comes down to a low 5 per cent (Seth 2015). A central concern in this study is to work out a criteria for evaluating the process of change in the gendered socio-technological spaces. How women's engagement with the IT industry worked to build gender sensitivity in employability and enabled rights to work in conditions of non-discrimination and freedom of mobility? Is there a process introduced and then halted to weaken institutional links with patriarchal positioning of women as secondary, unskilled or semiskilled workers on marginal economic returns and contributions to firms and society?

India's emerging middle class is a critical economic and social actor, largely because of its potential as an engine of technological change. Women and men of the middle class are seen to be engaged in a democratic change for an inclusive growth and transformation of discriminatory social norms related to gender, caste and ethnicity. This paper attempts to explore: does the NMC (new middle class) produce new norms about gender roles and relations, and more opportunities for women? Or, are seemingly progressive platforms created by the NMC of the IT industry influenced by claims for a moderate transition in gender roles and relations, where the majority of women are employed in subordinate income-earning, low-skilled jobs, and overburdened with social reproduction and unpaid care responsibilities? Feminist analysis have shown two central concerns: First, technology plays an important part in social action for change in gendered spaces. Second, any technology policy must respond to problems that emerge in the context of market-driven patriarchal forces which result in promoting women as a commodity that can be possessed by an individual or a collective force of masculinity (Harstock 1998, Patel 2010, Kelkar 2013, Cornwall 2014). In India and South Asia, the two areas of women's existence—the household and workplace—are seriously affected by patriarchal norms in society, the state neglect, and market fundamentalism. This study intends to explore the nature of change and use of power in the household and labour market, as a result of women's engagement with IT.

This study is informed by an earlier fieldwork conducted in 2005, 2009 and 2012 in the call centres of Bangalore, Delhi and Gurgaon, and interviews with the middle to senior management in NASSCOM, Infosys, and several other IT companies. Questioning the myths of detached neutrality and the objective findings through research, my perspective and positionality are influenced by well formulated theories of 'feminist standpoint' by Sandra Harding (1991) and the 'situated knowledge' by Donna Haraway (1988) about the context specific women's day-to-day experience of inequality in a variety of settings, ranging from the homes to the workplaces.

Unlike caste and other forms of domination, the doxa of gendered roles directly shapes and determines relations of power in our households and socioeconomic and political spaces. Usually it is within the household or family that girls grow up as women and learn to accept concepts of masculinity and male authority in decision-making. Of course, mother, like father, are complicit in forming such unequal social arrangements, these in turn are followed by a systemic degradation of women in marital homes by lovers of husbands and in the workplaces by employers. Feminist analysis sees the need for working out women's status in terms of sex, caste, ethnicity and class, and using this standpoint to understand patriarchy and develop a critical consciousness to resist male domination and attempt at gaining for women equal access to power and privilege both in the home and workplace.

Women's Inclusivity in the IT Industry: An Invisible Cliff

The percentage of women employees consistently measures from 21 per cent in 2003 to 36 per cent in 2008 and with an increase of 45 per cent in several companies in 2014-15 (NASSCOM 2003, NASSCOM and MERCER 2009, Seth 2015). Importantly, the percentage of women working in the human resources (for long an assigned career for women) dropped from 55 per cent to 25 per cent in 2008, which indicates an advance in women's options for non-gendered work preference. However, women professionals in mid-level roles constitute 12.5 per cent in IT industry, with National Institute of Information Technology (NIIT), Infosys, Wipro and Tata Consultancy Services having 17-29 per cent of women staff (Kelkar 2013).

The mid-senior level management positions in numerous IT firms did not see any rise in women's inclusivity. While discussing this stagnation of women at lower levels, the NASSCOM Regional Council meeting in Haryana in 2015 observed the four sets of reasons for 'an invisible cliff' in mobility of women from low to mid-senior management: a decline in career momentum after maternity; gender stereotypes or 'unintentional prejudices' of the majority of men from their houses to the workplaces; women's subconscious biases against their own capabilities; and deeply embedded gendered norms in society which limit education and growth opportunities for women (Seth 2015).

Notwithstanding women's concentration at low levels in the IT industry, the development of IT in South Asia has had a clear impact on women. Studies of 'village pay phones' in rural Bangladesh (Richardson et al. 2000), and computer aided technologies and teleworking in India (Mitter 2000, Gothoskar 2000) have observed that household income has increased, and women have more mobility and say in household matters. But women's work has multiplied, as professionals and lower level employees have continued with household work and care responsibilities.

Importantly, women's presence in decision-making positions as partners or entrepreneurs makes a difference to the recruitment and promotion of women in higher positions. A woman who is a partner in a growing IT company, said her physical presence at the interviews led to the recruitment of more women. Otherwise, even gender-sensitive men do not look for alternatives or other ways of recruiting women. The attitude of the people in charge of recruitment plays an important role in the number of women and their positions (interview with the author, Bangalore, March 2009).

IT is characterised by a production system of networking, outsourcing and subcontracting which requires individualisation of capacities. The nature of the work in the IT industry is different as compared to other industries. In the IT industry, labour loses its collective identity and individualises the capacities of workers. The positions of owners, producers, managers, and workers, are increasingly blurred in a production system of variable geometry of teamwork, networking, outsourcing, and subcontracting (Castells 2000). The networking of capacities required by IT increases women's capability to take decisions on their own and constructs greater space to enhance their agency, though within limited terms of culturally embedded, structural inequalities of women.

The Primacy of Domestic Work and Care

A major concern of feminist scholarship has been the impact of new technologies on women's lives (Cockburn and Furst-Dilic 1994, Folbre 1994, Kelkar and Nathan 2002, Omvedt and Kelkar 1995, Mitter 2000). It is not technology itself that has inevitable consequences but the economic and social situation in which technologies are introduced and the balance of forces at any time. Certainly systems to reduce the labour of cooking, cleaning and unpaid care may make it easier for employed couples to share domestic duties. But it is also possible for such technologies not to lead to such changes in sharing and maintaining gender division of work and notions of reinforcing it. While employment in the IT industry has decreased the time available to women for domestic work, their responsibility for these tasks has not diminished. Social norms are set for women to balance both roles in technology work, and cooking and caring at home. Most women depend on relations (mothers-in-law or housekeepers) to count on. Men do help in the housework, though this help manifests itself in women's absence when she is travelling or visiting relatives. In usual circumstances, cooking and caring remains the woman's responsibility and is unshared or minimally shared at its best.

The primacy of domestic work has adverse consequences for women who seek wage employment. Given the patriarchal structure of the Indian family, women are swamped in never-ending, fragmented demands of cooking and caring. This unjust division of work agitates many IT employees. A 30-year old woman employed in a call centre in Delhi reported, "I am frustrated when my unmarried junior colleagues are promoted. However because of my household responsibilities, I cannot work long hours and therefore cannot expect or progress at work" (author's interview, 2009). Burdened with the sole responsibility of domestic work and care, women have fewer locational choices than men do. This makes them less competitive with regard to exploiting the opportunities. Married women cannot spend a lot of time on commuting to work unlike single women and men who can. So they negotiate for a lower position in companies near their house. One woman in a call centre in Delhi said, 'Although the work is monotonous, I do not want to quit this job, because it is close to my house' (author's interview, 2005). A Dataquest—Jobs Ahead Survey in 2003 found that 52 per cent of the women (but 28% of the men) were 'not open to relocation' (Kalghatgi and Seth 2003).

There are, however, some innovative examples of attempts to understand the need for change in this gender-based division of labour, NIIT, with a large proportion of women employees, has instituted part-time and flex-time schemes for both women and men as some men were found to be involved in childcare. Paternity leave and part-time/flex-time work for men are also being instituted in some companies in Delhi, Bangalore and Gurgaon. Women's entry into the labour market and the changing nuclearisation of the households seemingly has helped to change the gender division of work.

Restrictions on women's mobility have increasingly loosened over the years and such mobility has a direct bearing on their ability to take up employment outside the house (Kalpagam 1992). While a large number of married women are still bound by domestic childcare responsibilities, single women seem to find a significant change in their mobility enabling them to take up jobs and advance their careers. However, women are not as mobile as men.

Surprisingly, women's lower mobility has influenced the recruitment policies in the industry in their favour. Several instances during my discussions at Delhi and Bangalore in 2009 made me realise that women (and men), who are unable to get into the more competitive areas of the industry, such as MNCs (multinational corporations) or large firms, join the IT-enabled sector. Therefore, they do not opt for more challenging and better paying jobs. Hence employers prefer married women with children, as they are not too mobile and would be willing to stay in 'a boring job' for reasons of domestic work and care responsibilities. Women were viewed as 'efficient in the work and would not leave the company as they get better opportunities' (author's interview with mid-level women professionals, Bangalore, 2009).

Empowerment and Complexities of the IT work

In common understanding, women's work in the IT industry is defined as 'money, mobility and independence' to voice their concern about familial relations, asset ownership and freedom to have unconventional dressing styles.

However, the male centred anxieties are reflected in statements such as 'young women are getting spoilt from earning their own income'; 'call centre jobs equal call girl jobs', despite such social questioning, why do women prefer to work in the IT industry? Based on a number of women's narratives on mobility and morality in the call centre work, Reena Patel (2010) noticed the following reasons for women's preference for the IT work:

- A IT job provides the means to support the household in terms of food, clothes, and schooling of younger siblings. My interviews in Bangalore suggested similar observations.

Of the 26 interviews with women employees who discussed their household finances with me, 18 were the primary supporters of their households, or gave a major portion of their income to support their mother and siblings (author's interview in a NASSCOM meeting, Bangalore, 2012).

- Some young educated women aspire to do IT work, which is different in terms of its global connectivity (i.e. connecting with offshore customers) and a fixed amount of work in the office. Given the responsibilities of cooking, care and housekeeping, many of the IT workers did not like to take work home.
- Enough money for spending, saving, and for starting new businesses. Many employees got enough money to shop for branded clothes, expensive mobile phone, and household items. In addition, a number of them were able to save money for their venture capital i.e. started their own businesses and non-profit organisations which provided skills to young women and men.
- With a few exceptions, the IT work shifts gave many girls and women legitimate reasons to escape the chains of immobility. They were able to leave the house at night to work in a collegial environment. They like the IT work because it provided them an opportunity for acquiring new skills, knowledge and freedom to socialise with other workers, female or male.
- A number of women employees preferred the IT work as it gave them freedom to organise a new way of life. i.e. single women living a life of their own and being free from marital obligations and having opportunities for skill acquisition, confidence building, and regular vacations. However, in numerous cases, this kind of living on their own was seen as 'strange' and a transgression of cultural norms. Some of these single women found it difficult to rent a place.

As noted in recent studies, many of the IT jobs in India have continued to be 'routine, monotonous, non-innovative, tedious, uncreative, less skilled, low end involving activities' (Noronha and

D'Cruz 2016: 433). This 'low end' of the IT industry work is seen as a result of the exclusion of Indian firms from the primary stage of conceptualisation and high level design.

Not surprisingly, there has been a high rate of attrition in the IT industry in India. This is largely caused by a lack of meaningful consultation with the employees, the rhetoric of non-hierarchical organisational structure, and demand for a sacrificial human-resources strategy in an environment of non-transparent system. Further, the collegial coping in stressful work in the industry reportedly involved resistance to the customer haste and abuse by pressing a mute button, and cursing the customer aloud and listen and enjoy with the team the customers' frustration and tirade (Noronha and D'Cruz 2016). There is no gender-specific data in such resistance patterns. However, given the high rate of women employees in the IT industry, I would safely make an intelligent guess about the women employees' participation in such resistance.

Like the nursing work in Kerala, which the Keralite communities disdain as 'dirty work', women working in the IT industry experience censure from the conventional social norms (for Kerala nurses study, see George 2005). This disdain comes despite earning a salary that in many cases is the sole support for the entire household. The actual context of their IT work is regarded as an easy job, done at night, and called 'the hooker shift' work. Women in general, and younger women and girls in particular, continue to be controlled by stricter gender regimes of surveillance. In a street play in rural Jharkhand in 2012, women presented how mobile phones were used as a surveillance device by migrant husbands to keep tabs on women's work, mobility and resource management.

It is important to note, however, when a large number of women start working a night shift, and economically upgrade themselves from earning a low wage, to a high wage, social norms that interpreted such work as 'hooker shift' work lose their hold on individuals and become ineffectual. The power of taboos on women's night work dissipate and tend to accept these women and girls as 'carefree' and 'modern'.

Towards Change in Structural Inequalities

In order to deal with the high attrition rates, much attention was paid to the potential of the IT industry for empowering women. In the beginning of 2003-04, a number of firms introduced measures that were likely to affect the gender balance, and thereby strategically enabling women to strengthen their negotiating agency in the ambiguity between seeming acceptance of social norms and agential strategising against patriarchal relations of assumed submissiveness and subservience to the male power, both in the home and in the workplace (Masika and Bailur 2015).

In 2003, Infosys, an Indian IT giant, set up a IWIN (women's inclusivity network) to keep women working longer in the company. Infosys provided women employees regular assistance and support for career life cycle through flexible working conditions, maternity leave, telecommuting, childcare leave, and satellite offices for new mothers. The impact of these gender-sensitivity measures was noted in the increase of women employees from 23 to 32 per cent in a 5 year period; and the attrition rate was reported to be at a 13 per cent low in 2008-09 (Ramesh 2009). IWIN was mandated to create a gender-sensitive environment with women's adequate inclusivity in employment and assist women to develop managerial and transactional roles through peer-counselling, professional counselling workshops and infrastructure support such as nursing stations/ lactation centres for employee mothers, transport services, grocery and drug stores at the Infosys campuses.

Through IBM DAKSH approach, the company has a strategic policy to retain and train women to undertake mid-senior management positions within the organisation. IBM DAKSH conducted an analysis of barriers against women's inclusivity in the IT industry, and in the following period, paid attention to assist women employees to overcome gendered cultural and social norms. Further, IBM DAKSH created policies and practices of gender sensitisation for mid-senior level management and built accountability for inclusion and diversity. Thus, the group ensured that women and other marginalised groups were enabled for quality performance and efficient working with flexible norms during the maternity and childcare periods (Kaul and Gupta 2009).

Importantly, Accenture invested in gender sensitisation programmes and conducted periodic workshops for its senior management and supervisors. The workshops and discussion groups such as 'leading a diverse workforce' and 'being gender sensitive' were/are regularly held to transform the gendered through processes and social norms held against women employees. Likewise, the Ford Technology Services in India, regularly organised workshops and discussion groups for gender-sensitivity in the workplace and trained women for leadership positions. An active forum called the ITWIL (IT Women in Leadership) was created to empower women through the development of leadership qualities with regular women-centric discussions in the workplace. The 'flexible work option' programme encouraged women with childcare or elder care responsibilities to work from home one day a week. These employees were issued a laptop with secure IDs to be enrolled in the plan. This programme was designed to give women 'the time and energy to balance their home and employment-related responsibilities' (Pulimood 2009).

In 2008, the Australia and New Zealand Banking Group Ltd (ANZ) launched the 'ANZ Women's Network', a global network constituting 10 regional networks known as *panchayats*. The *panchayat's* rationale was defined: 'women bring unique qualities to the table- in particular, great intuition, exceptional relationship-building skills, and an inclusive approach to decision-making' (Kannan et al. 2009). The result of the implementation of *panchayats* was noted in a 41 per cent rise in the number of women employees in the ANZ company in a couple of years. During the same period, the attrition of women employees had decreased more than 5 per cent. Data Quest set up a home-office system for some of the project leaders, it was important to the firm that women professionals would continue to provide knowledge of the office procedures and computer systems to the work organisation, and the firm does not have to duplicate these efforts through new recruitments (Nathan et al. 2016). There is a growing evidence of such flexible work systems being instituted in many firms in order to retain professional women's knowledge about the organisation of work.

Figure 5.1

India: Best Practices to Support Women at Work

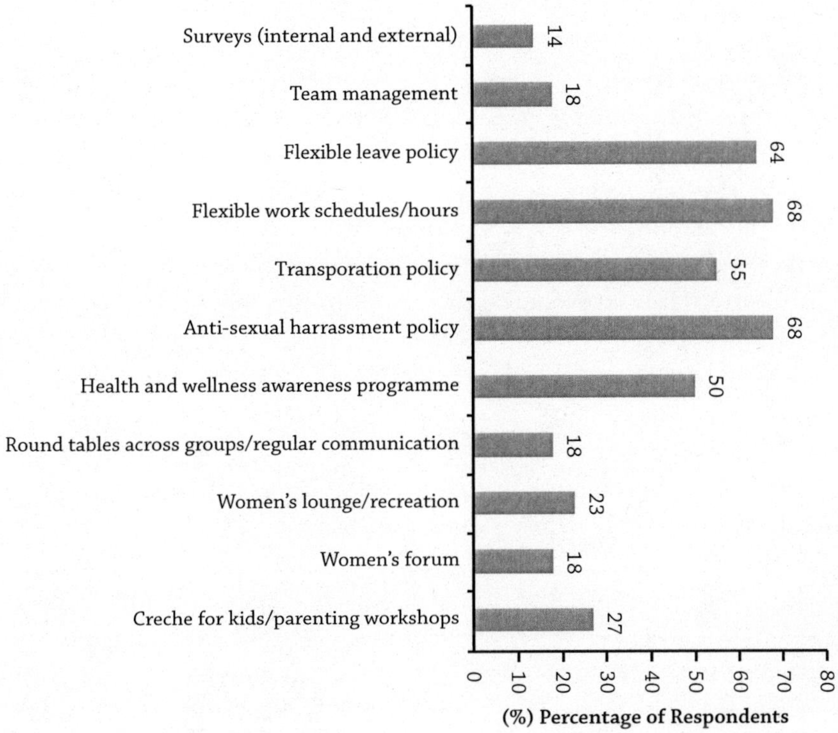

Source: NASSCOM-MERCER 2009.

Wipro Ltd, a global IT services and consulting company, has initiated 'Women of Wipro' (WoW) programme to bring together women executives for their personal and social transformation towards building sustainable careers. WoW's gender diversity approach has focused on three major themes: i) a speaking series on gender-sensitivity in the organisation; ii) flexibility of working hours to ensure women are enabled to balance work and personal lives with an opportunity to grow within the company. Some of these flexibility measures included extended maternity leave, transfers to ensure the family stays together, on-off-ramping (women leaving and coming back from maternity leave), working from satellite offices and telecommuting; and iii) empowerment with advancing career development through leadership grooming, formal mentoring by top management, and succession planning on women talent pipelines through 'career conversations' (Cherian 2012).

In exploring some of the good practices, it was noted that 70 IT companies in India have implemented policies on sexual harassment, flexible working hours, transportation policies and flexible leave usage as the most common policies, others (as shown in Figure 5.1) remain less common. Few companies provide a counsellor for women employees. There were others (45%) who have institutionalised 'gender neutral career advancement opportunities' followed by grievance management and reward an increase in women's inclusivity in the IT industries (NASSCOM-MERCER 2009: 17). As the Figure 5.1 shows, 68 per cent of women employees have flexible work schedules.

Importantly, there has been undeniable improvement in the social mobility and work participation rate of women in the IT industry. The nature of work (such as flex-time, tele-working and working from home), the tools, (such as email and internet) and the individualisation of capacities required by IT make women more capable of taking decisions on their own and construct greater scope to enhance their agency.

Women Organising through IT-enabled Work

Women individually and collectively in various parts of Asia and the world are able to keep in touch with each other through e-connections and mobile phones. The resulting networks of such organisations are able to work in close coordination in conducting campaigns on various issues such as asset rights and violence against women. Women's groups, indigenous people's organisations, Dalit people's rights groups and organisations protesting against large dams and other environmental concerns—all such organisations are now networking in a manner made possible by the new ITs. For instance,

Mahila Kisan Adhikar Manch (MAKAAM), a forum for women farmers' rights in 2014-15 has used email networking strategies to expand women's claim-making activities and membership base throughout India. Through 'feministsindia@yahoogroups.com' and e-consultations, women have mobilised to demand from the state to affirm its commitment to women's inalienable, independent and effective rights to livelihood resources, including land and clean technologies, and freedom from domestic violence and abuse in civil spaces.

M.S. Swaminathan Research Foundation, Chennai has set up an innovative programme for village knowledge centres in a number of villages in 18 districts of Southern India. Two major features of the programme are the inclusion of women from low socioeconomic groups in the management and training programmes run by these centres; and gender sensitivity (for example, considering the health and skill development needs of economically poor rural women) in assessment of the information needs of the local people. A significant outcome of the skills gained from the village knowledge centre is that many women in the age group of 20-40 years were able to take up jobs as computer teachers in the neighbouring schools, or as data entry operators in agri-knowledge centres. Reportedly women/girls "who were once diffident and had no exposure to the outside world, are today very happy that they can support their families with their own income. Besides this, they are now looked upon with respect and administration by the family and neighbours", and this has given them confidence and prestige in the communities (MSSRF 2010: 126). In a few cases where temples used their complex as IT centres, young women have continued to work in spite of objections raised by the temple authorities that they might be menstruating, which would pollute the temple space.

In Kuppam district of Andhra Pradesh, Hewlett-Packard developed a solar powered camera with an easy to carry small printer. This was given to women's SHGs (self-help groups) to help them to generate additional income by taking photographs at social events (Parthasarthy 2013). Feminist groups have made good use of social media by using Yahoo and Google Groups for raising awareness on sexual violence, hypocrisy in cultures about women and girls. They have set up a number of cyber forums, blogs, online sharing of research works and archives with photographic memoirs, reports, posters, diaries, songs, and documentaries on women's issues (Patel and Khajuria 2016). These have been used in mobilising both urban and rural women as well as men for coordinated action against sexism, gender-based discrimination and violence against women. They have produced videos that mock the notion of 'appropriate' roles for women and raise issues of rape, clothing, infanticide, marital relations, and women working in the night shifts. Women's engagement with the IT sector and social media, in particular, have created new spaces for women and girls to live in and work with dignity in various ways at the household, local, national and international levels. By changing their own conditions of work and lifestyles, they have become sources of inspiration for others.

The computer knowledge and skills introduced by IT does not however end power inequality but it does allow women and the disadvantaged groups more scope to project themselves and meet their livelihood needs. IT, therefore, constitute the basis of the redefinition of traditional gendered norms and supports a media of information, understanding and knowledge in which women's interests, opinions and rights are taken into account. Nevertheless, they function to bring about gradual and limited changes in social norms, and within the dominant interests of the market and the state. The IT industry therefore provides a non-threatening mobilisation of women's labour for the benefit of their families and communities. The concern to enhance women's agency has been missed in these efforts at inclusivity and diversity in the IT sector. Nor has it been possible for women in the IT industry to challenge and transform structural inequalities and gendered power relations.

Challenges in Change

Can women's engagement with IT play a leading role in bringing about change in gendered structures of power? IT, like any other technology, is likely to be shaped by the social, economic and political processes and institutions. It is the processes of gendered power and hierarchy of the economy, polity and society that determines technology itself. The relevant questions are: has the movement of women into the IT weakened the grip of patriarchy? Or, does it function within the confines of traditional structures of power and hierarchy between women and men?

We examined these questions keeping in mind women as employees in the IT industry. There is socially acknowledged role of women as income earners, which is different from their former and traditional status as dependent, contributing family workers. With the spread of IT, and more so, of mobile phone technology, women have learned new methods of work organisation.

With IT employment, women have gained greater prestige in the household and also have increased control over how their income is spent, which is what Amartya Sen's (1990) theory of household bargaining as cooperative-conflict would predict. In his analysis of gender and cooperative conflicts, Sen propose that household members do not necessarily share the same preferences and that they try to pursue their own interests and claims in the pluralistic level of existence. The household members face two types of problems at the same time: i) of working in cooperation and adding to total availabilities; ii) of conflict related to dividing the total availabilities among the members of the household. Arrangement regarding the division of paid and unpaid work, differential consumption patterns and decision making impact the combined problem of cooperation and conflict. If the household allocation of paid and unpaid work and asset ownership are not gender balanced, it may influence intra-household bargaining, inter-spousal decisions concerning production, consumption entitlement, formation of human capabilities and thereby accessing employment and entrepreneurial opportunities.

Further, the respective bargaining power of women and men within the cooperative existence depends much on their asset ownership (or its potential) through inheritance or employment earnings, including the social perception of their economic contributions and power outside the family/household.

As I observed elsewhere (Kelkar 2015), there are two challenging areas that resist a transformative change in gender hierarchy and power relations. First, the sex-based division of housework and domestic care. Public policies, social norms and familial grooming nurture men to be 'breadwinners' and household decision-makers. Generally, men are reluctant to undertake any responsibility with regard to housework and domestic care that is likely to affect their market work and potential advancement. This position of men within the household and outside in social, economic and political institutions provides them the power to disregard women's housework, its long working hours without any public recognition and economic remuneration. Housework and domestic care—so critical for the maintenance of human society—is condemned to remain invisible and sexually characterised as the women's duty. And, women's strategic interest for advancement with market work continues to be ignored. The feminist analysis of household work and domestic care considers it an important value in itself and the gender equality issue lies in its adequate recognition and its replacement with equal sharing by women and men.

The efficiency of the so-called productive (i.e., cash-income generating) activities is negatively affected by the other work being done, such as housework and food preparation, the care of children. Technology is not only about equipment and its operational characteristics but also about social arrangements that permit the equipment to be used and the so-called production processes to be carried on.

A second area of the continued challenge is the gender tag in the labour market: segregation of women and men in the market work and occupational structures. Employers tend to hire women for 'women's job' (often less skilled and with lower remuneration) and men for 'men's job' (skilled, supervisory work, with high remunerations), so that women do not lose utility from working in men's jobs and men do not lose utility from working in women's jobs. Firms generally consider that women are efficient in their traditional occupations (assistants and carers) and men do not feel threatened of giving up their skilled work or technological superior position, as happened in the case of keyboard operators in Kabyle society in Africa. The Kabyle society, studied by Bourdieu (2011: 60-61), shows that, 'women's entry into the publishing trades as the keyboard operators aroused formidable resistance on the part of men, who saw it a threat to their occupational mythology of highly skilled labour.' It was only after a long struggle by women that their keyboard operating skills were recognised. However, women's technological work was arbitrarily redefined as of lower quality, while maintaining the higher value of men's 'skilled work'.

Discussing how norms affect economic behaviour and choice of gender identity in labour market relations, Akerlof and Kranton in their recent study (2010) conclude that men do not generally dislike working with women. Their dislike is job-specific, for example, women as secretaries and men as executives. Therefore,

- Women invest in skills for jobs that are appropriate for women (education rather than business schooling or engineering).
- Women may have a lower attachment to the labour force because of wider gender norms (women are expected to stay home and raise children).
- The real problem is the norms that regulate that women and men should do particular jobs, irrespective of their individual tastes and abilities.

Generally, firms have limited interest in changing gender norms, which are generated within the household and then manifested in the labour market. Furthermore, whatever gains have come up as a result of the feminist critique of labour market relations and of conventional economic interpretations of work, they are likely to be at risk with the new forms of women's incorporation in global production systems.

To advance the struggle of women employers for equality-based working conditions, two major issues need to be confronted. First is that the gender differentiation of the labour force between a core of men who have better pay and more supervisory roles, and the flexible mass of women workers who do not have these conditions of work, largely organised on the basis of presumed skills. Women are kept out of skilled categories of work, and decision-making roles, even though skilled is classified as unskilled (Bourdieu 2001, Mason et al. 2000). In a recent report by Monster Salary Index, 30 per cent of the total IT sector workers in the country are women, and there is a huge gendered salary gap of 29 per cent. The gross salary of a male employee in IT work is ₹359.25 per hour, while a woman employee receives ₹254.4 per hour (*The Times of India*, 23 July 2014). The report further noted that men get promoted to supervisory positions more often than women workers in the IT sector.

The skill-based gender differentiation in employment and supervisory roles needs to be confronted and changed, if the conditions of women employees are to change. Second, since it is considered to be women's responsibility to do most of household labour, the enormous increase in women's work burden with their entry into income-earning needs to be tackled, if women are not to continue mining their bodies with much longer hours than men and more tedious work. The provision of sufficient infrastructure, like clean and efficient energy sources that would both reduce time in cooking and the health hazard from cooking, along with moves to bring about an equal sharing of household work, both together are part of a move towards enabling women to be better producers with skills, agency, and capabilities. Understandably, power is both restrictive and productive force. Power structures not only function at the level or ownership and control of material resources and technologies, but are also manifested in systems of social norms and cultural representation (Foucault 1977). The political economy of gender hierarchy and power has resulted in the creation of an entire category of human beings who are seen as secondary and devalued others.

Conclusion: Enhancing Women's Agency through IT

Women's subordination and marginality are enacted and embedded in the wider context of inequalities, hierarchies and social prejudices, which are pervasive in both the cultural domain of home and the technology domain of the workplace. Research shows that attitudes and norms about gender roles are passed from generation to generation and such cultural transmissions have implications for women in limiting their presence and position in the IT industry (Farre and Villa 2013, World Bank 2015). To improve women's agential power, it is critically important to bringing change in social attitudes towards the conventional role of women as secondary humans with only expertise for 'domestic duties' and 'unsuitable for decision-making'.

In a recently organised CEO meet on women's leadership and gender diversity in the IT industry, the NASSCOM Regional Council observed that the fundamental cause behind the inadequate numbers of women at mid-senior levels is gender stereotypes and 'unintentional prejudices' in their homes and the workplaces. Also, many women have internalised such 'subconscious biases where they put limits on themselves' (NASSCOM 2015). Nitin Seth (2015), Managing Director and Country Head of Fidelity Worldwide Investment observed,

> Even in our cities, where many women work, the expectations of relative contributions of women and men at home have not changed... unless we address this issue, we might not be able to move the needle significantly on diversity.

The panellists at the NASSCOM Regional CEO Meet in Haryana identified the following six areas of action for the IT industry to improve diversity at senior management level and deep-rooted problems about gender roles at multiple level: i) support for women after maternity; ii) peer networking and inclusion in senior management as well as sharing of good practices; iii) reach out to girls leaving colleges to shape mindsets; iv) address possible intake bias through mixed gender panels in hiring and promotions; v) raise awareness about 'unintentional prejudices' to change social norms and gender attitudes towards women; vi) support gender-focused business initiatives, such as Airtel which is opening all-women staffed 'Angel stores' (NASSCOM Regional CEO Meet Haryana, 2015)

Undoubtedly, these create challenges for the IT industry and threats from social norms, cultural institutions, and the state machinery and employment policies. Despite frequent declarations for mainstreaming of gender equality in the labour markets and the state policies, feminist analysis shows that traditional gender roles are reinforced not just by cultural norms but also by employment policies

(Sandburg 2013). The existing employment policies and the labour market relations encourage women the maintenance of traditional gender roles and do not encourage changes in the gender division of labour. Based on a panel study of income dynamics for 1891-2009, Elizabeth McClintock (2013) found that occupational interaction influences the gender division of work in the home. Her study points out that when men of the household are employed in traditionally female occupations (e.g. nursing, childcare or teaching), they spend more time doing housework compared to men who are employed in the traditionally male occupations (as machine operators, masons or supervisors). And that their wives or partners spend less time in caring and household activities. Further when married women or women in live-in-relationships work in traditionally women's jobs, they tend to increase the amount of time on housework and caring compared to when they are employed in traditionally male occupations.

While labour laws and employment policies tend to say that motherhood is the most important and difficult work of all, women who do this work get no reward or recognition for their contribution. In contrast, all the work related to motherhood is seen as the women's duty and not recognised as work. In most cases, women pay a big career penalty for raising the human resources for the future. In gender analysis of the labour market in North America, Stephen Rose and Heidi Hartmann noted:

> Controlling for education and hours worked, women's annual earnings decrease by 20 per cent if they are out of the workforce just for one year. Average annual earnings decline by 30 per cent after two to three years, which is the average amount of time that professional women off-ramp from the workforce (quoted in Sandberg 2012: 102).

Burdened with housework and childcare, women find it difficult to move up in the career. Once laid off, it is very difficult for them to be re-employed in any formal sector job; and they, therefore, have to seek informal employment with poor working conditions lacking any social security. Some preliminary steps towards economic empowerment of women require a bold and transformative change in discriminatory social norms that prohibit women (and also for Dalits and indigenous peoples) from accessing employment opportunities is also seen in the recent World Economic Forum report on the 'fourth industrial revolution' (Treanor 2016). Discussing the limits of women employed or seeking employment in the IT sector, Sheryl Sandberg (2013: 108) Chief Operating Officer of Facebook observed: 'Women must be more empowered at work, and men must be more empowered at home'.

Social norms are not a historical necessity, nor are they static. Change in social norms is part of an ongoing process of social, economic change. Women's movement, like any other social movement, creates its own culture and new social, gender norms. Such new social norms or cultural configurations also create social conflicts or possible contradictions arising from the existing and newly created norms. These new gender relations and norms operate in a dialectical way, introducing the germs of change that a new society may carry.

References

Akerlof, G and R. Karanton (2010). *Identity Economics: How our Identities Shape Our Work, Wage and Well-being.* Princeton, New Jersey and Oxford, Princeton University Press.

Bourdieu, Pierre (2001). *Masculine Domination* (Translated by Richard Nice). Stanford: Stanford University Press.

Castells, Manuel, (2000). *The Rise of the Network Society.* Oxford, Blackwell.

Cherian, S. (2012). *Women of Wipro (WoW).*WIPRO *http://www.iusstf.org/cms/newsimages/file/women-in-science/Wipro.pdf.* Accessed on 10 October 2016.

Cockburn, C. and Furst-Dilic Ruza (1994). *Bringing Technology Home: Gender and Technology in the Changing Europe.* Philadelphia, PA: Open University Press.

Cornwall, A. (ed.) (2014). *Feminisms, Empowerment and Development, Changing Women's Lives.* Zed Books, London and New York.

Nathan, D., M. Saripalle and L. Gurunathan (2016). "Labour Practices in India", *ILO Asia-Pacific Working Paper Series.* March. ILO South Asia and Country Office for India.

Farre, L. and F. Vella (2013). "The Intergenerational Transmissions of Gender Role Attitudes and the Implications for Female Labour Force Participation", *Economica* 80: 219-47.

Folbre, N. (1994). *Who Pays for the Kids? Gender and the Structures of Constraints.* London and New York: Routledge.

Foucault, M. (1977). *Discipline and Punish: The Birth of the Prison* (Trans. A. Sheridan). Harmondsworth: Peregrine.

George, S.M. (2005). *When Women Come First: Gender and Class in Transnational Migration.* University of California Press. Berkley.

Gothoskar, S. (ed.) (2000). "Nature of Teleworking in Key Sectors: Case Studies of Financial, Media, and Software Sectors in Mumbai", *Economic and Political Weekly* XXXV(26): 2277-92, June 24-30.

Haraway, D. (1988). "Situated Knowledge: The Science Question in Feminism and the Privilege of Partial Perspective", *Feminist Studies* 14: 575-99.

Harding, S. (1991). *Whose Science? Whose Knowledge? Thinking from Women's Lives.* Cornell University Press. Ithaca.

Hartstock, N. (1998). *The Feminist Standpoint Revisited and Other Essays.* Westview Press, Colorado.

Kalghatgi, M,.and R. Seth (2003). "Why Just a Few Women on Top", *Dataquest*, 30 June, Available at: *http://www.dqindi.com/content/strategy/hrd/103063001)*

Kalpagam, U. (1992). "Women and the Household: What the Indian Data Sources has to Offer", in L. Saradamoni (ed.), *Finding the Household: Conceptual and Methodological Issues.* New Delhi: Sage Publications.

Kannan, G., C, Mathur and S. Shetty (2009). *Gender Inclusivity Programmes and their Impact.* Australia and New Zealand Banking Group. *http://www.iimahd.ernet.in/grc/abstracts_9_11_09.pdf.*

Kaul, K. and V. Gupta (2009). *Building an Inclusive Workplace: An IBM Daksh Perspective. Gender Inclusivity Programmes and their Impact.* IBM Daksha *http://www.iimahd.ernet.in/grc/abstracts_9_11_09.pdf*

Kelkar, G. (2015). "Gender Regimes: An Assessment of Change", *IIC Quarterly* 42(2) (Autumn), April. New Delhi.

———. (2013). "At the Threshold of Economic Empowerment: Women, Work and Gender Regimes in Asia", *Asia-Pacific Working Paper Series*, December. ILO South Asia and Country Office for India.

Kelkar, Govind and Dev Nathan (2002). "Gender Relations and Technological Change in Asia", *Current Sociology* 50(3): 427-41.

MAKAAM (2016). *Declaration of MAKAAM's National Convention of Women Farmers.* Mahila Kisan Adhikar Manch. *http://www.makaam.in/about-us.html*

Masika, R. and S. Bailur. (2015). "Negotiating Women's Agency through ICTs: A Comparative Study of Uganda and India", *Gender Technology and Development* 19(1): 43-69.

Mason, A., S. Rozella, Xiao-yuan Dong and L. Zhang (2000). "Gender Wage Gap in Post Reform Rural China", *CCAP Working Paper Series* No: WP-00-E25. Chinese Academy of Sciences, Beijing.

McClintock, E.A. (2013). *Gender-Atypical Occupations and Time Spent in Housework: Doing Gender or Doing Chores?* Paper Presented at the American Sociological Association. August. University of Notre Dame

Mitter, Swasti (2000). "Teleworking and Teletrade in India: Combining Diverse Perspectives and Visions", *Economic and Political Weekly* XXXV(26): 2241-52, 24-30 June.

M.S. Swaminathan Research Foundation (MSSRF) (2010). *Human Dimesnions of ICR in Rural India-Reflections by Rural Women and Men.* Chennai.

NASSCOM (2015). *NASSCOM Regional CEO Meet Haryana.*

———. (2013). "The IT-BPM Sector in India", *Strategic Review.* New Delhi.

———. (2003). *Indian IT-Enables Service Providers Directory 2003.* New Delhi.

NASSCOM-MERCER (2009). *Gender Inclusivity in India Building: Empowered Organisations.* Bangalore.

Nathan, Dev, Madhuri Saripalle and L. Gurunathan (2016). "Labour Practices in India", *ILO Asia-Pacific Working Paper Series.* March. DWT for South Asia and Country Office for India.

Noronha, E. and P. D'Cruz., (2016). "Still a Distance to go, Social Upgrading in the Indian ITO-BPO-KPO Sector" , in D. Nathan, M. Tewari and S. Sarkar (eds.), *Labour in Global Value Chains in Asia.* Institute for Human Development Delhi & University of Cambridge, UK. Cambridge University Press.

Omvedt, Gail and Govind Kelkar (1995). "Gender and Technology: Emerging Visions from Asia'" *Gender Studies Monograph* 4. Bangkok: Asian Institute of Technology.

Parthasarathy, Balaji (2013). "The ICT Series in Bangalore, India: its Changing Structure and Characteristics", in Hirakawa, Hitoshi, Kaushalash Lal, Nacko Shinkai and Norio Tokumaru (eds.), *Servitization, IT-ization and Innovation Models: Two-Stage Industrial Cluster Theory* (Associate Editor: Shampa Paul). Chapter 5. London & New York: Routledge, Taylor and Francis Group.

Patel, R. (2010). *Working the Night Shift: Women in India's Call Center Industry.* Stanford: Stanford University Press.

Patel, V. and R. Khajuria (2016). "Political Feminism in India: An Analysis of Actors, Debates and Strategies-Country Study". *Mimeo*. Study done for Friedrich Ebert Stiftung, New Delhi.

Pulimood, F. (2009). *Ford Technology Services India: Gender Inclusivity Programmes and their Impact.* Ford Technology Services India. *http://www.iimahd.ernet.in/grc/abstracts_9_11_09.pdf*

Richardson, Don, Ricardo Ramirez and Moinul Haq (2000). *Grameen Telecom's Village Phone Programme: A Multi-Media Case Study.* TeleCommons Development Group, Canada (Available at: *http://www.telecommons.com/villagephone/index.html'http://www.telecommons.com/village phone/index.html* accessed on 20 October 2004)

Sandberg, Sheryl (2013). *Lean in, Women, Work and the Will to Lead.* New YorkL Alfred A. Knopf.

Sen, Amartya (1990). "Gender and Cooperative Conflicts", in Irene Tinker (ed.), *Persistent Inequalities.* New York, Oxford University Press. pp.123-49.

Seth, N. (2015). *Women in Leadership: NASSCOM.* NASSCOM Regional Council. Haryana

Treanor, Jill (2016). "Women to Lose Out in Technology Revolution as Robotics Threatens Jobs, Warns WEF", *The Guardian*, 18 January.

Varsha, Ramesh S. (2009). "The Business Case for Gender Inclusion: The IWIN Story", Paper presented in *International Case Writing Competition: Gender Inclusivity: Proposing New Paradigms*, held at IIM Ahmedabad, 14-15 November.

World Bank (2015). *World Development Report 2015: Mind, Society, and Behavior.* Washington D.C.

6

MARILENE DE PAULA

Jesus is Power! Neopentecostals and the New Middle Class in Brazil

On 17 April 2016, Brazilian population occupied the streets or waited by the TV to watch, directly from the Lower House, the historical vote for initiating the impeachment process against the President of Brazil, Dilma Rousseff. The 367 votes in favour of impeachment were more than sufficient to proceed with the process. Parliamentarians justified their decision by pointing to the electoral support they had received from evangelical groups , or with reference to the cities that they represented as mayors, or with an expression of professional solidarity with medical or military colleagues. 52 of them mentioned God, 270 mentioned their family and children, but only 6 of them made a direct reference to the 'manipulation of government finances', which was the fiscal crime that the president was accused of and which provided the purported rationale for starting the impeachment process. After Rousseff's suspension, the vote of the Senate on 31 August 2016, concluded the impeachment process.

These events marked the end of a political cycle of the Labour Party, in power for 13 years. In the course of the impeachment process, the role of the evangelical leadership in the National Congress became evident once more. At the end of his first speech as interim president, Michel Temer said, "What we want to do in Brazil now is a religious act, an act in order to reconnect all Brazilian society with the fundamental values of our nation." His words were also intended to please the important religious interest group.

The evangelical faction voted by a large majority for the impeachment of Dilma. After the ministers were sworn in, President Temer took part in a religious ceremony with some of the main leaders of the faction. His commitment to his evangelical allies and to their agendas made him have his first meeting as new President of the Republic with one of their leaders. Throughout the impeachment process, videos showing Temer together with Marcos Feliciano, one of the most controversial congressmen known for his racist preachings and statements against same-sex marriage and women's rights, strengthened Temer's alliance with this group.

But it were not only those now opposing the government who reinforced the alliance with the evangelical political leaders. President Lula himself, once demonised by the leadership of these groups, was publicly supported by the main churches during the 2002 and 2006 elections.

Political groups using the fundamentalist religious flag as an element of their political position have gained more and more space in parliament and in the government, forwarding agendas against sexual and reproductive rights of women and LGBT, same-sex marriage, and promoting the family-oriented view of society and, recently, the extension of religious study in schools.

Where does all this bargaining power and persuasion towards society come from? The power of these evangelical groups relies on the votes of millions of church members, not to mention an economic empire funded mostly by donations, tithes and sale of religious products. The socioeconomic profile of many of these church members coincides directly with what is called the 'NMC (new middle class)' in Brazil: poor working class people who had increased income, promotion to formal jobs, improvement in education and inclusion in social programmes.

During their government Lula and Dilma systematically used the expression 'NMC' to refer to a broad section of a poor population which, at least in media imagery, has comparable access to goods and services as the traditional middle class. For many researchers, however, what really happened was a broadening in the working class base during the Lula government (2003-2010). The minimum wage, primarily responsible for boosting the income of low-income earners and beneficiaries of social security, increased ten-fold over 20 years, mainly due to the increases passed during the Workers' Party government. Therefore, while there was a striking change for the poorest part of population, Brazil is far from effectively reducing its inequalities.

This essay briefly reconsiders some issues related to the concept of NMC. It also seeks to analyse one of the important variables to understand the profile of this sector and note closely one of the remarkable changes that occurred in Brazil in recent years: the role that neopentecostal religious belief plays in economic and social mobility of this group.

Now I am the New Middle Class!

By mid-2016, the expression NMC has largely disappeared from the vocabulary of the Brazilian media that had become fiercely critical of Dilma. Unemployment has increased to 10.9 per cent, so did layoffs in the construction sector, one of the main generators of jobs before; consumption of goods and services has decreased; the restraint of industry and other business sectors only show the economic crisis faced by the country. This directly reflected on the president's popularity, even more limiting her capacity to govern. The long-term strategy aimed at showing Brazilians and the rest of the world that Brazil could henceforth be a country entitled to a seat on the UN Security Council, a member of BRICS, and to move to another level in terms of improvement of living conditions did not mature and could not be sustained. In the last four years, all the formerly positive numbers came down.

The expression NMC had become popular when professor Marcelo Neri, economist and coordinator of the Social Policy Center of the Getúlio Vargas Foundation, one of the most respected thinktanks in the country, released a study determining the family monthly income of this segment between R$1.126 to R$4.854 (Neri 2011). This, at the time, would include 50.5 per cent of the population. From that moment on, the discussion started between those explaining this phenomenon with approval and those criticising this economic view mainly linked to the increased income of the population and not indicators as education, health, housing, etc.

In September 2012, the federal government released the book *The Voice of Middle Class* (SAE 2012), the result of a research project with the same title, in partnership with Caixa Econômica Federal and the United Nations Development Programme. The project had collected data and information on the portion of the population that experienced a significant increase in their income, leaving the stratum of extreme poverty and, thus, according to the document, becoming part of the NMC.

It may be controversial to determine a social class. But, despite the different views and explanations for the phenomenon, researchers agree that this group of people was included into the NMC category on the basis of consumption and not by asset ownership. Access to credit enabled them to purchase goods and services, such as mobile phones, home appliances, clothing, etc. In addition there was an increase in the number of formal jobs and of access to low-income housing units and scholarships in private higher educational institutions. For the first time in decades, a small decrease of social inequality was experienced in Brazil. The country's Gini index fell from 0.570 in 2004 to 0.515 in 2014.

Jesse Souza (2010), sociologist and former president of the Institute for Applied Economic Research (IPEA), has a critical position on this purely economics-based view. He states that, in fact, this social group consisted of a new precarious working class inserted into the job market through commerce, small industries and services, with a workload that, in many cases, exceeds 10 hours per day. Souza argues that 'this concept of middle class, which covers everything, is a mere mechanism to cover up conflicts and social injustices of all kinds. According to this dominant version, middle class is just a bunch of people competing on equal terms for scarce social resources' (Instituto Humanitas Unisinos 2013). In fact, it can be observed in the extremely unequal Brazilian society that the new working class does not have equal opportunities to compete and, moreover, has to face the barriers of the specific habitus of the game of privileges played by the wealthier classes in Brazil.

Kerstenetzky and Uchôa (2012), after analysing the data of the Household Budget Survey of the Brazilian Institute of Geography and Statistics (IGBE), found a lack of social and economic support structures (education, health, housing, etc.) that does not justify the inclusion of this group into the NMC. The data indicated that 9 per cent of the family leaders were illiterate and only 10 per cent held an undergraduate diploma, 71 per cent had no health insurance, 65 per cent of families had no credit card and 82.9 per cent had no overdraft protection agreement. According to the authors, this group did not present most of the criteria that characterises the traditional middle class.

But, in fact, what happened according to the interpretation of Souza, was the emergence of Brazilian 'strugglers', those who managed, after many personal and family sacrifices, to stay longer in school and perhaps attend university, and who are now in jobs that pay better than their parents' occupation. However, data show that although the new precarious working class is based on the idea of material prosperity, social and economic instability still characterised this group. An economic downturn, as currently experienced in Brazil, or some personal misfortune could quickly make this group even more precarious. All this is very different from the traditional middle class who have a network of contacts amongst their relationships which enables them to relocate into new jobs on equal conditions or provide benefits in obtaining public or private services; a middle class prepared and trained for professional practice, which means family orientation and proper education in order to maintain consumption levels and economic stability.

The Neopentecostal Wave

To discuss the NMC is to question a complex universe, with multiple variables that include the cultural, religious, social and economical conditions of this class. One of the most important variables is the evangelical religious belonging, which due to its symbolic universe is fully linked to the aspirations of change in this group.

For those living in the suburbs of the cities, especially in the southeastern states, it is common to come across an evangelical church nearby their house. These churches are everywhere, and their followers already total 22.2 per cent (42.3 million) of Brazilian population, a huge growth compared to 1970 when they were only 5.2 per cent (4.8 million), while Catholics represented 91.8 per cent. The last Census (IBGE 2012) gives us some clues to understand the growth of evangelical Christianity: Catholicism in Brazil suffered a significant decline of 12.2 per cent compared to the previous Census; today, Catholics represent 64.6 per cent of the population. The rise of new religious groups also demonstrates the religious diversity in Brazil.

The secularisation of the state, the end of the Catholic Church's monopoly as the official religion, as well as the state guarantee of freedom and religious tolerance, strengthened in the phase of democratic consolidation (initiated with the 1988 Constitution) created favourable conditions for a competition for religious hegemony to emerge. Other factors are important as well to understand the loss of membership of the Catholic Church. Between 1995 and 2010, the Catholic Church opened only an insignificant number of new parishes, at rates not higher than 2.4 per cent (CERIS 2011). The number of priests is low compared to the evangelicals.[1] Rural-urban migration has moved the population away from the traditionally rural Catholic Church, and the precarious urban life of those who live in suburbs provided an opportunity for the evangelicals to expand.

A range of religious denominations comprise the religious field, formed by several groups and trends that don't come any close to homogeneity. This means that the generic term 'evangelical' cannot satisfactorily explain all historical, behavioural, theological and aesthetic differences among these groups. But we can briefly point out that evangelicals historically originated from Protestantism which began in Brazil in the 19th century, with the Lutheran, Anglican, Presbyterian, Baptist and Methodist churches. In the beginning of the 20th century, the first evangelical churches arrived, thus launching the Pentecostals in Brazil. Having a missionary

1. There are 22,000 priests for almost 48,000 religious service centres—places where masses are celebrated, but not necessarily a full-fledged church—while nuns total 33,000 (Mazzitelli 2013).

purpose, they are distinguished by the baptism of the Holy Spirit, by speaking in strange languages, by spiritual gifts, etc.[2] However, the most critical changes took place by the end of the 1970s when the creation of the Universal Church of the Kingdom of God (1977) created a new religious profile with a deep impact on the population. The Universal Church of the Kingdom of God is present in 200 countries (even operating for 20 years in India, with 2 temples in Chennai, Tamil Nadu). Other churches should also be highlighted, such as the International Grace of God Church (1980, Rio de Janeiro), the Evangelical Community Heal Our Land Church (1976, Goiás), the Reborn in Christ Church (1986, São Paulo) and the World Church of the Power of God (1998, São Paulo), all founded by Brazilian pastors.

The number of these so-called 'neopentecostals', highlighted in this article, sharply increased in recent years. They managed to change the religious scenario by bringing in new ways of preaching. They abandoned the historical Protestant asceticism and changed the interpretation of customs and norms, making them fit better with modern, urban rules of behaviour. They constitute a success model for other churches, including the historical Pentecostalism or even the Catholic Church, which uses many of the evangelical formats in their Charismatic Renewal movement.

The neopentecostal churches are located in central areas, either in the suburbs or in urban locations with high visibility, available and in direct contact with potential followers, engaging an active evangelization. They are trying to attract people with the promise of solving their family, economic or emotional problems, as per the emblematic example of the Universal Church of the Kingdom of God proselytising motto: 'Stop suffering: we have the solution'.

2. Inspired by the US, the first two Pentecostal churches that settled in Brazil were the Christian Congregation of Brazil (1910), founded by an Italian missionary, and the Assembly of God (1911), founded by 2 Swedish missionaries. In the 1950s, another change occurred when two North American missionaries of the International Church of The Foursquare Gospel created the National Evangelization Crusade in São Paulo, mainly focused on preaching divine healing and attracting large crowds for their services. In 1953, they founded the International Church of the Foursquare Gospel (SP). In the wake of this kind of evangelization more churches—Brazil for Christ (1955 SP), God is Love (1962 SP) and the House of Blessing (1964, MG)—were created.

Their practices are magical, but also within a thaumaturgic Christian matrix, in a combination that brings them closer to the reality of their followers and facilitates the construction of a communal religious identity, in contrast to traditional Catholic practices where the priest during mass is distant from his faithful.

Once demonised by classical Pentecostalism, mass media are now being used intensively. Neopentecostal churches have a strong presence in the publishing and phonographic markets. 22 per cent of the Brazilian publishing market is aimed at religious literature (15% Catholic, 4% Evangelical and 3% Spiritists), with revenues of nearly R$458 million in 2012. At the same time, religious music accounts for 20 per cent of the market for music, and concerts are held throughout the country.

The evangelicals join a conservative mass that has been growing in Brazil in recent years. Corruption allegations, quackery accusations and dubious enrichment of some of its leaders were negative factors that helped to consolidate a negative view that described them as 'close-minded', fundamentalist, sectarian people. But Census data show that although their growth rate has declined,[3] this group becomes more and more important for political and sociological analyses on the Brazilian society today.

One example is parliamentary representation. The Evangelical Parliamentarian Front is composed of 75 congressmen and 3 senators, only a little smaller than the agribusiness faction. The evangelicals do not form a single group in Parliament, nor are they represented by only few parties. In the current parliamentary period (2015-2018), they are distributed over 20 parties of all political tendencies, though with a strong inclination for centre-right parties. The highest concentration is in the Brazilian Republican Party (PRB, 15 congressmen), the Social Christian Party (PSC, 9 congressmen) and the Party of the Republic (PR, 7 congressmen), all of which are linked to a particular church or religious order.

3. From 1980 to 1990 the evangelical growth rate reached a peak : from 36.3 per cent to 71.1 per cent. But from 1990 to 2000, there was a decrease and drop to 44.1 per cent (IBGE 2012).

Evangelical Profile and the New Working Class: Jesus is Power

But who is this public claiming to be evangelical? Among the 22.2 per cent evangelicals indicated by the last IBGE Census (2010)[4] including the evangelical churches' missions, of the neopentecostals and the undetermined churches—44.6 per cent are white, while blacks constitute 54.9 per cent. 36.3 per cent of the evangelicals earn between 1 (R$880.00—nearly US$273, in current figures) and 2 minimum wages, and 32.91 per cent up to 1 minimum wage. Schooling is low: 8.6 per cent are illiterate and 42.3 per cent have not completed elementary school. Most of the neopentecostal membership lives in the suburbs of cities. The traditional middle class is part of that group, but represents a smaller share; neopentecostalism is still not that much attractive for this group for whom Catholicism and spiritism, in addition to historical Protestantism, compete.

The growth among pentecostals is linked to the fact that their theological proposition and religious approach are based on the view that their followers are inserted into the consumer society to fully serve the current globalised world. So, living better not only means to be healthy or to pursue any other emotional/cultural values, but it necessarily means to have a better material life. The neopentecostals employ in their preaching the teachings of Prosperity Theology, which states that having material goods, being healthy, not having big financial problems etc. show one's faith and proves how God is working in one's life. Therefore, the neopentecostals became even more pragmatic and oriented towards the short-term, reversing the older theological logic that valued the suffering on earth, payment for the sins, and a better life in the kingdom of God (to come). For neopentecostal groups, prosperity is not something to achieve in the

4. Evangelical churches are divided by IBGE in three categories: Evangelical mission (Evangelical Lutheran Church, Evangelical Presbyterian Church, Evangelical Methodist Church, Evangelical Baptist Church, Evangelical Congregational Church, Adventist Evangelical Church, Other Evangelical Mission), or otherwise related to the historic Protestantism; the Evangelicals of Pentecostal origin (Assembly of God Church, Christian Congregation of Brazil Church, Brazil for Christ Church, Church of the Foursquare Gospel, Universal Church of the Kingdom of God, House of Blessing Church, God is Love Church, Maranata Church, New Life Church, undetermined Renewed Evangelical, Evangelical Community and other pentecostal evangelical churches) and a third classification are unclassified Evangelicals.

next life, but right here, now, in everyday life and, in this sense, it necessarily involves the exchange of 'material things' for 'material things.' To this end, the payment of tithes and donations to the church are crucial for demonstrating the members' commitment to the church and, mainly, to God; they evidence their spirituality and their faith in God.

According to Mariano (1999), this change of conception 'totally subverts the old Pentecostal asceticism', highlighting the need of donating money to receive blessings, and stressing that without this, there shall be no opportunity to change your life. Additionally, each church creates different ways to mediate this relationship with God in order to improve the financial life of its followers. The Universal Church of the Kingdom of God has the 'prosperity current', prayer meetings that states, "if you wish to boost your business, get the job of your dreams, set up your own business or finally settle your debts, join the prosperity current. Allow the Power of God to manifest in your life."[5] The World Church of the Power of God released the 'Hammer of Justice', an object that promises to 'break' the problems of their followers. But these promises of prosperity can only be achieved by those who were 'chosen by God'.

Solange Ramos Andrade (Wolfart 2012), however, states that the 'concept of religious efficiency is very important, because if a religious discourse is not efficient 'it does not work', losing its effectiveness, which is to offer answers to questions that are at the same time immediate and fundamental, as seen in the moment we face now.' Followers are interested in building a future for themselves that is, in economic terms, better than that of their parents; they also want to bequeath better conditions for their children. All this is not merely a desire or just a spiritual pursuit; this wish should come along with changes in everyday life, by investing time and money in education and professional development, but also in the reaffirmation of faith. In this sense, the ideas propagated by the churches can be a key stimulating element, from the religious perspective, arguing that people deserve

---

5. Available at *http://iurdmc.blogspot.com.br/p/reunioes_12.html* (accessed on 6 February 2017); see also Hanashiro (2013: 24).

a better life in this world, especially economically, and claiming to be a mediator to this end. For the evangelicals, to reaffirm their faith in these churches means to reaffirm a life strategy, and denying their faith would amount to denying these strategies and values.

The church also plays a fundamental role as an arena of social life, as it widens the range of relationships of its members; this can be a source of employment, of services and opportunities to find a new job. One may argue that providing a social arena with economic and social gains is not an attribute that pertains exclusively to churches. But it is important to emphasise the loyalty to an evangelical space. Participation in social work and other community activities takes place within these spaces, considered to be anointed by the solidarity and strength of faith. In this sense, the domain of Pentecostal churches can contribute to the weakening of other processes of social engagement, such as neighbourhood associations, mothers' clubs, NGOs, trade unions etc., once they compete with these to create their own networks of participation.

The growth of these churches is linked to the expansion of the public at the foundation of the social pyramid, where the precarious working class is located. For them, it was necessary to approach the religious logic present in the suburbs, which operates from religious mixes and the synthesis between Catholic rites, African-Brazilian cults and spiritualism.

Although African cults are demonised, still it is this from where many churches 'borrow' names and practices such as the 'discharge session' of the Universal Church of the Kingdom of God, the replacement of Saints Cosmas and Damian candies for 'Jesus sweets,'[6] as in the New Life Project Church in Rio de Janeiro; the acarajé[7] of Jesus in Bahia, a traditional Afro-Brazilian snack sold in the streets,

6. The Catholic saints San Cosme and San Damião are celebrated in Brazil in September. Devotees of these saints give candies to children in the streets of cities. This tradition was syncretised by the religious cults of African matrix, which associate it with the Erês or Ibejis, deities that represent children in Yoruba mythology. In fact they are responsible for keep this tradition alive.

7. The acarajé is a cookie made of beans, dried and fried shrimp in palm oil. Much appreciated in Bahian cuisine, it is a traditional delicacy linked to the cults of Yansã, one of the Gods of Candomblé.

now made by the evangelicals and not any more by the traditional black ladies dressed in traditional costumes of the Candomblé ritual[8]; the removal of demons or evil that would be harmful to the lives of the followers; the 'rue soap' for spiritual cleansing, that promise to end bad luck, to ward off the evil eye, etc.

Brazil is famous for its syncretic traditions, where one could go to church in the morning and visit a Candomblé courtyard or Umbanda centre by the evening, and to receive blessings on Thursdays in a Kardecist centre. This, and many other characteristics and expressions of Brazilian culture are now disapproved and rejected by the neopentecostal congregations. Of course, this does not necessarily mean that all will follow such prescriptions. But the goal is to increase participation in the evangelical congregation, to the detriment of all other religious experiences. Another important factor linking these churches is the inclusion and transformation of individuals who had no representation at all in their community or in the family (or at times were excluded due to alcoholism, drug trafficking, a morally condemnable life etc.). They now have recognition; by giving 'testimony' of the change that takes place in their lives, they become symbols of the power of faith and the strength of the church itself. The sentence 'Jesus is Power', used by some churches, is a good example of the empowerment given to followers. The recognition within and beyond the group creates a sense of self-esteem that makes them militate for the evangelical purpose, trying to bring to the church their family, friends and all those to which they somehow relate.

Sharing beliefs and world views makes it possible that the identification of being 'evangelical' can be invoked beyond the religious environment, thus creating fraternal and interest bonds. In some prisons, there are specific divisions dedicated to evangelical inmates. There are group meetings at schools and workplaces where those of the same religious belief get together; there is even the emblematic Evangelical Faction in the Parliament. But this logic

8. The traditional clothes of the vendors of Acarajé is a long and round skirt, turban and chalets, all whites. This clothing is also one of the dresses of the rituals of religious cults of African matrix.

also comprises the creation of dichotomies, such as 'us' and 'them', in a moralising speech that rejects those who does not adhere the church. Their relative sectarianism and the belief that they hold the monopoly of the divine truth and salvation, even nowadays, make interreligious and ecumenical dialogue very hard.

The conservative mode of speech, mainly based on the exhortation to return to the values of the traditional nuclear family, is another key thought to understand the strong appeal of these churches for this new working class. This speech rejects any type of sexual orientation other than the heterosexual, and condemns practices considered devious, such as abortion, drug use (alcohol or illicit drugs), adultery, etc. Thus, these churches serve as a moral barrier, strengthening the family relationship, and the integration and socialisation among people.

From the evangelical perspective, correct individual behaviour includes attending formal education, dressing properly, speaking without the use of profanities or vulgar language, respecting the members of the congregation brothers, etc.; in other words, it is a standardised set of behaviours that serve as social and economic support base. However, once the field is not homogeneous, the diversity includes both very conservative and flexible moral positions regarding the customs and behaviours of today's society. But there is a common point: they decisively contribute to bring together individuals with a common objective with regards to the improvement of their living conditions, in many aspects, including the economic.

But what can be seen as very positive—because we are talking about a socially and economically marginalised portion of population —also raises contradictions. Despite the common goal, the solution is individualised rather than collective. Prejudice against those who do not meet the moral standards of the group and the dichotomies between 'us' and 'them' are reinforced.

This moralising discourse is used by evangelical leaderships to justify their presence in media and in politics as a social good, and as a tool to fight contemporary social problems such as violence, family conflicts, drug addiction etc. At the same time, the struggles for power within the evangelicals' field and between their churches was one reason that motivated the construction of a broader political project. They realised that their power would be much higher, even though their political project is not a collective one at the moment.

The speech of Pastor Marcos Galdino de Lima, President of Assembly of God Ministry of Santo Amaro, on 2014 elections, is a good example of the compromise of leaders: "The people are now understanding and becoming aware not only of the word, but also of politics." And he adds: "We are involved so we can help to make the city improve in the aspects people need."[9] Evangelical leaders are attempting to convert the benefits of spiritual and social comfort provided by religious practices into a currency in the political market. And so far they have been successful.

References

Bomeny, Helena (2011). *Do Frango ao Avião ou o Que é Possível Dizer Sobre a Nova Classe Média Brasileira? Notas Exploratórias.* Rio de Janeiro: CPDOC/FGV & UERJ. Available at: *http://bibliotecadigital.fgv.br/dspace/handle/10438/8475?show=full*

Centro de Estatísticas Religiosas e Investigações Sociais (2011). *Censo Anual da Igreja Católica no Brasil: Análise Sociológica da Evolução Numérica da Presença da Igreja no Brasil 2010.* Rio de Janeiro.

Freston, Paul (1999). *Protestantismo e Democracia no Brasil.* Paris: Lusotopie. pp.329-40.

Hanashiro, Walker Umeki (2013). *A Igreja Universal do Reino de Deus e a Teatralização da sua Batalha Espiritual: Uma Construção Etnográfica da Sessão Espiritual do Descarrego.* Master dissertation. Universidade Federal de São Paulo, Escola de Filosofia, Letras e Ciências Humanas, Guarulhos. Available at *http://www2.unifesp.br/ciencias_sociais/dissertacoes-defendidas-versao-final/walker-umeki-hanashiro*, accessed on 6/1/2017).

IBGE (2012). *Censo Demográfico 2010: Características Gerais da População, Religião e Pessoas com Deficiência.* Rio de Janeiro.

Instituto Humanitas Unisinos (2013). *Nova Classe Média: Um Discurso Economicista.* Entrevista Especial com Jessé de Souza. 3 January. *http://www.ihu.unisinos.br/entrevistas/516686-nova-classe-media-um-discurso-economicista-entrevista-especial-com-jesse-de-souza.* Accessed on 15/1/2017.

Lamounier, Bolívar and Amaury de Souza (2010). *A Classe Média Brasileira: Ambições, Valores e Projetos de Sociedade.* Rio de Janeiro: Elsevier; Brasília, DF: CNI.

Mariano, Ricardo. (1999). *Neopentecostais: Sociologia do Novo Pentecostalismo no Brasil.* São Paulo, Ed. Loyola.

Martins, Rodrigo. (2012). "A Avalanche Evangélica", *Carta Capital*, 25 July.

9. "Pastor da Assembleia já Planeja 2014", *Journal Valor Econômico* (online version), Rio de Janeiro, 8 October 2012. *http://www.valor.com.br/eleicoes2012/2858964/pastor-da-assembleia-ja-planeja-2014*, accessed on 14 February 2013.

Matos, Teresinha (2007). "Caseiras Pentecostais: Mulheres Felizes", in *Último andar, Caderno de Pesquisa da Ciência da Religião* 16: 129-82, June. São Paulo.

Mazzitelli, Fabio (2013). "Brasil Tem Deficit de Mais de 20 Mil Padres", 17 February. *http://www1.folha.uol.com.br/fsp/mundo/94254-brasil-tem-deficit-de-mais-de-20-mil-padres.shtml*, accessed on 05 February 2016.

Neri, Marcelo (2011). *A Nova Classe Média: O Lado Brilhante da Base da Pirâmide*. Rio de Janeiro: Ed. Saraiva.

Revista Do Instituto Humanitas Unisino (2012). "Religiões e Religiosidade Hoje: Significados e Especificidades", *São Leopoldo* 407(XII), 05 November.

SAE (Brasil Secretaria de Assuntos Estrategicos) (2012). *Vozes da Classe Média*. Brasília: SAE.

Souza, Jessé (2009). *A Ralé Brasileira: Quem é e Como Vive?* Belo Horizonte: Ed. UFMG.

———. (2010). *Os Batalhadores Brasileiros: Nova Classe Média ou Nova Classe Trabalhadora?* Belo horizonte: Ed. UFMG.

Uchoa, Christiane and Celia Lessa Kerstenetzky (2012). *"É a "Nova Classe Média" Classe Média? O Que Diz a Pequisa de Orçamentos Familiares (2008-2009)". Texto para Discussão n.* 066. Rio de Janeiro: CEDE/UFF. p.10. See in *http://www.proac.uff.br/cede/sites/default/files/TD66.pdf*, accessed on 15 May 2015.

Vasconcelos, Paulo (2012). "Indústria da Salvação", *Valor Magazine:* 4-9. 28 December. Rio de Janeiro.

Wolfart, Graziela (2012). *Vitalidade e Criatividade: As Marcas da Religiosidade do Povo Brasileiro.* Revista On-Line do Instituto de Humanitas da Unisinos, São Leopoldo, edição 407. November. See: *http://www.ihuonline.unisinos.br/artigo/4737-solange-ramos-de-andrade*, accessed on 15 May 2015.

New Middle Class Politics

7

CÂNDIDO GRZYBOWSKI

Where are the New Middle Classes in Brazil?

In this beginning of the 21st century, Brazil, like other so-called 'emerging' nations, has seen the rise of a political and academic discussion regarding the NMC (new middle classes). Empirical evidence suggests an increase in income for the lower classes. Backed by the criterion of a per capita income of up to USD 1.25/day for extreme poverty and USD 2.50/day for the poverty line, there definitely have been significant improvements over the course of at least one and a half decades. The income level of millions of people has risen above these thresholds. Those who found themselves just above these basic levels, but who still had a low income, also obtained important benefits for a certain period. With higher incomes, there were changes in the market basket, and therefore in the market dynamics, with a highly significant financial impact, given the size of these groups, which comprise over 70 per cent of more than 200 million Brazilians.

Apart from better living conditions, what do those changes suggest? Would an increased income alone—many people have doubled their per capita income in actual terms—be enough to cause those changes in the structure and composition of social classes? Why use a single measure—financial income—and its continuous distribution along a pyramid as a means to define social classes? What about the extremely unequal distribution of wealth, which is more structural and has increased during the period in question? It can be stated that poverty has diminished among us, which in itself can be seen as a gain in terms of civilisation. However, as a phenomenon of social relations between the rich and the poor within a certain society, and not just the figure—below USD 2.50—we still have the same ratio of people living in poverty.

This essay seeks to contribute to the analysis of this process in Brazil, one of the so-called 'emerging' countries, but in a context of financial and geopolitical changes under the hegemony of neoliberal capitalist globalisation. Capitalism is fundamentally a social class system that generates inequalities. Social classes are not continuous, but rather modes of economic, social, cultural, and political organisation that are extremely different and dynamic in the history of each society, that create identities which develop their own interests, and that act as conflicting forces and tend to cluster in opposite and antagonistic poles. Middle classes then arise as a part of this set of forces with complex and somehow contradictory structures, and their existence is not entirely based on how large or small the average financial income is. Each class is in itself a contradictory summary of differentiated layers, distinguished by different situations, but that goes against other contradictory syntheses, which in turn are also elements of diversity.

Brazil: Contradictions in a 'Low-Intensity' Social Democracy

This article is based on the context in which Brazil is currently (November 2016) immersed, one of a huge financial and political crisis that is far from coming to an end. I do not intend to analyse this crisis. I am simply recording the currently observable massive dismantling of the economic, political, legal, and institutional conditions, both internal and external, that have enabled better income and consumption standards for millions of families and given rise to the discussion about the NMCs. As a citizen and social activist for radical democracy, I admit that we are facing a major political defeat, marking the end of a wave of democratisation among us. This moment demands fierce resistance against the possibility of the state power being entirely subdued by the interests of large economic and financial corporations that exacerbate exclusion, social inequality, and environmental destruction. We need to acknowledge our mistakes and learn from the recent past, testing the limits of our possibilities. At the same time, we must also construct, here and now, a newer, bolder mobilising thought that is capable of creating irrepressible civil movements and promoting the structural changes that are necessary for justice as well as social and environmental sustainability among us.

Hence, one must analyse what happened in Brazil over the course of its 30 years of redemocratisation, as well as the nature of the changes that have taken place, which is evinced by the current crisis. With regard to the issue behind these considerations—Brazil's new middle classes—it is worth highlighting some key processes within the aforementioned time period. They are complex and somehow contradictory processes. This article is not aimed at dissecting them, but they must be regarded as the infrastructure behind this entire historical period. The first one is the redemocratisation process itself, which was pushed forward by forces coming from within the civil society after its struggle against the military dictatorship and the wild capitalist expansion taking place at that time. It is worth mentioning the outstanding emergence of powerful labour movements in industrial, agribusiness, service, and financial centres (iron and steel workers, sugarcane cutters, drivers, merchants, bank employees, etc.), new peasant movements (such as the Landless Workers' Movement, squatters, rubber tappers, family farmers, among others), popular movements in slums and working-class suburbs, student movements, professional movements (engineers, lawyers, teachers, civil servants), and civil rights movements (such as political amnesty, feminism, racial equality, housing, etc.). Despite the enormous crisis and the structural adjustment imposed by the International Monetary Fund and the World Bank—the so-called 'lost decade' in economic terms—the fact remains that, in Brazil, this process gave rise to new collective political subjects, as well as a great democratic agreement towards inclusive citizenship: the Constitution of 1988, the legitimate judicial and institutional basis for 'social democracy' in the Brazilian style. It grants unrestricted political citizenship to everyone who is 16 or older and revolves around a set of cultural, economic, and social rights expressed through a guarantee of a universal system of education, health, and social security. As a result of this democratic impact, constitutional law, which imposes conditions for public budgets and government policies, thus became the centre of the political dispute in the redemocratisation process.

The second process that should be noted here is the creation of new political parties capable of disputing and exercising power. Given the legal facilitation and the political rules adopted at the time, many opportunistic parties came into play, leading to the current situation of about 30 political denominations, although most of them are inconsistent in their attempt to represent the diversity of Brazilian society. Nevertheless, a significant political polarisation was observed in Brazil during and because of the democratisation process between the Brazilian Social Democracy Party (PSDB, for its acronym in Portuguese) and the Workers' Party (PT), to which other relevant parties ended up associating themselves. Their social bases were different, but both parties helped to make it impossible for certain parts of the ruling classes, the middle classes, and the lower classes with less democratic and more conservative–or even authoritarian–profiles to compete for hegemony. PSDB and PT, the latter more than the former, presented themselves in the historical practice as ways to implement the 'social democracy' presented by the 1988 Constitution. The 2 political parties led all elections and held the political power during the 30-year democratisation wave that has now come to an end. Both forces are the biggest losers, PT more than PSDB, but both of them—PSDB's 8 years against PT's 13 years in power—were hegemonic and ruled the country through a 'conciliation of classes' in the name of governability. It was precisely this governability that gave them both the very justification they needed to actually 'buy' allies and fill the government with a wide range of smaller opportunistic parties, thus creating majority blocs that were not at all programme-oriented, especially in the National Congress, but also in state courts and local town halls nationwide. This is where the DNA for a low-intensity democracy lies: none of those coalitions made—or even attempted to make, in fact—any changes to capitalism in a way that prioritised citizens' rights over the accumulation of capital. These governments can be told apart based on the amount of social conditions they imposed onto the expansion of capitalism, or on the amount of incentives they provided so capitalism would grow, as long as it respected minimum democratic regulations and basic citizenship rights. The PSDB opted for a subordinate insertion in neoliberal globalisation, as long as it brought 'advantages' for Brazil. The Workers' Party chose to be more sovereign without denying globalisation, but taking advantage of its contradictions and believing in its own 'emergence' as a potential power and a strategic partner to the BRICS nations. In a way, the PT was more successful with its 'weak reformism', as described by Singer (2012), compared to the PSDB and its policy of building alliances with the 'owners of the world'.

This leads us to the third fundamental process in the entire period: the way global capitalism expands, its power, its geopolitics, and the imposition of a system that serves large economic and particularly financial corporations. Brazil's weak 'social democracy', apart from all internal contradictions, should be examined in the context of expansion and domination of a globalising neoliberal capitalism, which has nine lives. The first decade of democratisation in Brazil consisted of a search for ways to settle down and survive the radical structural adjustments imposed by the 'Washington Consensus' agenda, with all the International monetary Fund/World Bank (IMF/WB) measures embedded in their loans. Foreign debt was Brazil's weakness, which also holds true for all Latin American, African, and Asian countries, but the strategy was to subject the whole world to the free market project and its rules, as well as to neoliberalism as a global model of civilisation for all mankind. This process gave birth to the World Trade Organization and enabled the installation of a 'global economy' to serve large economic and financial corporations. A 'global casino' began to dictate the pace of things, subjecting capital goods to the logic of financial profit-seeking, which exploits and accumulates at the expense of the world, of all mankind, and of the planet. 'Emerging countries' then appeared during this process, at the time when the PT was already in power in Brazil, with China acting as the world's industrial maquiladora or sweat shop, and starting to assume the greatest burdens of environmental destruction and greenhouse gas emissions, while the other BRICS and secondary nations supplied commodities with their economies repressed. Is that a new form of colonialism? Yes, but one that uses armies only against breakaway groups, like Middle Eastern countries. In all other cases, the free market simply imposes itself, dispensing with the need for armies, although it does create exclusion and migration. Control has been maintained through powerful financial mechanisms and policies dictated by Central Banks—including money laundering in tax havens, as revealed by the Panama Papers—as well as espionage and the control of information and communications by new global corporations based on the new information and communications technologies.

Those were very contradictory processes, both in Brazil and in the rest of the world. However, it was in Brazil that the World Social Forum (WSF) was created amid worldwide demonstrations against the neoliberal globalisation of this era. The WSF, apart from contributing to the emergence of more progressive governments in South America, was primarily a catalyst for mobilisation within the civil society in search for 'another possible world', thus challenging the hegemony of neoliberalism and creating conditions for a new citizen-oriented political culture with global reach. The WSF lost both inspiration and capacity when it refrained from serving as a space for the incorporation of new political forces in view of the overwhelming crisis that has taken over the world since 2008. Nevertheless, it did leave behind a legacy of open possibilities that are currently threatened by the deep crisis within the civil societies of different countries. Finally, a few alternatives came up to face the contradictions of democracy itself against capitalism and its new aggressiveness, both in Brazil and in the rest of the world.

Taking these processes into consideration in order to analyse the changes in income and purchasing power for the lower classes, it is worth noting the impacts of the monetary stabilisation achieved in the 1990s—the Fernando Henrique Cardoso (PSDB) administration—and the important social conditions for the economic growth recorded from 2003 to 2015—the Lula and Dilma (PT) administrations—during the 2000s commodities boom led by China. The issue of the NMCs was fully embedded into Brazil's academic and political debate, especially after significant changes in income were observed during the PT administrations. It should be remembered that, although very important for a country marred by deeply ingrained inequalities, those changes were neither structural nor sustainable, as I have already stated in several occasions (Grzybowski 2004, 2012, and 2013). The current crisis completely reveals the limits of this low-intensity 'social democracy'.

Social Justice in Brazil: Important, Though Limited Developments

In Brazil's democratisation, even with the rise of the PT administration, no structural changes whatsoever were implemented in terms of distribution of wealth and power, and no changes were made to the bases of an economy that is highly dependent on the 'comparative advantages' resulting from the exploitation of natural resources across the country's huge territory since colonial times. However, one must acknowledge that there has been some progress in the search for more social justice in Brazil's historical context of tremendous inequality combined with racism, patriarchalism, and a patrimonial culture of privileges acquired by 'cattle and people owners.', I will attempt to spotlight some examples of this progress brought about by active social policies in a context of economic expansion.

The *Bolsa Família* ('Family Allowance') social welfare programme is a world-renowned conditional cash transfer programme that benefits over 13 million families who live below the poverty line, roughly a quarter of Brazil's population. The programme has nothing to do with a universal basic salary for all citizens—which would have been a radical and very transforming concept—but rather is aimed at those who are doomed to live in poverty and starvation. It is beyond doubt a programme with direct and immediate impact, one that is necessary from an ethical and democratic point of view, since it is unacceptable that people starve in the country that is currently considered the world's farm. *Bolsa Família* does not change the structures that generate hardships, poverty, and inequality. It simply avoids the worst-case scenario. It is nonetheless something to celebrate, considering Brazil's situation and how the poor, the black, and the excluded have been treated throughout history. Obviously, it was not the beneficiaries of *Bolsa Família* who moved up to a higher social class. The heralds of the NMCs keep failing to mention that.

Highly significant changes in the field of social justice that had an impact on Brazil's social structure were the millions of jobs that were created, including new labour laws and in particular, an actual increase in the minimum wage. About 20 million jobs were created in Brazil from the beginning of the century up until 2015. At the same time, there was an inversion in the ratio between informal jobs (roughly 60% to 40% of the labour force), without any rights guaranteed, and formal jobs (from 40% to 60%), with formal work contracts and the guarantee of labour and social security rights. However, it is important to point out that 9 in 10 of those people earned up to one and a half minimum wages (Pochman 2012), mostly in the service industry. Nevertheless, the real increase in the minimum wage had an even greater impact. Since its peak in the late 1950s, the legal minimum wage lost two-third of its actual value during the military dictatorship in Brazil. In the 1990s, it stabilised and showed some recovery, especially due to the stabilisation of the currency achieved during the Cardoso administration (PSDB), but it was during the PT administration that a strong recovery of the real value of the minimum wage occurred, with an increase of over 60 per cent. It should be noted that the minimum wage is a fundamental source of reference for the income of more than 80 per cent of Brazil's labour force, both in the formal and the informal sectors, representing the portion of the population that earns up to 3 minimum wages. The job creation policy and in particular the policy that increased the minimum wage were the most significant changes recorded in this period in terms of income. Due to the current crisis, however, many of these new jobs and increased wages have started to vanish. The signs of the crisis are visible on the streets of Brazil's largest cities.

Many other policies were put in place in the name of social justice which altered income and consumption standards, namely, extended social protection (a minimum wage—the basic reference for social security—for the disabled and the elderly), extended access to credit (payroll loans, the purchasing of durable goods), the *Minha Casa, Minha Vida* ('My House, My Life') subsidised public housing construction programme, and the National Family Farming Programme aimed at supporting small-scale family agriculture (with the public procurement of food for school meals and social assistance programmes), among others. The policy of affirmative action introducing racial and poverty quotas for admission to public universities, technical schools, and even the public service deserve special mentioning. This public programme might have had the greatest impact ever on Brazil's, excluding its social structure, as it dealt with class privileges associated with having access to higher-level academic and technical knowledge and to more stable and better paid public jobs. Moreover, more public universities and technical schools were created, and a funding programme for higher education was amplified. In this case, class privileges were indeed eradicated. More symbolically than in practical terms, it is also worth mentioning the creation of a federal ministry for women, racial equality, and human rights. The deep roots of social inequality started to at least be considered as a state and public issue, despite the pathetic public budget that was allocated to it. It is also symbolic that this same ministry was abolished in the current context of power seizure by the same old powers that be.

So, what are these changes? Only a beginning, although they are seen as a political threat to the privileges of other classes, especially the traditional middle classes and the ruling classes, nothing else. With regard to the development model, in fact, the same thing happened: the expansion of agribusiness and mining, the discovery and exploitation of large oil reserves, the resumption of large infrastructure works with the Brazilian Development Bank (BNDES) funding. In actual terms, Brazil has become more dependent on its natural resources, despite important developments in terms of technology that subsidises the extraction of minerals (mainly iron, aluminium and oil) and agribusiness (soybean, sugar and ethanol, coffee, eucalyptus/paper pulp, meat), all of which comes hand in hand with a great concentration of property and wealth. In Brazil, social and environmental justice is just a façade, seeing that the country is actually going in another direction.

This kind of exacerbation in structural terms ended up leading to the consolidation of an essentially urban country with large cities. Statistically speaking, almost 85 per cent of Brazil's population lives in cities, although in practical terms, it is estimated that nearly 35 per cent of them still depend on the health of agriculture, or agribusiness in this case, even though they live in cities. What really matters is that, from a social and democratic perspective, the country is increasingly marked by the favelas, by the urban slums. In reality, Brazil has a highly segregated urban country with symbolic walls that materialise geographically: slums versus paved neighbourhoods, poverty versus wealth, black versus white, in different territories, where some have virtually nothing while others are super-equipped. All Brazilian cities contain super-wealthy areas and luxury condos, private zones, some of which are heavily armoured and protected by private security personnel, whereas some of the poor areas are fully militarised and subject to the 'occupation' of private militias, drug cartels, and the military police.

Still regarding the meaning of the recent changes, I would rather align my opinion with that of analysts such as Souza (2015, 2013, and 2010) and Pochman (2012), who do acknowledge the changes, but also state that they have failed to modify the foundations of Brazil's social class structure. There has indeed been more access to new consumption standards, usually based on precarious jobs, double shifts, and a lot of effort, combining paid work and entrepreneurship of all kinds, mainly in the service industry. We are talking about the new 'strugglers', in the words of Souza, as well as about a new form of poverty for those who are self-employed. In fact, we are far from anything that could be regarded as actual social and citizen emancipation, having merely reached a milestone of civilisation within a system of socially excluding and environmentally predatory capitalism. What really happened was a full-scale change, whereby the poor started to earn more and therefore gained access to assets they had previously been denied. Other classes also experienced an increase in income, such as the traditional middle classes, but more importantly, the wealthy got a lot wealthier. Wealth and power inequality increased instead of decreasing.

Social Classes and Democracy in Today's Brazil

The theoretical and political clarity of the concept of social classes is crucial for this analysis. It served as a practical, dynamic, and historical notion long before it was adopted as a theoretical concept in social sciences. People identify with a certain social class and act as such. Analysts are responsible for looking into the actual practice, breaking it down and rebuilding it as a conscious synthesis, as an analytical concept. The opposite path leads to confusion and a certain mystification of reality, something that is very common in the social sciences, which are limited to functional empiricism.

The first piece of evidence is thus outlined: people do not see, or think of, themselves as located somewhere on a continuous scale, but rather based on the differences and oppositions, they themselves perceive or that others exert towards them. We are this, not that: we are poor, not rich; we live in slums, not in paved neighbourhoods; we come from the outskirts, not from the upscale part of town; we are farmers, squatters, natives, rural workers, not landlords or agribusiness magnates; we are workers, not bourgeoisie; we make our own living, we do not need to exploit others; we are black, not white; we are women, not men. We can be neither this nor that, but we feel we belong to a group or layer. However, we never truly are or see ourselves as just an average in the social scale. This is human life, complex and wondrous, oppressive or liberating, joyful or sorrowful. The truth is that we are socially localised; we occupy predetermined places, whether assigned to or conquered by us. Not continuously, but with contradictions and oppositions.

Social classes make sense historically, and therefore theoretically and scientifically, only when they express the historical experience and practice as all-encompassing collectives, as groups that share the same conditions, situations, desires and struggles. Social classes exist in sociological and political terms only when specific groups are integrated and identified as part of a larger block, as part of a larger set of similarities, however different they may seem, as opposed to other blocks or social classes. For this reason, the best concept of social classes in my opinion is the one that defines them as a historical social block of collective subjects living under the same conditions and holding the same position in the social structure who, at the same time, perceive themselves and act as such. To simplify it: social class is defined by the position in the social structure plus political will, with identity and interests (Gramsci 1978).

Using that as a point of reference, in order to analyse the changes in social classes that took place in the context of economic and political changes during the Brazilian democratisation process, I believe it is essential to examine and assess those changes as part of how they are perceived and how the people who experience them live. It is important to see the process through which, based on those changes and perceptions, they arise as collective subjects and form social classes. This sort of analysis goes far beyond the present essay, in which I attempt to demonstrate the total theoretical and political inconsistency in the understanding of the changes to the base of Brazil's social pyramid—viewed in a continuous scale of distribution, considering a single variable: income—as a process through which the NMCs emerge.

I hereby reiterate a theoretical perspective that has guided me in my role as political sociologist and activist. Structural changes are a necessary condition for the appearance of new social classes or fractions of classes within a given society, but they are politically insufficient to the extent that social classes and fractions thereof ultimately need to emerge as such in politics. This implies the creation of their collective identity, their values and their visions on society, a process that takes place by means of social and political struggle, being capable of generating political autonomy or subordination to another class or fraction of a class. In this sense, it is also important to analyse how they organise themselves as a collective subject and the complex issue of leadership and political representation by and for themselves. Furthermore, this analysis can only be carried out in a context of relationship of forces. From a radical democracy perspective, to which I adhere, analysing the political and social changes for the poor and the excluded—as is the case in this pathetic debate on the NMCs—is important only insofar as it demonstrates their social and political emancipation as emerging classes.

As a matter of fact, many uprisings and resistance movements were seen during Brazil's democratisation process. I have already pointed out those political forces that explain democratisation itself, as well as the birth and consolidation of the PT. The intensification of the process of capitalist expansion inwards went along with an intense 'reprimarisation' of the economy, focusing on production and export of agricultural and natural resource commodities, which then led to an aggravated process of occupying and taking over territories and natural resources. This was and is a source of conflicts. The Landless Workers' Movement, consolidated during the redemocratisation process, polarised the resistance to agribusiness in the entire country. However, indigenous groups appeared as collective subjects, in their own way showing strength and legitimacy in opposition to the expansion of large construction projects in their territories for agribusiness or energy generation (hydropower dams in the Amazon). Another important resistance front that is full of contradictions relates to public territories versus excessive mining, which leads to privatisation and destruction. However, these are practical and historical examples of struggle and civic awareness against the exploitation imposed by large corporations. Those undertakings have obviously generated changes in the working class. Even with low wages, workers often build alliances with large corporations in order to defend...well, their own jobs. Contradictory? Yes, but this analysis is much more important than the masking to which linear statistical analyses lead, while failing to take into account all the conflicts and actual struggles behind all the numbers.

In large cities, the working class was considerably reduced in size—through technification, increased productivity, and reduction of the industry's relative importance for the economy, Brazil increasingly built industries and a modern service sector of its own. This led to the consolidation of urban centres with 100,000 to 1 million inhabitants outside of major metropolitan areas. This has become a challenge for the trade union movement, the basis of the PT. The movement was not renewed at the same pace as the profile of services and industrial labour changed, which caused the 'working class' to split and even lose its legitimacy to represent the trade union movement in actual struggles. In recent years, before the current political crisis, more significant strikes took place as a means to question this very representation of the trade unions.

Nevertheless, I want to draw attention to those 'strugglers' that come from slums and ghettos, comprising roughly half of the Brazilian population, who experienced some improvement in their living conditions, however small, when compared to two decades ago. Their political emergence is complex, even though most of them voted for the PT in this context, as stated by Singer (2012). Identities emerged, but with a flair of individualism, a search for personal success, and the conservative values of the new Pentecostal churches, this group's main social and political expression outlet. They represent a large portion of the working class, despite being poorly organised and having no previous organisational experience whatsoever, which makes for a contradictory presence in the social and political arenas. They are by far the most connected to the mainstream media, especially TV, their main source of information and their main tool of including themselves into the social imaginary. This affects their values, the way they see and consume, and even their moods. The new resistance in slums and ghettos, especially when the youth are involved, obviously does not follow that pattern. The new information and communication technologies and the sharing platforms enabled by them have led to new forms of social and political expression in the field of culture and in the new student movements. That is where the sons and daughters of the 'strugglers'—in most cases young people who have to start working prematurely to help their families—show society the emergence of something very new that is taking place within their social class, which I call 'the new workers'. The major demonstrations that took place in Brazil's largest cities in 2013, right before the World Cup, constituted an 'explosion of citizenship' (Grzybowski 2013). Some movements, such as the Landless Workers' Movement, are manifestations that brought about changes to the old perspective of a dominated, exploited working class. This demands serious investigation, as well as the whole popular Pentecostalism that preaches individualistic and conservative values. More consistent analyses on the subject have only just begun to surface. In the case of events that challenge the status quo, our attention is drawn to a common trait that can be seen in many countries today: the practice of direct democracy and the refusal to grant legitimacy to any kind of representation, as shown in the articles published in the special edition of the *Nueva Sociedad* magazine (Penny et al. 2014).

In this regard, it is worth noting how the 'traditional' middle classes evolved. In my understanding, traditional middle classes consist of self-employed professionals, lawyers, engineers, architects, physicians, professors, public policy-makers and 'white collar' employees, politicians, both elected and party members, media professionals, artists and cultural producers. They need to be regarded as a collective subject in their diversity, full of contradictions both internally and in their relationship with other social classes. Their political role as a class, however, must not be ignored or minimised. Alone, they might not drastically change structural situations, but without them, without their involvement, the ability to change is also reduced. Their voting capacity and the way they influence public discussions, the development of mobilisations and the construction of political agendas, all of that penetrates virtually all areas of society, social movements and political parties. The traditional middle classes have obviously also experienced changes. Perhaps not a change in social class as such, but they have at least faced political challenges in this new reality of changes to the foundations of society and how they affect politics. The role played by the middle classes in the major demonstrations against the Dilma administration during this crisis scenario still deserves a lot of attention. The current crisis has shown an alarming bias of the traditional middle classes towards a more conservative, right-wing ideology in an attempt to defend those privileges that these changes to the foundations of society seem to threaten.

Finally, we are definitely still going through economic, social, and political changes. The old Brazil can no longer be sustained, and the new one has not been able to fully emerge yet. However, in the name of democracy and a new wave of democratisation, one that is more radical and able to make structural changes, a lot of inspiration and a renewed, bolder political will are required. This is not a fact, only a possibility. Social classes in Brazil need to reinvent themselves as they crumble to the ground.

Conclusion: The Collapse of Brazil's New Middle Classes

In Brazil, the debate on the NMCs was deep and relevant, especially in academic circles, with a clear political and ideological motivation (see the essays in Bartelt 2013). Based on this debate, it was possible to observe that there was, and perhaps still is, a political project for 'other social classes', as well as active forces in the official arena for the creation and co-opting of new potential collective subjects as forces that are subject to their projects. The PT administration, by adopting a strategy of 'reconciling classes' with the powers that be, failed to conceal the intention to use their poverty reduction and social inclusion policies as a diffuse idea of creating NMCs, US style. By renouncing a programme of deeper changes in the economy and power towards a more socially and environmentally just society, the PT failed to promote changes to the social or political structure that would break their centralising, excluding, and destructive logic. The crisis brought an end to the government and likewise to the illusion of NMCs.

Nevertheless, it is possible to resist and start over. We need to start over by assessing the experiences and contradictions that have come up. However, if we want to dream of a new country and if we want to build a road that will guide us there, we must go back to thinking strategically about what should be done in order to ensure the social and political emancipation of millions upon millions of strugglers, they themselves being key active players in this task.

References

Bartelt, Dawid Danilo (org.) (2013). *A Nova Classe Média no Brasil como Conceito e Projeto Político*. Rio de Janeiro: Heinrich Böll Stiftung.

Gramsci, Antônio (1978). *Maquiavel, a Polĩtica e o Estado Moderno*. 3 ed. Rio de Janeiro: Civilização Brasileira.

Grzybowski, Cândido (2004). "Cidadania Encurralada", *Democracia Viva* (23): 8-14, ago-set. Rio de Janeiro.

________. (2012). *Como criar as Condições Para a Grande Transição*. Rio de Janeiro, Ibase. Available at: *http://www.canalibase.org.br/brasil-como-criar-as-condicoes-para-a-grande-transicao*

________. (2013). *O 'Estouro' da Cidadania nas Ruas*. Available at: *http://www.canalibase.org.br/o-estouro-da-cidadania/*

________. (2013). "Que Brasil Estamos Construindo", in Dawid Danilo Bartelt (org), *A Nova Classe Média no Brasil como Conceito e Projeto Político*. Rio de Janeiro: Heinrich Böll Stiftung. pp.96-105.

Güemes, Cecília (2016). *Classes Medias na América Latina: Mitos e Relidades*. São Leopoldo: IHU/ UNISINOS. Available at: *http://www.ihu-unisinos.br/noticias/533986-classes-medias-na-america-latina-mitos-e-realidades*.

Penny, Laurie et Alli (2014). "Contra o Sistema?", *Jovens, Lutas e Dissidências no Século* XXI. Nueva Sociedad (Edição especial da revista em português), Buenos Aires, dez.

Pochman, Marcio (2012). *Nova Classe Média? O Trabalho na Base da Pirâmide Social Brasileira*. São Paulo: Boi Tempo Editorial.

Singer, André (2012). *Os Sentidos do Lulismo: Reforma Gradual e Pacto Conservador*. São Paulo: Companhia das Letras.

Souza, Jessé (2010). *Os Batalhadores Brasileiros: Nova Classe Média ou Nova Classe Trabalhadora?* Belo Horizonte: UFMG.

________. (2013). "A Invisibilidade da Luta de Claees ou a Cegueira do Economicismo", in Dawid Danilo Bartelt (org), *A Nova Classe Média no Brasil como Conceito e Projeto Político*. Rio de Janeiro: Heinrich Böll Stiftung. pp.55-67.

________. (2015). "Entrevista: Para Gilberto Maringoni", *Desafios do Desenvolvimento, Brasília* 12(85): 10-16.

8

PARANJOY GUHA THAKURTA

Political Preferences of India's Middle Classes

Introduction

While the definition and composition of the middle classes in India have been and remain subjects of discussion and debate, there is no doubt that this demographic segment has become increasingly important in the country's politics because of its expanding numerical size and the influence it wields. India's middle classes have historically been considered influential. From social, cultural and religious reform movements in the 19th century to anti-colonial struggles leading up to India's political independence in 1947, this section of the population has consistently provided a pool of leaders and thinkers who have scripted and altered the narrative of politics in the country. After independence too, people belonging to the middle classes have extended their hold over to the political leadership, the bureaucracy, professional groups and the media, influencing electoral choices and trends. However, any generalisation about India's middle classes is fraught with the risk of oversimplification. Far from being a monolithic entity, this segment of the population is different from the middle classes in many other countries because Indian society is extremely heterogeneous and often deeply divided not merely along lines of class, religion, region and language but also on the basis of caste and ethnicity. Not surprisingly then, the political preferences of the Indian middle classes are frequently divergent.

During the 2014 general elections, large sections of the middle classes supported Narendra Modi and the right-wing, Hindu nationalist Bharatiya Janata Party (BJP) he leads. His candidature was favoured for, among other things, his promises of providing efficient and clean governance, which was in sharp contrast to the perception that the Indian National Congress-led United Progressive Alliance (UPA) government had been brazenly corrupt and afflicted by policy paralysis. Yet, the same middle classes were enamoured of Manmohan Singh, who was India's Prime Minister for 10 years and who was considered the architect of economic liberalisation in India in his earlier avatar as Finance Minister between 1991 and 1996. What swung the mood of the middle classes in favour of Modi in 2014? Why did the same section that jettisoned the Congress government so decisively in 2014 also reject the 'India Shining' campaign of the BJP-led National Democratic Alliance (NDA) led by Atal Behari Vajpayee a decade earlier in 2004? The answers to these questions reveal the shifting patterns of the political preferences of India's middle class, which mix elements of continuity and change.

The proportion of people who may be considered to belong to India's middle classes has grown in recent decades. Various estimates would place the size of this amorphous section of the country's population at roughly a fourth of the total population or approximately equal to the total population of the United States of America. While in the past, it was believed that most families belonging to the middle classes in India resided in urban areas, after economic prosperity spread across rural areas, more relatively well-off families are now found in small towns and villages.

With Modi and the BJP captivating large sections of the middle classes, the issue of identity politics resurfacing in the political choices of the religious majority needs to be revisited. During and before the phase of 'Mandal' politics from the early-1990s which saw the ascendancy of those belonging to the OBCs (other backward classes) or intermediate castes, the BJP made Hindutva and the so-called appeasement of minorities major ideological planks for electoral polarisation. (The Mandal Commission, headed by Parliamentarian B.P. Mandal, was set up in 1979 with the mandate to identify 'socially and educationally backward' sections of the population to consider whether these sections could benefit from reservation of seats in educational institutions and in government jobs; more than 10 years later, in 1990, the Indian government headed by V.P. Singh sought to implement some of the Commission's recommendations.)

The new Modi brand of muscular Hindutva is different in that it has been accompanied by promises of economic development and jobs for the 'aspirational' sections of the middle classes, especially in private enterprises. One group of analysts argue that larger sections of India's middle classes are becoming less self-absorbed or insular and are now more concerned about issues that impact the lives of the public at large. The manner in which women and men from the middle classes agitated on the streets of the national capital after the gang-rape of a young woman in December 2012 is cited as an example of this phenomenon. People from the middle classes contributed to the anti-corruption movement spearheaded by Anna Hazare in 2012 and 2013. But this is hardly the first time this has taken place. In the mid-1970s as well, middle-class students and their parents actively supported the political movement led by Jayaprakash (JP) Narayan against the imposition of the Emergency by the Indira Gandhi government. Many from this section also supported Vishwanath Pratap Singh when he mobilised political support against the Rajiv Gandhi government. There are commentators who claim that such agitations are matters of convenient public posturing rather than serious political engagement, but others disagree and contend that sections of the middle classes have become more politically active and socially conscious than before.

Through the decades of the 1950s, 1960s, 1970s and much of the 1980s, the Indian state played a central role in the working of the country's economy. During this period, the middle classes were dominated by government employees and those working for public sector corporations besides small traders and businesspersons. From the 1980s onwards, as the growth rate of India's GDP (gross domestic product) picked up, the middle classes started prospering materially. More people belonging to this segment of the population began to benefit from higher education, became proficient in using the English language and gained from job opportunities in the private sector with the relative decline in the importance of the public sector in the Indian economy. In terms of caste affiliation, the OBCs were an important part of this upwardly-mobile demographic segment while much smaller sections of the SCs (scheduled castes) or Dalits and STs (scheduled tribes) or adivasis also benefitted.

The exponential growth of television as a medium of mass communication from the early-1990s inwards (coinciding with the beginning of the phase of economic liberalisation) and the growing access to modern technology—especially the use of computers and mobile phones—dramatically impacted the aspirations of the country's middle classes. Since the middle classes were far from monolithic, the impact of technology was uneven. Even as many from the middle classes participated in the growth of India's computer software and IT (information technology) enabled services sector, some remained 'cyber coolies' while others became 'knowledge workers'. As media consumption rose, more belonging to the middle classes perceived themselves as important players in the country's social, economic and political life. A sign of this development is the manner in which Arnab Goswami, the lead anchor of one of the most popular television news channels in English, Times Now, frequently refers to the nation. He repeatedly uses the phrase 'the nation wants to know' in a hectoring tone despite the fact that his audience belongs largely to the upper and middle classes.

Many from India's middle classes have become obsessed with material betterment with an almost-complete absence of social obligation or civic responsibilities. This is manifest in attitudes towards ecologically-sustainable development strategies, for instance, issues like the relative importance of public transport *vis-a-vis* the use of personalised motor vehicles. Yet these sections are not entirely indifferent to environmental concerns: poor air quality in cities affects the middle classes as much as any other section of the population.

The electoral behaviour and political inclinations of India's middle classes are not uniform. This segment of the population does not emerge as a self-conscious class beyond fragments. In India's capital, Delhi, which is dominated by the middle classes, voters emphatically supported Modi and the BJP in the general elections that concluded in May 2014. The same electorate rejected the BJP (as well as the

Congress) in the Delhi assembly elections that took place nine months later in February 2015 by voting overwhelmingly in favour of a 2-year-old new political outfit, the Aam Aadmi Party (AAP) (that was born out of an anti-corruption movement).

Amidst talk of a weakening of identity politics in India, are the middle classes ready to rewrite the language of political discourse with new idioms and paradigms of development and governance? How integrated are these sections with the concerns of their global counterparts in developed and developing countries on environmental issues? Can those from the middle classes exert greater pressure on those in positions of power and authority to hold them accountable for their actions? Can India's middle classes compel politicians and government officials to rework and rethink their approaches towards curbing corruption, checking electoral malpractices, reducing political malfeasance and making corporate entities and large organisations more socially responsible? The answers to these questions are not clear nor simple.

Constituents of Indian Middle Class (or Classes)

The Difficulty of Identifying It and 'Classes' within Class

In a sting operation of a conversation made public on 11 March 2014, it was heard that the AAP convenor and (the then former) Chief Minister of Delhi, Arvind Kejriwal had sought to influence the portrayal of his image in a television interview by being careful about how the middle class perceives him. The video of the sting operation opened with Kejriwal speaking in Hindi to a well-known journalist of a TV news channel about why he does not want to talk about the 'corporate-wala' (or a person who represents the corporate sector) because the middle class would turn against his party, the AAP. Kejriwal says, "The middle class will turn against us, (and believe) that we are against the private sector, against companies, which is why I'm not getting into that." This statement raises a question: Is the middle class identifiable as a homogeneous entity in India now and can its political thinking be cubby-holed into a discernible category? If not, has Kejriwal not made a flawed assumption, or a partial one, about what constitutes the middle class in India?

In absolute numbers, it is now generally accepted that the size of India's middle class has shown impressive growth in recent decades, particularly in the post-economic liberalisation phase. However, there are intra-group differences within this broad social category which make it a diverse and hence, complex segment to analyse. Social scientist Richa Singh (2014) writes of three primary reasons which shape the complexity of this class. First, it is a highly heterogeneous social category, and differences are rooted not just by income, education, occupation, but also by caste, language, religion, age, gender, ethnicity, rural or urban location. It has also been argued that the dominant role is played by the NMC (new middle-classes) who have come to embody India's transition to liberalisation—the prosperous, young, metropolitan, invariably upper caste and Hindu, white collared professionals—working in the private sector, who feel as 'at home' in India as in the West, with a consumption pattern similar to their Western counterparts. So the defining (or rather differentiating) attributes of this 'class within a class' is lifestyle, consumption and social distinctions. Leela Fernandes, a sociologist at the University of Michigan, describes the NMC in India like a 'Napoleon layered cake' or a cake with many layers of dough and cream merging into one another, with those born after economic liberalisation took place in the early 1990s stacked on top of the old one without replacing or blending with it. Perhaps eminent sociologist André Béteille had this sub-group in mind when in an interview in 2014, he said that the middle class in India "tends not to occupy the middle of the pyramid. It merges with the elite, because it's the privilege stronghold" (Bouissou 2014).

Second, in the post-liberalisation phase, it's important to note the key elements which shape a common political outlook of this social group despite internal differences. Singh (2014) argues that the heterogeneity within the middle classes, their priorities, their ideologies, their relationships with the state and their politics, differ depending on the subgroup they belong to. Hence, the NMC that works in the private sector, reposes its faith in that sector and does not depend on the state for jobs or public services such as education or health. But, political interests of significant sections of this class could be entirely different. They conceive of the state in a central role in their world view and seek solutions through politics and the state. Despite the generalisation addressed earlier wherein it was suggested that the middle class is invariably upper-caste, there is a section of the middle class coming from historically marginalised sections: for them, the state remains an important centre where they gain or lose power, and hence continue to depend on the state and its framework of social justice, rights and entitlements, and on representative democracy.

However, what's interesting is that even relatively prosperous sections of this class have people who have been beneficiaries of state interventions and are favourably inclined towards the role of the state in public services and resource management. According to Professor Eswaran Sridharan of the University of Pennsylvania, between 58 per cent and 75 per cent of its members depend on the state, either from subsidies or employment. That is a remarkable contradiction which the middle class in India reflects. "As a whole, it benefits from the economic liberalisation", Sridharan underlines. "It has access to a range of services and products that didn't exist before. But that doesn't mean that it unanimously supports all liberal measures, such as privatization or cuts in public spending".

Singh (2014) also warns against confusing the middle class way of life with that of the NMC. In this context, it's important to know sub-sections of middle classes living in smaller cities, towns, rural India, are not what we mean by 'new' middle class. Though they may share the aspiration of their metropolitan counterparts (depending on their caste, religion and other locations), their consumption pattern and location in the economy is not the same. They do not have the same proximity to power, nor the same visibility as the dominant urban middle classes.

Third, middle classes are also a statistical construct when defined in economic terms, using income levels, consumption patterns, and ownership of assets. The National Council for Applied Economic Research (NCAER) surveyed and identified 153 million people in this category as per the 2001 Census data, each with an annual disposable income varying between ₹200,000 and ₹1 million ($4.380-$21.890) a year. According to the estimate made in 2011, the NCAER stated that by 2016-17, this 'consuming segment' would be growing to 267 million. However, such estimates have not found favour with many sociologists. Satish Deshpande has offered the most thorough critique of both the figures (he took a critical view of an earlier NCAER survey which predicted that middle class population would be 520.5 million by 2007) and the logic behind the classification. He has also advanced a larger non-economic definition that involves seeing the middle class (composed mainly of the intelligentsia and the managerial-technical professional elite) in terms of their dominant ideological, cultural and social roles. For instance, he attributes the middle class elite's nationalist awakening and interest in the development and modernisation of their countries with an increase in state-funded research, or "at least into willing co-operation with externally sponsored research efforts". His historical study of the middle class in Lucknow in *Contemporary India: A Sociological View*, has defined the colonial middle class as one that prides itself for its distinctive middling position (between the *taluqdars* and the lower orders) and draws upon its ability to become cultural entrepreneurs, defining itself thus through the public sphere and a web of preoccupations that include questions of gender, religion and nationalism.

There is also a view that the NMC is emerging as the 'moral majority' despite being a small section of India's electorate. By punching above its weight, it is playing a dominant role in public discourse by being well-represented in the media. As an ideological construct, the NMCs have come to occupy a hegemonic position, and their world view, aspirations and values are influential far beyond themselves. They have come to project what India wants to be in the 21st century: educated, upwardly mobile, with a Westernised consumption pattern. However, being in the NMC in India may suggest a far more privileged position than what the middle class expects in the West. While incisively attacking the convenient sense of moral outrage shown by the urban middle class during anti-graft agitation led by Anna Hazare, journalist and novelist Manu Joseph (2012) observed:

> The Indian middle class (the not-poor and everything above) does daydream about lining up down market politicians and shooting them, but they simply cannot be angry enough and angry too long. What reasons do they have really to be angry in this paradise of the middle class? They are, after all, the easy beneficiaries of India's inequities. It is not just about the maids, the baby maids, the cooks, the gardeners and the drivers, who come at laughable rates. The comfort is much deeper. As long as one is from a certain background, one does not have to be exceptional to go a long way in the private sector, academics, arts, media, anything really. In fact, one can even be a low-grade tennis player and still be considered a sports star in India.

In this context, it is relevant to note that Indian middle class concerns about cheap household staff—the same class in Europe barely have access to cheap household help and the use of servants is deemed aristocratic or bourgeois, not 'standard' Western middle class. Furthermore, basic services—facilities like roads, water, power supply, centres of higher education which are still state controlled—are now being generally supplemented by an increasing assertiveness about land use for 'public' purposes. How the state can facilitate that demand for 'public' which is synonymous with religious use for middle class endearment is also significant to note in this context. In a country where the use and construction of religious sites can earn individual leaders considerable political capital, such religious inclinations can also be used by political parties to win popular support for itself in any debate on proper land use—often at the peril of environment and local development interests. It somehow also goes well with grandiose of modern consumerism which has percolated in how middle classes perceive public monuments. Anthropologist Sanjay Srivastava took a critical look at how executives, and later the judiciary too, looked the other way when land use was diverted for construction of grand Akshardham temple complex in eastern part of Delhi as if it was some tribute to religious identity of a majority wedded with its new found fascination for architectural grandeur—an extension of unbridled consumerism. Srivastava recalls that during 2003-04, newspapers reports suggested that the ruling National Democratic Alliance (NDA), of which BJP was the dominant partner, had smoothed the way for Bochasanwasi Shri Akshar Purushottam Swaminarayan Sanstha (BAPS) to take over the land by violating or amending building and planning norms. In general, there was a general belief that 'Hindutva leanings' of NDA had been critical factor in facilitating the construction of the Akshardham temple complex. However, in 2005, the Supreme Court in its verdict said that the construction was 'lawful' and all 'Land Use Plans' had to be adhered to. The point is whether the violation or the verdict wasn't subjected to enough debate because middle class had been won by the promise of grand religious statement. At a different level, similar logic can deployed in the instance of the Art of Living organisation led by Sri Sri Ravi Shankar using the floodplains of the Yamuna River in Delhi to stage a controversial cultural extravaganza.

While much vagueness is likely to persist regarding the composition and political outlook of the middle class, because of its diversity and also because of socioeconomic forces unleashed by economic liberalisation in the 1990s, there is also a growing realisation that some degree of convergence is visible in the aspirations of divergent sections which constitute the middle classes in India.

Hindus and Elements of Continuity and Change

Whither the Appeal of Hindutva for the Political Imagination of Middle Classes?

In the aftermath of the right wing BJP getting a resounding majority on its own (and evident middle class support) in the 2014 Lok Sabha elections—something happening for the first time after 30 years in the country's electoral history—commentators sought to explain the middle class endorsement of Narendra Modi in different ways. By extension, the role of the Hindutva as an ideological plank for mass mobilisation of religious majority was also analysed, particularly with reference to middle class political inclinations. Sociologist Shiv Vishwanathan argued that Modi's brand of refreshing decisiveness was cathartic for a middle class which felt that the hypocrisy of secularism was repressive for the religious sentiments of country's majority. Vishwanathan remarked that the vote was a backlash against a kind of secularism that enforced oppositions in a way that the middle class felt was apologetic and under-confident about its beliefs and perspectives. Being drawing room discourse, secularism was seen by the middle class as something which excluded them because they were inept at it. It became a repression of the middle class. The secularists misunderstood religion and by creating a scientific piety, equated the religious with the communal.

This school of post-election commentary was of the opinion that for a generation of middle class voters, Modi sensed this unease, showed it was alienating and nursed that alienation. He turned the tables by showing that secularism—rather than being a piety or a propriety—was a hypocrisy, or was becoming a staged unfairness which treated minority violations as superior to majoritarian prejudice. From a middle class perspective, he was noted as: "Modi was therapeutic for a generation that felt that elite modernisation was a hypocritical affair conducted by groups which used words like 'secular' to dismiss the thought processes of a middle class more rooted in religion. This NMC wanted to feel at home in its home-cooked religiosity and its extension, nationalism. By articulating such anxieties, Modi soothed their wounded subconscious. And this 'wounded class', tired of pseudo secularism, elite cronyism and majoritarian hypocrisy, voted him to power".

This view does not cohere with other ways of looking at the 2014 electoral verdict. For instance, political scientist Pradip Kumar Datta is of the view that such arguments could have been considered in the 1980s, the decade of ascendancy of political Hindutva, but it cannot explain middle class voter behaviour in 2014. Datta views the Modi brand of communal mobilisation as very toned down and moderate, and argues that the winning formula for Modi was the promise of development and efficient governance which the BJP strategically juxtaposed against the middle class view of the UPA as scam-tainted, tardy, 10-year old regime afflicted with 'policy paralysis'. As a sign of the middle class warming up to Modi's image as an efficient administrator, he cites the example of how the quick clearance given by the Gujarat government under Modi to the Tata groups Nano car project in the state endeared Modi to a section of the middle class which values private investment-driven growth. It was also interesting to note that with this stroke of decisiveness, Modi blunted the critical stand that the Tata group had taken against communal politics in Gujarat. Notwithstanding the fact that the Tata group funds Tata Institute of Social Sciences (TISS) which has promoted several critical studies on communal politics and the Gujarat communal riots of 2002, group head Ratan Tata had publicly admired Modi for the efficiency of his investment-friendly regime.

In the pre- and particularly post-Mandal political discourse, in which the upper castes had considerable influence but castes belonging to OBCs, SCs and STs also made their presence felt in different degrees, the RSS and the BJP's Hindutva ideological catchment area extended considerably to middle classes. The BJP's success as the lead partner of the NDA, which had 2 brief and one full stint in power at the Centre from 1996 to 2004, was, among other factors, made possible by middle class support (particularly in urban segments of the northern and western parts of the country).

But did the surprise defeat of NDA in the 2004 polls indicate a shift in the way the middle class was making its political choices? Did the blend of soft Hindutva with right-wing economic policies lose its sway over the BJP's core constituency? Datta advises caution before jumping to such conclusions. He argues that although the re-formation of the middle class may have happened over the last two decades of the 20th century, the middle class has shown signs of stabilisation. The NDA government may have faced electoral reverses in 2004, but this was not the consequence of a substantial change in the middle-class affiliation to Hindutva. He attributes the average four per cent drop in the social groups that voted for it (in the 2004 elections in comparison to the 1999 elections) to a range of factors: the reversal of policies regarding small-sector industries; the Gujarat pogrom, which gave rise to discomfort in an elite that is not fully willing to shed the Nehruvian heritage of secularism, and which is also sensitive to international opinion because it does not want to scare away foreign investors, and so on.

So what message did the middle class voter have for political parties and what message did the middle class get from elections results? According to Datta, the election results indicated that the middle class will have to reckon with a lesser degree of political fragmentation among subaltern social groups, who generally disapprove of the economic policies that are enthusiastically endorsed by the middle class and which constituted the core value of the 'India Shining' campaign of the BJP before the 2004 elections. However, as far as the middle class in India is concerned, the consolidation of forces supportive of Hindutva may ultimately depend on how long and how deep the process of subaltern consolidation will be. Far from being dogmatic in its world view and committed in its political preferences, Datta finds that in its imagination of politics, as the history of the national movement demonstrates, "India possesses a singularly flexible, accommodative and pragmatic middle class." Perhaps it was this pragmatic political attitude of the middle classes which found promises of development and decisive governance to be attractive enough reasons to vote for Narendra Modi (rather than merely endorsing Hindutva politics) in 2014.

Perceptions and Projections

Middle Class Voter and Mass Media

While the diversification of mass media and IT-driven highways of news and views in India may make it difficult in the years ahead to 'manufacture consent' in the sense Noam Chomsky and Edward Herman used it in the context of the political economy of the US media in 1988, the Indian news media had a profound influence on—and in turn is influenced by—middle class preferences. As the largest consumer of news and views on current affairs, the middle classes in India are vulnerable to be moulded by what it reads, listens to and sees on mass media while making political choices. For instance, it can be convincingly argued that in the 16th general elections in India, the Narendra Modi-led BJP benefitted from wide and favourable media coverage and also spent a lot on advertising on the media. In an article for the South Asian journal, Himal (30 June 2014), this author had argued that a distinctive feature of the elections was the manner in which large sections of the mass media extended whole-hearted support to the candidature of Modi, who led the BJP to power, by winning more than a majority of seats in the Lok Sabha, the lower house of Parliament in the world's largest democracy. The media, in turn, was greatly benefitted by an unprecedented advertising campaign launched to promote Modi—the scale of the campaign was unparalleled in Indian history not only in the traditional media (print, radio, television and outdoor banners) but even more so in the new media (internet websites, blogs and social media platforms like Facebook and Twitter).

It has always been an intriguing question to ask whether the middle classes shape media discourse or are shaped by it. The perception wars have become integral to the electoral strategies in India and are often fought on the media turf infecting media with vices like 'paid news' or clandestine payments for masquerading advertising as independent news. How far do these sections actually affect the script of political contests, draw and redraw the narrative of public image in terms of their preferred perceptions? There is hardly any empirical evidence to show such causal patterns. However, as middle classes are the prime audience and readership target groups for a major section of media, one is entitled to assume that media could be one of the prime instruments of seeking an advantage in how middle classes think about people, politics and issues.

Middle Class Electoral Behaviour: Important Statistical Observations[1]

Over a period of 5 years, did the BJP really succeed in making deep inroads into electoral choices made by middle class? Is there any statistical evidence to support the claim? And if so, what was the nature of the shift in political preferences in favour of the Modi-led NDA regime? These are some of questions to which the Centre for

1. Made by National Election Study (NES)-Centre for Study of Developing Societies (CSDS-Lokniti).

Developing Societies (CSDS) tried to provide some statistical clues in a study done by E. Sridharan (2014). The study observes that a significant difference between 2009 and 2014 was the turnout of the upper-middle and middle-classes, both in terms of proportion of the total population and hence the share of the total vote constituted by these 2 classes (47% from 26% in 2009, Table 8.1) and also in terms of the overall turnout increase from 58 per cent to 68 per cent (Table 8.2). The class configuration of the party preferences made by voters is shown in Table 8.3.

Table 8.1

India: Class Composition, 2009 and 2014 (NES 2009, 2014) (%)

Class	*2009*	*2014*
Poor	41	20
Lower	33	33
Middle	20	36
Upper	6	11

Source: a) *http://www.lokniti.org/national_election_study2009.php*;
b) *http://www.lokniti.org/nes.php*

Table 8.2

Class-wise Turnout, 2009 and 2014 (NES 2009, 2014) (%)

Class	*2009*	*2014*
Poor	57	60
Lower	59	68
Middle	60	69
Upper	57	67
Total	58	67

Source: a) *http://www.lokniti.org/national_election_study2009.php*;
b) *http://www.lokniti.org/nes.php*

The overall picture provided by these figures is partly due to the 'definitional' effect of the cut-offs for class, definitions remaining the same, and hence providing for a much larger percentage of the sample falling in these 2 classes. Turnout by the poor at 60 per cent is significantly lower than the 68 per cent turnout by the 2 richer classes (Table 8.2), this pattern resembling the demographic pattern of voters in Western countries wherein the better-off and more educated sections turn out to vote in higher proportions of the electorate than the poor. Turnout by the upper middle and middle classes is equal to that by the lower class and much higher than the poor class regardless of their location in rural areas, small towns or in cities or metropolitan areas.

Table 8.3

Class-wise Party Preference, 2009 and 2014 (NES 2009, 2014) (%)

Class	*Congress*		*BJP*	
	2009	*2014*	*2009*	*2014*
Poor	27	20	16	24
Lower	29	19	19	31
Middle	29	20	22	32
Upper	29	17	25	38
Total	29	19	19	31

Was the upper middle and middle classes shift towards the BJP part of a Hindu consolidation on an anti-minority platform? The responses to questions on equal treatment of minorities, and on special provisions for minorities indicate that it was not an anti-minority shift since an above-average solid majority of the upper middle (68%) and middle (62%) classes strongly or somewhat agree on equal treatment of minorities, and only 16 per cent strongly or somewhat disagree, and an above-average majority of the upper middle (61%) and middle (58%) classes strongly or somewhat agree on special provisions for minorities and only 19 per cent strongly or somewhat disagree. Although in response to a question on whether in a democracy the majority community's will should prevail, a majority agree, a large percentage of the respondents fell in the 'Don't Know/ Can't Say' category, this view cannot automatically be interpreted as anti-minority. However, the CSDS-Lokniti exercise did not segregate responses regionally.

It is just possible, though not at all certain, that in the Hindi-speaking belt in the northern and western Indian states, attitudes might be anti-minority as a whole (with under 20% 'strongly' or 'somewhat' disagree on the acceptability of equal treatment and special provisions for minorities). However, it is also possible that attitudes on minorities might be somewhat less favourable in the pro-BJP regions than what the overall average indicates. Overall, one can say that in 2014, the class-wise gradation of pro-BJP responses, with pro-BJP sentiment rising as we go up the class hierarchy, as well as the caste hierarchy, indicate support for the emergence of a loose, not compact, 'new social bloc' of class and caste privilege. This supports the Iversen-Soskice (2006) finding that majoritarian electoral systems tend towards a top-middle alliance in the absence of a corporatist economic structure.

Compared to previous elections, recent studies and data indicate that a sizeable chunk of voters have emerged as rightward leaning on economic issues. The BJP was also able to put together this coalition of social and economic conservatives at least in part because of the administrative failures of the Congress-led UPA in the years preceding the 2014 elections. While the UPA government introduced several schemes that could potentially benefit a large segment of India's population, the corruption and inefficiency with which it did so limited the electoral gains that the UPA could potentially have drawn from these schemes. The administrative failures of the UPA government in managing the economy played a catalytic role in the emergence of the economic right as an electoral force. Third, a large 'Modi effect' propelled the BJP to victory in the 2014 elections. Modi's image as a Hindutva icon and pro-business reformer contributed substantially to the BJP's appeal. During the campaign, Modi played up the idea that he was responsible for Gujarat's economic growth and proved himself to be an efficient administrator capable of helping the BJP to attract the economic right. While it's not clear whether such statistical evidence holds any seminal relevance for the course that middle classes have charted for themselves in India's political landscape, what is becoming increasingly evident is that they will become an even more important arbiter of India's political narrative.

References

Bouissou, Julien (2014). *The Myth of India's Middle Class.* 21 March, *http://www.worldcrunch.com/culture-society/the-myth-of-india-039-s-middle-class/liberalization-globalization-state-caste-poverty/c3s15318/* (orig. in Le Monde)

Datta, Pradip Kumar (2006). "Hindutva and the Re-formation of the Indian Middle Class Subject", in Mary E. John, Praveen Kumar Jha and Surinder S. Jodhka (eds.),*Contested Transformations: Changing Economies and Identities in Contemporary India.* New Delhi: Tulika Books.

Deshpande, Satish (2003). "Mapping the Middle: Issues in the Analysis of the Non-Poor Classes in India", in *Contemporary India: A Sociological View.* New Delhi: Penguin Books.

Iversen, Torben and David Soskice (2006). *Electoral Institutions and the Politics of Coalitions.* Boston: Harvard University Press.

Fernandes, Leela (2011). "Hegemony and Inequality: Theoretical Reflection on India's 'New' Middle Class", in A. Baviskar and R. Ray (eds.), *Elite and Everyman: the Cultural Politics of the Indian Middle Classes.* Routledge.

Manu, Joseph (2012). "The Obituary of a Movement", *Open Magazine.* 9 August. *http://www.openthemagazine.com/article/india/the-obituary-of-a-movement*

Srivastava, Sanjay (2011). "Urban Spaces, Disney-divinity and the Moral Middle Classes in Delhi", in A. Baviskar and R. Ray (eds.), *Elite and Everyman: the Cultural Politics of the Indian Middle Classes.* Routledge.

Singh, Richa (2014). *New Citizen's Activism in India: Movements, Moments, and Mobilization.* The Centre for Democracy and Social Action. February.

Sridharan, E. (2014). "Class Voting in 2014 Lok Sabha Polls", *Economic and Political Weekly*, 27 September.

Thakurta, Paranjoy Guha (2014). "Mass Media and the Modi 'Wave'", *Himal*, 30 June.

Visvanathan, Shiv (2014). "How Modi Defeated Liberals Like Me", *The Hindu*, 26 May.

9

RICHA SINGH

The Rise of the 'Aam Aadmi'

The New Middle Class and its Politics in India

The Hindi film *Satyagraha* (non-violent resistance, 2013, Prakash Jha) serves as an interesting entry point into the politics of the new middle class in India. Inspired by the middle class-led anti-corruption movement of 2012, the film depicts the rising anger of the '*aam aadmi*' (ordinary citizen, also translates as every citizen) against a corrupt and unjust system that leaves them with no recourse but to form a spontaneous movement to renegotiate 'real democracy'. At one point in the film the protagonist Manav, a software engineer, is addressing a public gathering and is asked about his vision for India's future. In response, he points towards a young protester Ravi Kumar and says:

> He is the future of India. Ravi Kumar's parents were rural labourer who did not send their son to the dilapidated government school in their village but struggled to pay for his private education. They took a loan and paid for him to train in computer operations. Today Ravi Kumar works in a call centre in the city and earns forty thousand rupees. Unlike his forefathers, he does not believe in the '*mai-baap sarkar*' (the 'nanny' state). Instead he considers himself as a client of the government. He pays fee to the government in the form of taxes and in return expects the government to provide him with services. If the government fails to deliver those services, he will stop paying the fee (taxes) like any other client.

This vignette in many ways captures the emerging political narrative of the new middle class in India. The middle class has been an important historical and sociological grouping in India, but focus on it, has intensified ever since liberalisation. Suddenly, the middle class is on television, in popular cinema and in the newspapers, in scholarly analysis, market discourse on potential consumers, and in the government projection of India's progress. The middle class is the visible *aam aadmi* activist on the street—the common man and everyman. All of this tells of the dominant presence the middle class enjoys today, and the influence it has in shaping cultural politics, policy, and national and international agendas.

Notably middle class in India is a highly heterogeneous social category with wide internal differentiation. What we have thereby are middle classes. On one end are the new middle class who embody India's transition to liberalisation—the prosperous, young, metropolitan, invariably upper caste and Hindu, white collared professionals who feel as at home in India as in the West, and have consumption patterns similar to their Western counterparts. This section does not depend on the state for jobs or public services such as education or health but seeks to reinvent its relationship with the state as a 'client' to protect its own interest. On the other end are other middle class grouping such as those who come from the historically marginalised or rural background who articulate a different world view and continue to depend on the state and its framework of social justice, rights and entitlements.

However, among the different subsection of middle classes, not all social groups enjoy equal dominance. The hegemonic position is occupied by the 'new middle class' that, though lacking numerical strength in proportion to the total population, nevertheless represents the new 'moral majority' (Deshpande 2006) in so far as their world view, aspirations and values are influential far beyond themselves. They have come to project what India wants to be in the 21st century: educated, upwardly mobile, with a Westernised consumption pattern (but not necessarily Westernised values) and it is their values and aspirations that have become hegemonic. Hence notwithstanding the heterogeneity and contestations within middle classes, there is a homogenisation of aspirations. What we thereby have is a project of 'middle-classisation' unfolding with contradictory tendencies. On one hand, there is a growing social polarisation between new middle classes and others, when it comes to practice (consumption patterns, lifestyle, living spaces, on issues of affirmative action and social justice etc). At the same time, these lines become increasingly blurry when it comes to aspirations. This is becoming evident in Indian cities, where much of urban politics can be located within this Janus-faced project of 'middle-classisation' (Mooji and Lama-Rewal 2010: 83).

In this essay, I examine the new middle class, the source of its socio-cultural economic power, and its politics. It is divided into two sections. The first looks into the composition of middle classes, its political evolution and changing relationship with the state through three phases–the pre-independence phase during which the middle class emerged under colonial rule, the post independence phase when the middle class expanded and diversified under a state-led process of nation building and command economy, and the post liberalisation phase when the new middle class emerged and gained dominance. The second section focuses on the political activism of the new middle class and goes on to present in a summary form the anti-corruption movement as a case study (Singh 2014) to highlight key features and characteristics of middle class politics in India.

India's Middle Classes, and What is 'New' About it

Defining the Middle Classes

The middle class is an ideological construct across the world. Although it suggests a singular social category, it is differentiated internally by income, education, and occupation. In India, the middle class is further differentiated by language, caste, religion, gender, ethnicity, and rural or urban location. In the popular understanding, there are two concrete classes—the rich and the poor. Everyone else in between becomes middle class. Not surprisingly, then, defining who constitutes the middle class has been tricky. Moreover, in the popular sense, the middle also represents a safe location that avoids the two concrete extremes. It is common in India for many people to identify with the middle class location—be it a school teacher or the first Prime Minister of India, Jawaharlal Nehru who stated that, "I am, of course, a middle class person." Similarly Narayan Murthy, an IT Industrialist continues to drive his old Fiat car as a beacon of middle class values. Is 'middle class' then to be defined as an economic category or by its values and aspirations? Or is middle class a proper noun—as political scientist Yogendra Yadav (cited by Baviskar and Ray 2011: 7) suggests, a term by which the ruling class prefers to call itself?

Conventionally, the middle class has been defined from an economic perspective, using income, consumption pattern, and asset ownership. Based on these criteria, the National Council for Applied Economic Research (NCAER) identifies 153 million people in this category as per 2001 data, with a disposable annual income of ₹200,000 to ₹1,000,000 ($4,380–$21,890; the numbers have gone up since the survey was last conducted). These numbers are not definitive, for the exact number of the middle classes in India has been much debated, and estimates and projection vary. However, as a number of analysts (Gupta 2000, Sreedharan 2004, Fernandes 2006, Baviskar and Ray 2011, Jodhka and Prakash 2011, Venkatesh 2013) point out, the middle classes make for a complex group. In defining the middle classes in contemporary India, Sandhya Venkatesh (2013: 1) argues:

> The middle class in India is today a complex group; complex in its classification, its identification, its heterogeneity, its politics, location and other factors. It comprises multiple locations across class, caste, religion, gender, occupation, and age; although in large part it consists predominantly of upper castes and dominant religions. It is not surprising then that the ideological base and priorities of the group vary, depending on the subsection. Notwithstanding the heterogeneity, it is a class that is in large part defined through the language of liberalisation, and finds its identity not merely in its economic base but through its social and cultural capital. Its visibility, and through that its influence, is linked with its social distinction, lifestyle and consumption patterns; and the class consequently actively engages in protecting and leveraging its social privileges and cultural capital. It is through such protection that differentiation from, and hegemony over, other sections of the population, is often sustained. There are of course exceptions, and some subsections of the middle class do speak out for equity and justice.

Clearly, the middle classes in India today are comprised of diverse subsections, even as there is a hegemonic middle class. To understand the dynamics of middle classes in India, their evolution becomes significant and can broadly be seen through three phases: pre-independence, post-independence, and post-liberalisation.

Evolution of the Middle Class

In India, the middle class emerged under colonial rule as an administrative class (rather than a manufacturing class, as in the West) in the Presidency towns of Calcutta, Bombay, and Madras, to staff the colonial administration. Modern English education would turn this class of persons into English in taste, morals, opinions, and intellect, as stated by Lord Macaulay in his 'Minutes on English Education', 1835 (Varma 2002: 2). Notably, Macaulay used 'English' to mean upper-class English, a fact that had long-term implications in defining the traditional middle class, and its often being seen as the elite in India.

In this initial phase, the middle class was characterised by homogeneity. Its members were mostly from financially comfortable, upper caste families; had received English-language education abroad or in India; were employed in the administrative services of the British Government or were lawyers, journalists, teachers, or doctors. What distinguished them from the other classes was their dependence on employment through education—unlike the richest strata and the vast majority. The richest strata (big landlords, aristocrats, industrialists) did not need employment. The vast majority comprised the agricultural poor, unskilled and semi-skilled manual workers, craftsmen, and lower-rung employees under the British such as soldiers, clerks, postmen, among others (Mahapatra 2009: 126). However, with modern education came the influence of ideas of liberalism and democracy, which had gained ascendance in the west since the French Revolution. Soon, the middle class in colonial India began championing internal social reform and also emerged as the leaders of the freedom movement against colonial rule. However, though this class represented the modern, it also participated in identity movements and played an active role in strengthening boundaries across religions and communities (Jodhka and Prakash 2011). Partha Chatterjee argues that since the middle class in India was invented through colonial education, but structurally lacked the basis for economic expansion in the context of colonial control, it was different from the bourgeoisie in the West, and did not really bring about a social transformation. An upper-caste Indian who had access to traditional education could now simply avail the opportunities of English education and become this new class without losing 'his' caste moorings. Understanding this upper-caste mooring of the Indian middle classes helps us understand their existence, values, and politics. One obvious reflection of this mooring is in how the Indian middle classes distance themselves from any physical labour—in the household or elsewhere (Chatterjee 1992: 24).

The second moment of middle-class evolution began after Independence in 1947. The middle-class leadership of the nationalist movement now became the new democratic leadership of the independent nation. Given the state-led command of the polity and economy, the middle class retained its dominance. The older bureaucracy continued, and expanded with the steady growth of the developmental state that sought socioeconomic development through centralised planning (based on the soviet model of planned development). During this period, the salaried and professional class constituted the middle classes, which relied on the state and were not directly involved in trade, commerce, or industry. They received limited salaries and enjoyed a number of institutional perks and, therefore, austerity rather than consumerism characterised them (Jodhka and Prakash 2011). Their power came from their control of the state apparatus, particularly, the bureaucracy. This control enabled them to appropriate policies in their own interest and to claim that they represented the interests of the nation in the task of nation building. The middle classes during this period at one level represented the Nehruvian notion as described below:

> To be middle class was to inhabit a particular orientation towards modernity. It meant being open-minded and egalitarian; following the rule of law and not being swayed by private motive or particularistic agenda; being fiscally prudent and living within ones means and embracing science and rationality in the public sphere. It demanded setting aside the primordial loyalties of caste and kinship and

> opening oneself to new affinities and associations based on merit and to identities forged at the workplace (Baviskar and Ray 2011: 6).

At the same time, the middle classes continued to retain their particularistic characteristics based on ethnic and social location of its members, such as caste, religion, and linguistic and regional identities. An important development in this phase was the expansion of middle classes, and further differentiation within it. With the Green Revolution in agriculture in some parts of India, there emerged sections of farmers ready to enter the fold as the rural middle class—changing, in effect, the urban-centredness of the middle classes. Affirmative action by the state and the institutionalisation of electoral politics also led to the entry of historically marginalised sections (SCs [scheduled castes] and STs [scheduled tribes]) in state institutions, public sector jobs, educational institutions, and therefore into the middle class fold, thus diluting its upper-caste nature. Facing resistance from the upper caste, this segment became the voice and leadership for assertion from marginalised castes and the demand for social justice (Jodhka and Prakash 2011).

The third phase in the evolution of the middle classes in India came after liberalisation and gave them centre stage as never before. It is against this background that the actual size of the middle classes began to be first debated, as they came to be viewed in terms of consumption or as a consumer goods market. It marked the emergence of the new middle classes of today. Leela Fernandes argues that this social class is not new in terms of structural or social basis, and that its newness is characterised not by new upwardly mobile entrants but through its embodiment of India's transition to liberalisation (Fernandes 2011: 69). The new middle class works in the private sector, has its faith in the market, and does not depend on the state for employment nor for services. It expresses itself in consumerist terms to articulate its style and identity, and believes in efficiency, merit, and competition. Sandhya Venkatesh points out:

> Since...post liberalisation growth was based on educated and technically skilled human resources, it led to the creation of a class that was based outside the state system and was empowered with education and skill resources, employed predominantly in the private

> sector. These attributes, education, skills, facility with language, confidence, social networks and the ability to access a certain type of job, became the cultural capital of the middle class, through which it came to be identified. Carrying the identity of a consumer, this was in large part a self-serving class focused on the protection of their own interests, and emphasising the values of merit, competition, and efficiency. (Venkatesh 2013)

The new middle classes today are both producers as well as consumers who drive economic growth. In addition, the software industry, which grew independent of the old economy, has also shaped a section of the middle classes into a transnational global class. In its composition, the new middle classes are characterised by continuity with the older pattern of middle class formation (upper caste, Hindu, urban). However, it assumes that market principles of merit and competition rather than affirmative action, social justice, and redistributive principles of an interventionist state will enable other segments to join. It differs from the Nehruvian middle-class values of austerity and in its conceptualisation of the state's role and responsibilities. It believes that the state should not 'do' but simply steer or ensure; should not play a redistributive role but a managerial one; and that solutions lie outside politics with the technocrats.

However, given the heterogeneity of the middle classes along lines of caste, religion, regional, gender, and occupation, this formation does not include every section of the middle classes and is confined to the 'dominant' or 'hegemonic' middle class. This section has gained dominance as their interest converges with the market, media, and an increasingly neoliberal state. All of this takes them closer to the centres of power; and enables them to represent the hegemonic ideas and shape the culture, economy, politics, and society in India today. Although this section does not depend on the state for much, it relates to the state as clients primarily to serve its own interest. It is an anti-political class, and supports working democracy on the principles of the market with the NPM (new public management style of governance rather than then what it perceives as the messiness of politics.

However, large sections of the middle classes articulate a different world view and seek solutions through politics and the state. For middle classes coming from historically marginalised sections, the state remains an important centre where they gain or lose power. Hence, they continue to depend on the state and its framework of social justice, rights, and entitlements, and on representative democracy. This is in sharp contrast with the push for efficiency, completion, and value-neutral meritocracy by the dominant middle classes, and creates for contestation on issues such as affirmative action policies, representative vs. direct democracy, and notions of equality as sameness vs. substantive equality. Similarly, subsections of the middle classes who live in small towns and cities of rural India do not exemplify the new middle classes, because while they may share the aspirations of their metropolitan counterparts (depending on their caste, religion, and other locations), their consumption pattern and location in the economy differ. They have neither the same proximity to power nor the same visibility as the urban dominant middle classes. For instance, protests in non-metropolitan cities by sections of the middle class—be it against rape in Guwahati (Assam),[1] or against Reliance Fresh retail business in Bhubaneswar (Orissa)[2]—hardly makes headlines or similar impact as protests by the dominant middle classes on the metropolitan street. Notably, the post-liberalisation phase has also been one that witnessed the rise of Hindutva (Hindu right wing nationalism) with the support of large sections of national and transnational middle classes. This phase has witnessed violence and the alienation of minorities, and has particularly marginalised the already small section of Christian and Muslim middle classes (Engineer 2011).

Clearly, liberalisation has sharpened intra-class contestations between segments of the middle class. However, as stated earlier,

---

1. "Protests Rife in Assam Over Rape", *The Shillong Times*, 28 November 2013. *http://www.theshillongtimes.com/2013/11/28/protests-rife-in-assam-over-rape/* (Accessed on 30 June 2016).
2. "Reliance Fresh Orissa Debut Hits a Hurdle", Business Standard, 26 September 2007. *http://www.business-standard.com/article/economy-policy/reliance-fresh-orissa-debut-hits-a-hurdle-107092601103_1.html.* (Accessed on 30 June 2016).

there is a dominant new segment constituted of the dominant communities in India. This new middle class, as Jodhka and Prakash (2011) argue, is globally mobile, inhabits modern spaces, uses the language of modernity and, simultaneously, participates in articulations of identity politics of both dominant majorities and minorities, depends on patronage, and perpetuates the patronage culture. At one level, this section isolates itself from other middle classes, builds gated communities, indulges in a more lavish lifestyle. On the other, its values and world views have become hegemonic and is projected as 'India's future'—blurring the distinction with other middle classes when it comes to 'aspirations'.

Political Activism of the New Middle Classes

Given the internal diversity within the middle classes, their varied relationship with the state, market, media, and the growing contestations within, it is not surprising that the political activism of the middle classes are articulated in varied frames. At one level is the not-so-visible activism of the less dominant middle classes in different urban settings—such as on the issue of privatisation of water and electricity, price hike, or on the question of loss of livelihoods because of the entry of large retail chains. Over the past decade, a number of middle-class citizens' interest groups have been formed to take up issues where they have had immediate stake in combination with larger societal interests. Some instances of these are:

- The Association of Victims of Uphaar Tragedy (AVUT) was formed in Delhi by grieving families of the Uphaar fire tragedy in 1997. They had came together to fight for justice against the powerful Ansal corporate lobby. Ultimately, their personal tragedy turned into a political battle to augment central accident and trauma services and highlight the issue of safety laws in public places.
- Environmental and consumer groups, such as the Citizen Consumer and Civic Action Group in Tamil Nadu which raised the question of electricity governance.

- Neighbourhood committees, such as in the K-East Ward of Bombay, where the voter identity of the bloc became the rallying point for waging struggle against water privatisation, and where alliances were built across *jhuggi* (slum) clusters and middle-class residential areas. In Delhi, the issue of hike in electricity tariff and privatisation of water saw the emergence of platforms of resident welfare associations, such as United RWAs Joint Action (URJA), Joint Front, which built alliances with civil society groups like Parivartan and Right to Water Campaign.
- Large citizen platforms where middle-class citizens came together with other civil society groups for a common cause, such as the Save Goa Campaign against SEZ (special economic zone). This campaign brought together an alliance of professionals, retired government officials, churches, village committees, and NGOs.
- Middle class–urban poor alliance against retail. In many cities and towns of Odisha, Uttar Pradesh, and Jharkhand, alliances were forged between small traders, grocery shop owners, and vegetable vendors to protest against entry of Reliance Fresh and large retail business which threatened their livelihood.

Notably, most of these activisms (with a few exception such as AVUT, protests against retail or in cases where there was common interest) were articulated in the discourse of civic responsibility and in the framework of consumer-citizen–not in the framework of rights, entitlements, or social justice. As a result, many of these initiatives tended to be hostile towards poor and marginalised groups. Environmental activism, for instance, around beautification and cleaning of cities (or 'bourgeois environmentalism', according to Amita Baviskar (2011)) has been against the urban poor, hawkers, and slum- and pavement-dwellers. Similarly doctors of the All India Institute of Medical Sciences (AIIMS), a prestigious medical institution, organised against reservation of seats for Dalits and historically marginalised communities. However, the modality of political activism in all these instances was similar to traditional forms of political mobilisation—there were common lines of interest, an organisational structure, a set of clear demands, and planning and preparation. Moreover, given the non-hegemonic location of these segments of the middle classes, they were not choreographed as spectacular events. They nevertheless set the ground, and the tone, for the more visible and audible protests of the new middle class on the urban street that soon followed.

The more spectacular middle class protests first began in the city squares of Delhi in 2006 with a huge media-led outcry against the initial court verdict in the murder case of Jessica Lal—under the glare of satellite television and news and social media. In the same year, young, professional middle classes took up cudgels against the system that had let sons of rich and powerful politicians and bureaucrats off scot-free in two other cases of Priyadarshini Mattoo and Nitish Katara. In all these cases, the dominant middle classes in megacities took up the cause of the victims from among them. It led to the reopening of each of these cases against the powerful political elite. This was the beginning for what followed was bigger middle-class activism in the anti-corruption and the anti-rape upsurges which spilled over from city squares to urban streets and became large movements–drawing participation from cross-sections and becoming more amorphous, even though they remained predominantly middle class. Against this background, a new political party emerged with its genesis in the anti-corruption movement and the urban middle class—the Aam Aadmi Party (AAP). In a relatively short course of time, AAP won the Delhi Assembly election and came to form the government. In the course of its journey, the AAP transformed from a middle class movement to a 'catch-all' political party, expanding its base across different urban classes. While a detailed discussion on the AAP is beyond the scope of the essay, it would be sufficient to mention here that despite huge difference in consumption patterns, lifestyle, income of the urban voter, what for the moment has clicked for AAP is urban India's 'aspiration'.

To draw attention to some of the key features of new middle class politics, the following section presents the case of the anti-corruption movement.

The Case of Anti-Corruption Movement: TV, Tweets and the Streets

Overview

In 2011, there was an upsurge in India on the issue of corruption. It was triggered by an indefinite hunger strike in New Delhi by Anna Hazare, a civil society activist from Ralegaon Siddhi, a village in the Western state of Maharashtra. At the beginning, there was something little unusual about the movement. The issue of corruption was hardly new for India where endemic corruption has been rampant, and there had been many earlier attempts to fight it. Yet, this time, when Anna Hazare sat on a hunger strike demanding the passage of an anti-corruption legislation, the event sparked off a momentous groundswell in urban India that forced the government to accept many demands from civil society.

The immediate context of the anti-corruption movement was a series of scams within the government that had hit the headlines, such as scam in the distribution of telecom licenses, estimated at $40 billion; corruption in the Commonwealth Games held in Delhi that had resulted in a revenue loss of $38 million; illegal selling of mines in the state of Karnataka costing $3 billion to the exchequer; among others. Fuelling public outrage was the government's silence at these large-scale scams taking place within it and its failure (perceived as resistance) to create institutions to check it. What was staring the public in the eye was clear evidence of crony capitalism, which until now had been working with stealth.

At the heart of the anti-corruption movement was the demand for anti-corruption legislation called the Lokpal Bill. Developed on the model of the Ombudsman of Sweden, the proposed legislation sought to set up a national institution or the Lokpal, to look at control, and remedy corruption in India. Attempts to bring about such legislation had a long history but had been left pending. However, in light of these high profile corruption cases, the demand for a Lokpal drew extraordinary attention and became a popular rallying point. Finally the government was compelled to bow down to demands of civil society, and draft out a Lokpal Bill.

The Net and the Square: Cities and Cyber as Space of the Campaign

The anti-corruption movement began in the national capital Delhi, and soon spread to other megacities, smaller cities and towns—marking a significant shift from the rural base of social movements to an urban one. The most visible sites of the protest were the familiar dissent spaces—Jantar Mantar in Delhi, a space almost designated for civil society groups and citizens to converge for any agitation; Ramlila Grounds where Anna Hazare sat on a hunger strike, is associated with large political rallies during the nationalist movement and afterwards. However, the movement in these spaces differed from other civil society movements in two significant ways. First, the protesters were unusually diverse and self mobilised. Second, though there was centring of the movement in these spaces of *dharnas* (sit-ins) and fasts, it also spilled over to sites of social life in neighbourhoods, market squares, metro stations, and city streets which began to witness spontaneous marches, sit-ins, and gatherings. Another significant development was the use of cyber space. Citizens used social media platforms, e-groups, blogs, Facebook pages, tweets, SMS and mobile technologies to connect as well as to register protests. Outside India, in New Jersey, New York; London where there are sizeable population of immigrant Indians, protests were held outside the Indian High Commission.

Choreographing a Leader

The anti-corruption movement was symbolically led by Anna Hazare, who occupied the centre stage. Under continuous media coverage, Anna (literally, elder brother) came to be projected as an elderly next door neighbour who was putting his life at stake for the cause of the nation. Anna became the signifier of all that is good against all that is dirty with Indian politics and yet remained as someone familiar who was part of the everyday in popular perception. This image of Anna was successful—almost inspirational in mobilising youth and the middle classes, and Anna became synonymous with the identity of ordinary citizens demanding an end to corruption.

However, even as Anna remained the face of the movement, the leadership had more to it. When the movement was seeded, the initial platform of India Against Corruption (IAC) included a diverse range of social activists, prominent individuals, religious, and spiritual leaders who came from varied background. The IAC built a oppositional, competitive platform against the government on the issues of corruption. However, as the movement grew, so did differences over issues such as the use of 'fasting unto death' as a method to oppose the government with some sections feeling that this was akin to 'blackmailing' the government. Differences also arose over the way the movement went beyond opposing the government in power to questioning representative democracy, and positing vs. direct democracy. Gradually, the real leadership came to rest around a core group, popularly referred to as 'Team Anna'. Its key figures were RTI activist Arvind Kejriwal, ex-police officer turned development activist Kiran Bedi, and activist lawyer Prashant Bhushan. Over time, differences also surfaced within Team Anna. Anna Hazare and Kiran Bedi went separate ways, and Arvind Kejriwal and Prashant Bhushan floated a new political party the AAP that later went on to win the State assembly elections in Delhi.

Participants of the Movement

Initially, the protesters were mostly the vociferous middle class in megacities—professional executives, the upwardly mobile, students, young men, and relatively fewer women in the 15–35 age group who came out to oppose the government, framing the struggle as 'citizens' against all politicians. However as these protests spread and became more street like as well as 'spectacular' (aided by the visual and social media), it grew into a movement and became simultaneously more amorphous. While retaining its middle class character, it came to be peopled by school children, migrant workers, teachers, auto-rickshaw drivers, college students, film actors, farmers from neighbouring states, cadres of the extreme right wing organisation as well as student organisation of the far left. In Mumbai, the *dabbawallas* (lunch box carriers) broke their 120-year-old tradition of never going on a strike, as 1,200 *dabbawallas* struck work for the first time to march in solidarity with the Anna and the anti-corruption movement.

While the leadership came from developmental civil society and some sections became important constituents of the movement, such as the National Alliance of People's Movement (NAPM), Bhopal Gas Survivors, there were others who did not join. A notable gap was the absence of minorities and Dalits in the movement. According to Paul Divakar of the National Campaign of Dalit Human Rights, Dalits and marginalised sections did not join the movement. 'The anti-corruption movement reminded one of the anti-Mandal agitation[3] by upper castes in the 1990s. Corruption was also given a narrow meaning within the movement, wherein the issue of social inequality was excluded from being a parameter of defining corruption. The bias against the marginalised in policies—for example, the diversion of development-related SC and ST Funds, Multi-Sectoral Development Funds for Muslims or the bias of the judicial systems which target Dalits and Muslims—did not seem to bother or find a place in the elitist definition of corruption' (Divakar 2011). Thus, though the anti-corruption movement created a wave 'virtually' and in the cities, it tended to be dominated by the urban upper caste, the Hindu middle class, and was less able to include or become a tool for marginalised communities to fight corruption and access their rights.

Slogans and Symbols

The anti-corruption movement worked with a catch-all strategy, bringing in organisations, slogans, ideologies from far right to far left. Hence the campaign did not always speak in one voice. There were divergent projects competing—from right wing agenda, to issues of land acquisition by corporate and there were divergent understanding of 'corruption'. This was reflected in the symbols, and slogans of the movement, which also tended to be deliberately nationalistic. On one hand, Anna and India seemed to have merged into one—reflected in slogans such as 'Anna is India, India is Anna';

---

3. Protest by upper caste students in 1990 against reservation in government jobs for historically marginalised castes.

or in use of nationalist slogans such as *Vande Mataram, Bharat Mata ki Jai* (salute to Mother India) in an anti-corruption movement. At another, any and every individual experience of corruption tended to have found embodiment in the image of 'Anna', voiced as 'I am Anna/ Mein Anna Hoon'.

Method and Strategies of the Movement: Fasting and Harvesting of Anger

The anti-corruption movement was a non-violent upsurge that used the 'fast unto death' stratagem (popularised by Gandhi, and often used as a method of protest in India) as its key method to oppose the government. In that sense, there was nothing novel about the method of hunger strike. What proved critical was how it was used it to tap into popular anger, mobilise ordinary citizens to build support and alliance to 'compete' against the ineffectiveness of the government, and then to later negotiate. While the government had drafted its own Lokpal Bill (alleged to be weak), the movement promoted its own 'alternative' draft called the Jan Lokpal Bill (People's Lokpal bill)[4] to compete with the government. The Jan Lokpal (People's Lokpal) was circulated at protest sites, on websites, social media to seek inputs and support, and then used to pressurise and negotiate with the government. When the government showed lack of interests, Anna Hazare used the method of 'fast unto death' to pressurise the government to adopt the Jan Lokpal—raising debates if fasting was 'blackmail' and an illegitimate method in a democracy, or was it a legitimate non-violent method of civil society's social action. It nevertheless put the government on the back-foot, creating subsequently space for different sections of civil society who also drafted other drafts versions of Lokpal Bill and submitted them to the legislature.

The anti-corruption movement had a strong populist tone, and was specially designed to target the middle class and the media—the

4. The proposed Jan Lokpal bill included establishing a central government anti-corruption institution called Lokpal, supported by Lokayukta at the state level; independent appointment of Lokpal; bringing all anti-corruption agencies under the Lokpal; Lokpal to have complete power to investigate and prosecute all officers, judges, politicians (including Prime Minister).

two vehicles in contemporary India which could make it audible/ visible and push it closer to centres of power. It thereby used what was termed as 'smart media strategy' which proved to be the tidal wave on which movement could ride.

Role of Communication Technologies: Social Media, Media and Mediatised Politics

> Media weren't just doing their job... they are now part of the movement (Arvind Kejriwal, 28 August 2011, Ramlilla Grounds).

The movement against corruption marked a dramatic shift, both in terms of its usage of information and communication technologies, and the unprecedented media coverage. Media became integral to the discourse, and to understanding of the event itself, leading some to argue that the upsurge was fuelled, if not created by the media (Murlidharan 2011, Sengupta 2011).

In terms of coverage by visual media, Anna Hazare, Team Anna, every aspect of the protest dominated satellite television and was beamed 24x7. In the earlier phase of Anna's hunger fast in April, coverage totalled 5,576 news clips, of which prime time news coverage numbered 1,224 clips across 152 hours, with an ad value of ₹52.47 crore. New channels raked in advertisement revenues news of ₹175.86 crore over a nine-day period. Classifying the news clips by their tone, 5,592 were positive towards Anna and his cause, while 92 were characterised as negative (Murlidharan 2011). In the second phase of the movement, from 16 to 28 August, according to a monitoring exercise done by Centre for Media Studies (CMS), the 2 Hindi channels, Aaj Tak and Star News had devoted 97 per cent of total news time during prime viewing hours (7 to 11 p.m.) to the Anna fast. For the English channels, CNN-IBN and NDTV 24x7, the corresponding figure was 87 per cent. Besides, national print media was not too different when it came to coverage. Newspaper covered minute details of the movement providing detailed description of every move taken by Anna, about every aspect of his public life, his earlier work. Some of the newspapers even carried banners appealing to people to join the movement, such as '*Ek saptha desh ke naam, Anna ke saath utariyae'* (give one week for the nation, join Anna, according to Navbharat Times).

The usage of social media was phenomenal. With the help of a dedicated group of software professionals associated with IAC, the Anna-Team was able to spawn off a number of social media programmes that were immensely popular and which were then copied and worked upon by others. There were more than 150 Facebook pages related to Anna on Facebook, several online signature campaigns, more than 4 lakhs 'liked' the IAC Facebook page; there were also several Anna Hazare fan pages, as well as several videos posted on YouTube by supporters (Ohri 2011). Comprehensive SMS campaigns were launched across the country and attracted huge number of responses. A special campaign involving people to ring up a particular number to express solidarity with the movement, allegedly clocked 1.3 crore (Nabanita 2012). Corporations hooked on to the bandwagon and designed online computer games around Anna, one even came out with an IAC phone application to keep cell phone users updated with the events of the 'IAC'

Media–social and mainstream worked to inform and spread what was happening on the ground, as well as a means of getting people on the street. It contributed to the emergence of a heavily connected public space and streets, that was in a web of satellite television, the internet, round the clock circulation and movement of images, sounds, and affective experiences.

However, to view the movement simply from the prism of technology and as being media created would be inadequate, because there was an entire socioeconomic-political context that created the rise of the anti-corruption movement. However, the protests on the ground were being 'mediaised' in the ways images with commentaries were projected by the media. Between what was happening on the street, the images on televisions screens, the social networking sites, there were complex forms of 'mediations' that were shaping public gatherings, setting the scene, constructing a different kind of an emotional/public space—connecting diverse individual with little common bonds or interest.

Notably, the mainstream national media has hardly paid attention to other social movements, protests, causes of marginalised groups. As Aruna Roy (2012) argued, 'there is never a TV shot shown of tribals who are mobilised for their causes.' There are thus conditions to the role played by media and ICT—the constituency of the middle class which finds common grounds with the media; the ownership of ICT and all the possibilities it offers, the urban setting which in the midst of television and ICT web. As all these conditions met in the anti-corruption movement, media and ICT became critical enablers, as well as part and parcel of the anti-corruption protests.

No Ideology

Though Anna Hazare and the other leaders came from different civil society formation, and represented proximity to one kind of political ideology or another, the predominant stand of the movement was anti-political class, and of posturing the *aam aadmi* (ordinary citizen) vs. corruption, from a moral position rather than a political or ideological position. This seemed to find resonance with the middle class, and the mainstream media. The mass of the people who 'collected' at the sites of protests or demonstrated in support of the movement were not contained within any specific civil society formations or political parties or any political ideology. They stepped out as 'individuals', spoke in disparate voices that cut across class, political views, and disclaimed identification with any ideology or political party. What was unfolding was a 'politics of chaos' where who was representing whom or who was speaking for whom was not clear. It was India' against corruption; where everyone was 'Anna' protesting against corruption, or where the *aam aadmi* or ordinary citizen was partaking in politics. The focus in this domain of politics was the individual citizen—stepping out in the streets, protesting, making placards in his/her home on the back of used calendars or notebooks. The 'bonding' was loose, often ephemeral—forged through cyber groups on social media. What was moving the protesters to act though was affect and emotional narration, stirred by the mainstream and social media.

The movement also saw the participation of some political organisations that included both the left and the extreme right ideological groups. Its dominant strain however remained that of 'no ideology'.

To conclude, the anti-corruption movement had far reaching ramification. At one level, the movement brought the issue of corruption to the centre stage and forced the government (for the first time) to bend backwards to accommodate civil society demands, acknowledge corruption[5] and formulate a Lokpal Bill (though critiqued as too weak) with inputs from civil society. The movement left the government walking on a tight rope—unable to grasp or adequately respond to the large mass swell on the ground. It was significant moment of redefining state-civil society relations, the impact of which is still unfolding. At the level of civil society, the movement propelled civil society as an active and powerful player vis-à-vis a strong state—giving it huge prominence where for the moment, civil society found itself filling in the 'democratic vacuum' that prevails in the country. At the same time, it raised a number of critical questions about the role of civil society, its legitimacy and accountability, its methodologies of social action in a functioning democracy. The movement also surface the idea of '*swaraj*' (self rule) implying direct democracy/direct participation of people in decision making and popular control of power—revealing the cracks in the functioning of representative democracy in contemporary India. Within civil society, the movement also established the emergence of a new form of social mobilisation—an activism of a new generation, a middle class that is self-organising through new mediums—social networking sites and social media—connecting as individuals and yet spilling into the streets for a collective cause. This is a class that has come to enjoy political, economic and cultural dominance in India beyond its relatively smaller numerical strength, and its activism has been proving to be a game-changer in government–civil society

5. For the first time, the 12th Five Year Plan of India devoted a section on combating corruption in formulating plan for the country.

relations in India, a dynamics has critical implication for civil society and democracy at large in the long-term.

References

Baviskar, Amita (2011). "Cows, Cars and Cycle-Rickshaws: Bourgeois Environmentalism and the Battle for Delhi's Streets", in Amita Baviskar and Raka Ray (eds.), *Elite and Everyman: The Cultural Politics of the Indian Middle Class.* Delhi. New York: Routledge. pp.391-418.

Baviskar, Amita and Raka Ray (eds.) (2011). *Elite and Everyman: The Cultural Politics of the Indian Middle Class.* Delhi. New York: Routledge.

Chatterjee, Partha (1992). "A Religion of Urban Domesticity: Sri Ramakrishna and the Calcutta Middle Class", in Partha Chatterjee and Gyanendra Pandey (eds.), *Subaltern Studies VII.* Delhi: Oxford University Press.

Deshpande, Satish (2006). "Mapping the Middle": Issues in the Analysis of the Non-Poor Classes in India", in Mary E. John, Praveen Kumar Jha and Surinder S. Jodhka (eds.), *Contested Transformations. Changing Economies and Identities in Contemporary India.* New Delhi: Tulika Books. pp.215-36.

Divakar, Paul (2011). *Presentation at Civil Society Conversation: Anna/Anti Corruption Phenomenon: Its implication for Democracy, Civil Society and Policy Making.* CDSA. 13 September.

Engineer, Asghar Ali (2014). "Indian Muslim Middle-Class Must Play a More Active Leadership Role", Interview to Y. Sikand: *Countercurrents. http://www.countercurrents.org/sikand180311.htm.* Accessed on 10 January.

Engineer, Asghar Ali (2001). "Muslim Middle Class and its Role", *Secular Perspective*, 16-31 May.

Fernandes, Leela (2006). *India's New Middle Class: Democratic Politics in the Era of Economic Reforms.* Minneapolis: University of Minnesota Press.

———. (2011). "Hegemony and Inequality: Theoretical Reflection on India's New Middle Class", in Amita Baviskar and Raka Ray (eds.), *Elite and Everyman: The Cultural Politics of the Indian Middle Class.* Delhi. New York: Routledge.

Fernandes, Leela and Patrick Heller (2006). "Hegemonic Aspirations: New Middle Class Politics and India's Democracy in Comparative Perspective", *Critical Asia Studies* 38(4): 495-522.

Jodhka, Surinder S. and Aseem Prakash (2011). *The Indian Middle-Class: Emerging Cultures of Politics and Economics.* International Reports. Berlin: Konrad-Adenauer-Stiftung.

Mahapatra Sujit (2009). "Explosion of the Middle Class", in Neera Chandhoke and Praveen Priyadarshi (eds.), *Contemporary India: Economy, Society, Politics.* New Delhi: Pearson. pp.121-138.

Mooij, Jos and Tawa Lama-Rewal (2010). "Class in Metropolitan India: The Rise of the Middle Classes", in Joël Ruet and Tawa Lama-Rewal (eds.), *Governing India's Metropolises: Case Studies of Four Cities.* Routledge.

Murlidharan, Sukumar (2011). "Media as Echo Chamber: Cluttering the Public Discourse on Corruption", *http://sukumar-md.blogspot.in/2011/09/media-as-echo-chamber-cluttering-public.html.* Accessed on 4 January 2014.

Nabanita, M. (2012). 'Gandhian Crusader Anna Hazare, Now Turns A Web Warrior', *http://www.oneindia.com/2011/08/18/gandhian-crusador-anna-hazare-now-turns-a-web-warrior.html.* Accessed on 29 August 2011.

Ohri, Kapil (2011). 'How Powerful is Anna Hazare on Facebook and Twitter', originally at *http://www.afaqs.com/news/story.html?sid=31413_How+powerful+is+Anna+Hazare+on+Facebook+and+Twitter.* Accessed on 29 November 2011, but later unavailable. Copy at *https://www.flickr.com/groups/1760843@N21/discuss/72157627486122312/.* Accessed on 2 July 2016.

Roy, Aruna (2012). "Hazare's Movement Lacked Ideological Tethering", *The Hindu*, 21 January.

Sengupta, Pritam (2011). "How the Times of India Pumped up Team Anna", *http://wearethebest.wordpress.com/2011/08/31/how-the-times-of-india-pumped-up-team-anna/.* Accessed on 3 January 2014.

Singh, Richa (2014). *New Citizen's Activism in India. Moments, Movements and Mobilisation.* Delhi: Centre for Democracy and Social Action/Heinrich Böll Foundation.

Sitapati, Vinay (2011). "What Anna Hazare Movement and Indian Middle Class Say About Each Other", *Economic and Political Weekly* XLVI(30), 23 July.

Sridharan, E. (2004). "The Growth and Sectoral Composition of India Middle Class : Its Impact on the Politics of Liberalisation in India", *India Review* 3(4): 405-28

Varma, Pavan K. (2002). *The Great Indian Middle Class.* New Delhi : Viking

Venkatesh, Sandhya (2013). "Engaging with the Middle Class and Youth on Issues of Dignity and Social Justice: A Scoping Study" (Unpublished Report supported by Oxfam Publication, New Delhi).

New Middle Class Consumption and Green Politics

10

NITA MATHUR

Indian Urban Middle Class Youth's Engagement with Consumer Culture

Restraints, Constraints and Freedom

In many discussions, consumer culture is associated with ostentatious and luxurious lifestyle, renewed confidence in selfhood, and predominance of market forces in people's personal life and urban landscape. One cannot but be awed by its pervasive nature even as, willingly or hesitantly, everyone feels compelled to participate. While the 'lower class' struggle hard to catch up with conspicuous consumption, the 'upper class' find new avenues of consumption and new ways of engaging with them. The centre stage, however, is occupied by the new middle class (hereafter middle class) that is numerically significant, sets the agenda for marketers, and terms of reference for the government. This chapter does not present an ethnography of the middle class in the broad framework of consumption. Rather, it examines the complexities of the everyday life of urban middle class youth as they negotiate their aspirations, anxieties and consumer sovereignty within the restraints and constraints that surround them. The objective is to examine the complicated relation between identity, ideology and consumption practices in the middle-income section of society.

This chapter is informed by a comprehensive survey carried out between March and September 2008 at shopping malls and traditional markets in New Delhi. There were 377 survey respondents in the age range of 15 to 43 years belonging to the middle class in Delhi. The material serving as a basis for discussion here, however, is largely confined to sub-sample of 275 respondents (113 women with average age of 23.4 years and 162 men with average age of 24.7

years) between 15 and 29 years of age representing the youth sample[1] with average monthly income of ₹15,500. Inclusion of both youth and middle aged people in the comprehensive survey provided the advantage of marking the trajectory. The survey was supplemented with in-depth interviews largely with youth (focusing on their spending and saving patterns, aspirations, anxieties, restraints and constraints and strategies they use to deal with them). This was followed with a few interviews with middle-aged people (i.e. those between 34 and 43 years) on their viewpoint regarding youth's engagement with consumption.

Subsequently, between February and March 2016, I revisited a few middle class families, discussed the data and their analysis with them to, first, affirm their validity and reliability; and second, renew insights into everydayness of consumption. Following the ever-rising importance of environmental concerns, particularly so after the Copenhagen Summit of 2009, I carried out fresh interviews in order to develop an understanding of whether and in what way shopping decisions accommodate green choices. The specific interviews were based on three key areas of interest: priority of green products in the practice of consumption; personal viewpoints on the pressing global issue of concomitance of consumption and environmental degradation; and the extent to which mundane consumption decisions contribute to environmental degradation. The perspective and findings of the study were discussed with other scholars and with the respondents in order to obviate inconsistencies in the arguments presented here.

The central argument presented here is that the middle class in India relates with consumption equivocally. A sense of 'feel good' and one of 'overall loss of virtue' coexist. People view consumption as a threat to morals and values, a source of many evils in society (e.g., corruption, demand for dowry, rising indiscipline and intolerance). But alongside, they treat it as a liberating force that enables them to throw away the shackles of conservatism and positions them next

1. The Ministry of Youth Affairs and Sports (2014), in its National Youth Policy, defines youth as those in the age group of 15-29 years.

only to the transnational community in a general sense and India's upper class in particular.

Thus, first, this chapter contributes to the ongoing discussion on the nature and extent of consumption by the middle class in third world countries. Second, in light of empirical data, it examines the popular perception that urban middle class youth in India are uncritical of consumption. Third, it reflects on how consumption profiles and aspirations are negotiated in everyday life of people.

Profiling the Middle Class: Size, Composition and the Propensity to Consume

Far from being homogeneous in size and composition, the middle class constitutes a contested terrain in academic discourse. Among others, a significant point of contention is the basic criteria used for defining the middle class.[2] Two positions are imminent. The first defines the middle class in relative terms as "people who are beyond the poverty line but not in the category of the rich" (Lahiri 2014: 37);[3] the second defines middle class in absolute terms by measure of income or wealth (Asian Development Bank 2010, Kharas 2010, Banerjee and Duflo 2008, Bhalla 2007). With shifting grounds for its delineation, middle class eludes precise estimation. Circumscribing the middle class as those whose per capita income per day lies within the bracket of $10 and $50 measured in 2005 PPP (purchasing power parity), Meyer and Birdsall (2012) estimate the size of middle class in India as 70 million or less than 10 per cent of the population. Kharas (2010) defines the middle class as the section of households with daily expenditure between $10 and $100[4] per person on PPP terms and projects that the middle class would comprise 90 per cent of the population in 30 years time.

In the same vein, McKinsey Global Institute (2007: 13) defines the middle class as comprising two economic segments: seekers

2. This section does not make a distinction between new middle class and old middle class, for it is based on a review of studies that do not segregate the two.

3. More specifically, Easterly (2000), for example, defines the middle class as those lying between the 20th and 80th percentile on the consumption distribution.

4. Kharas defines the middle class in terms of US$.

with real annual household disposable incomes of ₹200,000 to ₹500,000 ($4,380 to $10,940 or $23,530 to $58,820 at PPP) and strivers at ₹500,000 to₹1,000,000 ($10,940 to $21,890 or $58,820 to $117,650 at PPP)[5] and foretells that by the year 2025, the middle class will constitute 41 per cent of the population of the country. The definition of the middle class by the National Council of Applied Economic Research (NCAER), done between 1995-96 and 2001-02 and was adapted by McKinsey Global Institute in its 2007 report, was confined to annual income figures. It incorporated households with annual income between ₹2,00,000 and ₹10,00,000 (i.e., $4,444 and $22,200). On this basis, the size of the middle class was estimated to be 10.8 million households in 2001-02 i.e., around 5.7 per cent of that year's population and projected to be 28.4 million households by 2009-10 i.e., 12.8 per cent of that year's population (Bery 2005). Interestingly, as Shukla (2010) mentions, over a period of 2 decades, NCAER's classification of the middle class whilst retaining income has taken cultural parameters (e.g., education, patterns of consumption and ownership of selected consumer goods) into account. Further, a report by the Centre for Macro Consumer research of the NCAER extrapolates that by 2015-16, the number of middle class households would be 53.3 million or 267 million people. This would increase to 113.8 million households or 547 million people by 2025-26 constituting 20.3 per cent and 37.2 per cent of the population by 2015-16 and 2025-26 respectively (*The Economic Times*, 6 February 2011).

Departing from purely economic criteria, Joshi (2010) argues for the importance of cultural capital and human agency in defining the middle class. He maintains that in colonial India, people who identified themselves as the middle class engaged with new cultural politics, participated actively in public debates and in doing so shaped political and social life in a major way. Deshpande (2003) suggests that, in a general sense, the social significance of the middle class is due to its marked influence in 'ideological matters'; being 'projected

5. McKinsey clarifies that the labels and cut-offs that it has used are similar to those used by the NCAER (2004). The specific brackets have been re-calibrated for the time period examined.

as an 'average' class that best represents the whole of society' (p.128); being treated as 'stable centre of society and polity impervious to extremes' (p.129). More specifically, in the context of contemporary Indian society he establishes 2 general features of the middle class: in terms of absolute numbers, it cannot be considered as a very large class against the backdrop of world standards; and it constitutes a very small portion of the Indian population. Jaffrelot and van der Veer (2008) concur that despite being numerically far from robust, the middle class, in effect, sets the terms of reference of Indian society, not only because of its development but also because it is the most favoured in the official discourse and of policy makers. Also, by self-ascription, Indian society is, by and large, middle class-centred. Public discourse surrounding the middle class has mostly projected it as a promising consumer market. A large section of people belonging to the middle class consolidate their self-identity around consumption.

The McKinsey Global Institute (2007) estimated that (i) within a generation, the number of upwardly mobile middle class households given to consuming goods ranging from high-end cars to designer clothing will increase significantly; (ii) by the year 2025, the per capita consumption in India will rise from US$ 334 to US$ 1064; and (iii) in about 2 decades, India will be world's fifth consumer market.

Spending and Saving

The report of the 68th round of the National Sample Survey (NSS) on 'Household Consumer Expenditure in India' carried out by the National Sample Survey Office (NSSO) for the period July 2011 to June 2012 records an all-India MPCE (monthly per capita consumer expenditure) of ₹2,630 for urban India (₹1,121 for food i.e., 42.6% of total and ₹1,509 for non-food items i.e., 57.4% of total). Apart from education, and fuel and light (adding up to 13.6%), major non-food item groups were conveyance (6.5%), clothing and footwear (6.4%), miscellaneous goods and entertainment (5.8%) and durable goods (5.3%). The share of discretionary spending exceeds spending on basic goods. Buoyant consumer confidence and soaring aspirations of the middle class are fed by an overall sense of consistent improvement in economic and social life situation. Liberalisation of the economy, and delicensing, among others, have not only provisioned stiff competition leading to addition of more commodities and as also their variants on the shelf but also laid more disposable income in the hands of people. Importantly, some of the high-brands that earlier catered to choices of the rich and elite sections of society have launched cheaper variants that are accessible to the middle class. The middle class, in turn, celebrates its ownership of such brands and stretches hard to reach out to more expensive variants. There is 'now a lot more to buy, it is cheaper, and what's more, it is better than ever before!' Bijapurkar (2007: 5). There is unwavering rise in consumer durables sector revenue in India. According to the India Brand Equity Foundation (IBEF) update of July 2016, it reached US$9.7 billion in FY (financial year) 2015 and is expected to US$12.5 billion by FY 2016. The urban population contributes about two-third of the total revenue (the remaining one third is generated from rural population). The consumer durable market is expected to grow at CAGR (compound annual growth rate) of 13 per cent between the FYs 2005 and 2010.[6] According to Shukla (2010), while the top 20 cities in India[7] account for only 10 per cent of the total population of the country, this population contributes 31 per cent to the country's income and spends 21 per cent thereby generating surplus income of 60 per cent.

In most middle class households, a large part this surplus income is of easy access to youth. While many of them maintain that the access to surplus income of the family makes them feel independent, confident and empowered to take decisions, they relate with it ambivalently. Notwithstanding the fact that they aspire to make big money and lead a luxurious life, money is not regarded as the be-all-and-end-all of life. They assign tremendous importance to money for its propensity to fulfil their dreams and simultaneously treat it, as they say, '*haath ka maiel*' i.e., dirt of the hand (which awaits being washed off). This understanding emphasises the spattered and

6. *http://www.ibef.org/industry/indian-consumer-market.aspx*

7. Top 20 cities in India comprise 8 megacities (Delhi, Mumbai, Chennai, Kolkata, Bangalore, Hyderabad, Ahmedabad and Pune), 7 boomtowns (Surat, Kanpur, Jaipur, Lucknow, Nagpur, Bhopal and Coimbatore) and 5 niche cities (Faridabad, Amritsar, Ludhiana, Chandigarh and Jalandhar).

ephemeral nature of money. A few individuals willingly surrender enviable economic gain sufficient in a job in favour of the virtues of conscientiousness and commitment to the family and community at large. Of the IT workers in Hyderabad, Radhakrishnan (2011: 158) writes:

> Consumption patterns that uphold, reinforce, or add status to the family are acceptable and do not signal materialism, while leisure practices that spend money irresponsibly, outside the purview of the family, signal an unacceptable morality.

Spending money on commodities that would benefit the members of one's family is appreciated while splurging on oneself is criticised. A fairly large section of youth noted that forced into consumption by the peer group, they compromised branded commodities, particularly clothes and accessories, by buying look-alikes, flaunted their credit cards (but refrained from using them), and as, many put it, 'ingeniously managing to project an image of a compulsive consumer'.

Against this backdrop, spending on consumer goods and services is curtailed even as saving is facilitated. In contrast to the older generation who saved money incrementally for several years, sometimes decades, to buy a house and/or consumer durable goods (e.g., a refrigerator, television set, motorcycle, or an air conditioner), youth seek to make big purchases (such as a car and/or house) early in their career. Much of their optimism comes from the provision of EMIs (equated monthly instalments) offered by the retail sector and the hope to earn and save enough money to pay the instalments. It is important to note that whilst being careful and wary of buying on credit, the youth segment does not use the credit card with ease but remains sanguine about EMIs which, in effect, is a form of credit. By and large, they restrict the use of credit cards for making mundane and frequent purchases but avail the EMI facility for purchase of durable household effects. Evidently, use of EMIs is less frequent than credit cards but involves long duration repayments. The contradiction in spending patterns is resolved in the understanding that present-day youth are realistic and draw long-term plan for the future. In a way, this is a sort of diversion of resources from current consumption to future asset base augmentation. The youth choose to slog in the present so that they can have a more comfortable life later. Interestingly, this tendency increases as age advances.

The Paradox

Discussion on urban youth tends to centre chiefly around education, unemployment, unrest, overseas migration, and generational conflict. They are often dismissed as a generation given to materialism, hedonism, individualism, and moral corruption. An informed understanding, however, indicates that their aspirations, change in values and lifestyle are underlain by newly founded economic empowerment and freedom to make choices that came with economic reforms of 1991. For urban youth, economic reforms and subsequent pay commissions paved the way for consumerist ideology, widening of the spectrum of choices available on the shelf, and renewed pressure to showcase individual achievement and performance even as social and economic security got compromised. In comparison to their predecessors, urban youth now have a wider and diversified range of, not only commodities, but also education and employment opportunities, leisure-time engagements, in sum, lifestyle options to choose from. There is greater preparedness to take risks and own responsibility of failure (if any). Even as they gear up to take control of their lives, parents worry about interfering relatives and societal pressures to conform. They, in turn, feel burdened by the anxiety of their parents.

Youth do not deny a sense of community but they remain wary of intrusion of others into their personal life. They fashion their identity, among others, on consumption choices, mainly commodities and services. Each individual strives to stand out and be distinctive in the peer group. Personal narratives are replete with initiatives in this regard. A close look at these narratives, however, presents a composite design of life that is, by and large, standardised. The paradox lies in youth revelling in the freedom to choose but driven to make choices within a common frame provided by a set of common lifestyle choices, decisions and behaviour. Drawing on insights obtained from more than a decade-long series of interaction with urban youth in different parts of the country, Titus (2015: xv) concludes:

> The diverse youth in the country who are qualified by differentiating variables like language, ethnicity, religion, caste, community, etc. were all merging into one chunky mass at the surface...The particular outcome of convergence I focused on was consumption behaviour, and consistent with what was emerging, consumption patterns too were flocking together...

Finally, the young were patronising either similar or the same products and brands. In certain categories, a gaggle of brands was being bought with acute loyalty; in others it was products.

Four key points emerge from freedom of choice. First, it privileges self-expression and construction of the notion of self. Second, it provides a common platform for interaction with peers. Third, it serves as a gate pass for contemporary youth culture constituted of those with similar ideology and choices. Fourth, it equips youth to navigate through consumption opportunities.

Urban youth attract marketers not only because of their aspirations, longings and anxieties, but also because they have income from allowances and/or salaries to realise them. Additionally, they influence the consumption profile of their families. Youth try to present carefully managed images in professional, social, and personal realms. Projection of managed images is becoming a means of self-expression. Their ideas about fashion and style are largely obtained, among others, from the internet and the social media, television, movies, and magazines. Aggressive advertising and other marketing strategies fuel their aspirations a great deal. Of critical concern is young people's experience of consumption and the negotiation of their agency in dealing with it. Their aspirations are supported by relatively higher starting salaries, easy availability of finance and purchase policies such as buy-now and pay-later, and free add-ons. Interestingly, the same youth who seek to be extraordinary and exclusive in everything they do and own, also tend to revive their belief in tradition albeit in a renewed form. Evidently, urban middle class youth haplessly oscillate between demands of consumer culture (particularly show of new fashions and styles, ownership of luxury commodities and treating them as determinants of happiness, fulfilment and a meaningful life) and sufficiency (i.e., modest but adequate scale of living). In fact, a few elements of tradition are becoming commercialised in being available as commodities off the counter e.g., ayurvedic products, and art and craftwork. The middle class is acutely aware that success awaits hard work and conscientiousness. As Sinha (2011: 20) notes, middle-class merit has the potential to transform ordinary lives into extraordinary ones. A large section of youth concurs with this view. More specifically, middle class are "striving to activate their destiny rather than resigning themselves to a pre-ordained fate. A pursuit of extrinsic values has a rightful place in their lives today. They have realised the criticality of pushing to the limits and closing the last lap, of not letting up until they reach the finish line. They are pursuing individual extraordinariness as never before. In this pursuit, they are making tradition an essential part of their success strategy".

Green Choices

Urban youth in India are projected as increasingly self-centred and given to a lifestyle that pursues comfort, luxury and opulence. Expectedly, business models that seek to make the most of the fire of desire in the youth meet with limited success. The intriguing issue then is one of framing, what lies at the root of their consumption choices. There are two major currents that run through consumption choices of urban youth: one that pushes for consumerist lifestyle and the other that prioritises 'simple living'. The seemingly opposing trends are, in fact, complementary to each other. Bijapurkar (2007: 171) notes that socialism coexists with free market economics. Further, "The future of Consumer India, therefore, must be thought of in terms of coexistence, fusion, loosening of rigid structures and new ways of doing old things." The interface between socialism and free market economics has prepared ground for an ideology of consumption that engages with environmental issues on an everyday basis. Of critical concern is the pertinence of green consumption to reflexivity and negotiation of self-identity.

Much of general discussion among the middle class is surrounding the unsustainability of the nature and magnitude of consumption in the present day and the pressing need to 'do something about it'. Such discussions, however, do not inspire people to prioritise green product choices. In India, ethical concerns are often overshadowed by other personal and economic ones in shopping decisions. These are neither commonly mentioned on products on the shelf nor are they sought after by consumers and policymakers as of now. A person buying a pair of shoes, for example, is hardly aware of safety norms or working conditions under which they were manufactured. Similarly, customers seldom look for organic label on tomatoes or other vegetables. Many people buy vegetables from street vendors or local markets. Whether and to what extent pesticides have been used, however, is of limited concern to few of them and awareness campaign is going on by civil societies. From consumer's side, two lines of related arguments surface in this regard. First, doing 'something' about the environment and ethics of production and dissemination of a product is the responsibility of the state and not of an individual. Second, it is the aggregate rather than individual consumption that determines environmental gains or quality. So of what good is an individual's initiative to ride a bicycle rather than a car or purchase free trade products? Defeatist arguments remain popular with many, for there is an overall sense of ignorance or apathy about one's surroundings and the environment; and green products come at a premium and are not readily available. It is rather uncommon to find people who self-define themselves as green consumers in terms of being driven by green subjectivity in all product purchases. Green consumption is reflected in limited product choices.

In the present day, green product choices are determined by either personal gain (as in the case of choice of organic food that is known to contribute overall well-being) and/or concern for environmental gain/quality. Importantly, irrespective of the reason(s), the section of the middle class making green product choices is constituted largely of the youth and the middle-aged who are aware about environmental issues. Also, the inspiration for green consumption is inextricably tied with the struggle to establish an identity that projects one as benevolent and upbeat about social concerns of which threat to environment is central.

Interviews with youth suggested that their purchase decisions are greatly influenced by two factors. The first is celebrity-led advertisements and social media endorsements. In fact, celebrities' endorsement is a lucrative means of developing awareness, credibility and confidence in the green products and services. The dividend is higher when the consumer believes that the celebrity actually uses the product and/or service himself/herself. One way ahead then is to get celebrities to promote (and preferably use) such products and services. The second is government-led initiatives. Often, youth wait for government-led initiatives rather than leading initiatives themselves, for as one of them stated that their small-level initiatives would need financial inputs that are usually not forthcoming from either the peer group or the state. Also, there was likelihood that their small, localised initiatives would never get aggregated to make a big difference. Government-led initiatives, on the contrary, are financially secured and designed to experience and showcase the effect. The recent odd-even policy of the Delhi government allowing alternate day use of a car met with much support from the middle class. Despite the inconvenience of travel, most of them said that this was a necessary step in the direction of ensuring air quality. According to Barik (2016), there could be three policy options: moral suasion, command and control, and economic incentives that influence decision-making of consumers.

Environmental responsiveness among the middle class awaits robust leadership and appropriate strategies of resource management. It would be worthwhile to adopt a disaggregated approach provisioning opportunity for policymakers, members of the civil society and laypersons to focus on those aspects of a measure that would have the largest impact on the specific section of people. The number of green consumers and the extent of green consumption is likely to impact growth of fair trade and recycled products' markets as also organised resistance or anti-consumption movements in India.

Conclusion

The discourse on consumption of urban middle class youth is both complex and intriguing. They value freedom and individuality and at the same time, remain connected with family and friends, are bold in the face and at the same time, extremely sensitive and guarded, are care-free in attitude and at the same time, cautious about how their appearance, and live in the present and at the same time, worry about the future. One of the most powerful ways in which consumer culture mediates between the contradictory strands in youth is by way of generating ideas for construction of self-identity affording the freedom to individualise a commodity that is available on the shelf for anyone to pick up, to connect with family and friends at will and protect their personal life from gaze, and to wear what is in fashion in a way that the no-cares attitude remains intact. Iqani (2012: 166) contends,

> Despite the emphasis that has been placed on the public nature of consumer media, the private and personal also plays a fundamental role in the seductive power of their messages. The personal plays out in the consumerist public in more ways than one. The persistent individualisation of readers and viewers, the ongoing appeals to their unique sense of personal identity, and the invitation to sexual fantasy, all imbricate the personal, individual and private into consumer discourses.

The practice of consumption is impelled by Gandhian ideals of self sufficiency, restraint and austerity even as consumerism is disavowed. Reflexive deployment of these ideals makes consumption a contested terrain for youth. Equipped with higher disposable income than their predecessors and confronted with larger variety of commodities to choose from, and easy payment options, urban middle class youth seem to be caught between traditional (anti-materialist) and consumerist (opulent) ideologies. Fernandes (2006) argues that these antithetical ideologies shape identity politics and construe individual identities of people. More specifically, Saavala (2010: 147) concludes, "However, most people do not see themselves or their close ones as crazed by the new consumer society, but rather manifest a very moralistic discourse on mass consumption. Only a very small fraction of the upper-middle class is able to dive wholeheartedly into the consumerist way of life; most people who consider themselves middle class have to try and make ends meet and orchestrate growing needs for consumption along with the most important middle-class expenditures—children's schooling and daughters' marriages." Such compulsions and the naturalising and ubiquitous nature of consumer culture are mutually constitutive and feed each other.

The unignorable and pervasive presence of consumer culture calling for, among others, ownership and display of luxury commodities and an extravagant lifestyle marks a shift in focus on virtues of humility, self-restraint and nurturance to individualism and conspicuous indulgence in consumption. This shift in focus, however, is not totalitarian in the sense that traditional values, ideology and way of leading one's life are not overlaid by new ethos and practice of life that accords centrality to conspicuous consumption in social construction of identity. Rather, the process, while emphasising selective and individualised strategy of acquisition of commodities and maintenance of lifestyle itself remains pinned to traditional values. It is widely accepted that a sense of personal meaninglessness has set in the psyche of people in the present day (Giddens 1991, Lasch 1985). Arnould and Price (2000) demonstrate how consumers use self-referential behaviour that they feel reveal or produce 'true' self and collective displays with the objective of inventing or refashioning cultural traditions to restore a sense of community, tradition and self. More specifically, in individualising a commodity picked up from a shelf where it, and others of its kind were available for anyone to buy, youth create self-narratives around it. The self-narrative of an individual serves to imbue uniqueness to the commodity projecting it as customised for her/him.

Urban youth are mature consumers who remain watchful of mindless consumerism. Interestingly, one of the ways by which many of them seek to balance out their indulgence with consumption celebrating a sense of the self is by helping others in a myriad of ways—giving money in charity to individuals, religious organisations, and NGOs, engaging with social issues as activists, running skill development/enhancement programmes for the economically weaker sections of society. Personal narratives of youth combine multiple images of the self that render comprehensible the relationship between self and community, and the techniques that individuals use to cope with the pressure to consume. Also, they relocate selective tradition-specific practices and motifs in the context of consumer culture in a way that they appear more relevant and amenable (see Mathur 2014 for details). Consumption portfolios of urban youth in India seems to be a bricolage in which "innovation within tradition, as creativity within conformity, and as novelty within the familiar," to borrow words from Thompson (2000: 132), are used to create new identities and refurbish old ones. It is envisaged that in the time to come, there is a possibility that the strong wave of consumerism would loosen the grip of virtuous morality holding back the psyche of Indian middle class. The challenge before society lies in integrating consumer culture with traditional wisdom in a way that a sense of renewed identity is constructed.

References

Arnould, Eric J. and Linda L. Price (2000). "Authenticating Acts and Authoritative Practices", in S. Ratneshwar, David Glen Mick and Cynthia Huffman (eds.), *The Why of Consumption: Contemporary Perspectives on Consumer Motives, Goals, and Desires.* Routledge: London and New York.

Asian Development Bank (2010). "The Rise of the Asian Middle Class", in *Key Indicators of the Asia and the Pacific 2010.* Manila. Also available at: *http://www.adb.org/sites/default/files/KI2010.special-chapter.pdf*

Banerjee, Abhijit and Esther Duflo (2008). "What is Middle Class about the Middle Classes around the World", *Journal of Economic Perspectives* 22(2): 3-28.

Barik, Kaustuva (2016). "Road Rationing and Economic Gains: An Assessment of Delhi's Odd-Even Formula", *Economic and Political Weekly* LI(2): 12-14.

Bery, Suman K. (2005). "Foreword", in *The Great Indian Market: Results from the NCAER Market Information Survey of Households.* New Delhi: NCAER and Business Standard Limited.

Bhalla, Surjit S. (2007). "Second Among Equals: The Middle Class Kingdoms of India and China", Available at: *https://ssbhalla.files.wordpress.com/2015/08/second_among_equals_omega_august- 25-2015.pdf.*

Bijapurkar, Rama (2007). *We are Like that Only: Understanding the Logic of Consumer India.* New Delhi: Penguin Group.

Deshpande, Satish (2003). *Contemporary India: A Sociological View.* New Delhi: Viking.

Easterly, William (2000). 'The Middle Class Consensus and Economic Development", *Policy Research Working Paper* 2346. World Bank, Washington, DC. Available at: *http://elibrary.worldbank.org/doi/pdf/10.1596/1813-9450-2346*

Fernandes, Leela (2006). 'Nationalizing 'the Global': Media Images, Cultural Policies and the Middle Class in India", *Media Culture and Society* 22(5): 611-28.

Giddens, Anthony (1991). *Modernity and Self-Identity: Self and Society in the Late Modern Age*. Polity Press: UK.

Indian Brand Equity Foundation (IBEF) (2016). *Indian Consumer Market, Economy, Indian Middle Class, Market Size.* Available at *http://www.ibef.org/industry/indian-consumer-market.aspx.*

Iqani, Mehita (2012). *Consumer Culture and the Media: Magazines in the Public Eye*. Basingstoke: Palgrave Macmillan.

Jaffrelot, Christopher and Peter van der Veer (2008). "Introduction", in Christopher Jaffrelot and Peter van der Veer (eds.), *Patterns of Middle Class Consumption in India and China*. New Delhi: SAGE.

Joshi, Sanjay (2010). *The Middle Class in Global India*. New Delhi: Oxford University Press.

Kharas, Homi (2010). "The Emerging Middle Class in Developing Countries", *Working Paper* No. 285. OECD Development Centre. Available at *http://www.oecd.org/dev/44457738.pdf.*

Lahiri, Ashok K. (2014). "The Middle Class and Economic Reforms", *Economic and Political Weekly* XLIX(11): 37-44.

Lasch, C. (1985). *The Minimal Self: Psychic Survival in Troubled Times*. New York: W.W. Norton & Co.

Mathur, Nita (2014). "Modernity, Consumer Culture and Construction of Urban Youth Identity in India: A Disembedding Perspective", in Nita Mathur (ed.), *Consumer Culture, Modernity and Identity.* New Delhi: SAGE.

McKinsey Global Institute (2007). *The 'Bird of Gold': Rise of India's Consumer Market.* Available at *https://www.mckinsey.com/locations/india/mckinseyonindia/pdf/India_Consumer_Market.pdf*

Meyer, Christian and Nancy Birdsall (2012). *New Estimates of Indian Middle Class: A Technical Note.* Centre for Global Development. November. Available at *http://www.cgdev.org/doc/2013_MiddleClassIndia_Technical Note_CGD.Note.pdf*

Ministry of Youth Affairs and Sports (2014). *National Youth Policy*. Government of India. Available at *http://yas.nic.in/sites/default/files/National-Youth-Policy-Document.pdf*

Radhakrishnan, Smitha (2011). *Appropriately Indian: Gender and Culture in a New Transnational Class.* New Delhi: Orient Blackswan.

Saavala, Minna (2010). *Middle-Class Moralities: Everyday Struggle over Belonging in India.* New Delhi: Orient Blackswan.

Shukla, Rajesh (2010). *How India Earns, Spends and Saves: Unmasking the Real India.* New Delhi: SAGE and NCAER-CMCR.

Sinha, Dheeraj (2011). *Consumer India: Inside the Indian Mind and Wallet*. New Delhi: John Wiley and Sons (Asia).

The Economic Times (2011). "India's Middle Class Population to Touch 267 Million in 5 Years", *The Economic Times.* 6 February.

Thompson, Criag J. (2000). "Postmodern Consumer Goals Made Easy!!!!", in S. Ratneshwar, David Glen Mick and Cynthia Huffman (eds.), *The Why of Consumption: Contemporary Perspectives on Consumer Motives, Goals, and Desires.* Routledge: London and New York.

Titus, Ray (2015). *Yuva India: Consumption and Lifestyle Choices of a Young India*. Gurgaon: Random House.

11

ASHISH KOTHARI

Consumerism and the Indian Middle Classes

Walk down any big city centre in India today, and the dominant image is of an explosion of global brands, with in-your-face adverts by companies convincing you that life is worthless unless you own one of their products. Gurgaon outside New Delhi takes the cake in the sheer concentration of glitzy shopping malls, but every city of indecent size has its fair share of these orgasmic centres of retail, many of them, ironically, lined up along a Mahatma Gandhi Marg. You'd have to excuse anyone who wonders whether India is still poor. The way a section of Indians is spending its money, with collective consumer frenzies during festivals and individual ones on birthdays and weddings and anniversaries, it would seem that the image of emaciated people in rags that so characterised the country is history. Nothing, of course, could be farther from the truth.

In April 2015, I circulated a news item announcing that the Government of India had set a Sustainable Consumption Line, and all those consuming above that line would have action taken against them. Several readers wrote to me asking for more details, some even wanted to write to the Government congratulating it for the bold step. Eventually, of course, people figured out it was a spoof.

But my intention was more than using April Fool's Day for some fun. It was a light-hearted attempt at addressing the issue of rising consumerism amongst India's rich including its middle classes. What percentage of India's population is middle class and above, is disputed, but what is clear is that the absolute numbers are huge (the middle class figures ranging from 70 to about 200 million, depending on definition used). This number of people with high or relatively high buying power, makes for an impressive amount of consumption, a fact long ago recognised by both Indian and foreign brands, the latter using the opportunities offered by the 'opening up' of the economy in 1991.

There is here a need to distinguish between consumption per se, and consumerism. Every human being needs to consume to stay alive, be healthy, fulfil basic needs. Consumerism, on the other hand, stems from the desire to have more and more ('*dil maange more*'), way beyond one's basic needs, and where a combination of social and psychological factors leads even luxury items to appear to be needs. Of course the dividing line may sometimes be fuzzy and very subjective, mixed up with the complexities of today's urban lives; I might say, for instance, that owning a refrigerator is being consumerist, but a couple working through the day to make ends meet in a city may consider it a need so they can cook once in a couple of days and still come home to a readily available meal. Most people would agree, though, that the desire to change a basic fridge to one of the new-fangled ones that offer multiple compartments one of which can store your *aam ras* (mango puree) for a year, moves over the line into consumerism.

But why is this an issue at all? Should we not be celebrating higher consumption, given that it stimulates higher economic growth rates, and is supposed to be a key driver in any nation's move out of underdevelopment?

Why do we Need to Limit Consumerism?

There are many reasons to interrogate the rise of consumerism globally, and in India. One is that it is part of the forces trashing the earth. Collectively, humanity has in many ways already overstepped the ecological limits that the earth places on us. In 2005, the Millennium Ecosystem Assessment already found that "60 per cent (15 out of 24) of the ecosystem services examined ... are being degraded or used unsustainably, including fresh water, capture fisheries, air and water purification, and the regulation of regional and local climate, natural hazards, and pests." In 2009, a large team of scientists led by Johan Rockström of the Stockholm Resilience

Centre concluded that of 9 'planetary boundaries', "humanity has already transgressed three ... for climate change, rate of biodiversity loss, and changes to the global nitrogen cycle." The Global Footprint Network estimates that we are already on 'planetary overshoot', consuming what the earth provides us 50 per cent faster than can be replenished with horrifying implications for both future generations and those in current generations who are victims of environmental damage. The currently prevalent form of human development is, clearly, unsustainable and unjust.

While sheer numbers of people are certainly one factor behind this trend, an equally or perhaps more serious factor is the wasteful consumption patterns of industrial countries and of the rich in so-called developing countries. Profligate consumerism and the destructive production processes linked to it are stripping the earth. If you've got a car, air conditioner, refrigerator, electrical appliances in your kitchen, a home theatre and stereo system, or exotic food items that have come from half-way across the world, or if you simply use a new disposable plastic bag every time you shop, or (like me) take flights across the world (to conferences about saving the world!), chances that you are part of this class that is treating the earth like a giant extraction machine and as big a dump.

We Don't all Consume the Same

Rich (industrialised or urbanised) countries of the world are today consuming far above their fair share of the earth's resources. Each average citizen in the United Arab Emirates needs over 10 global hectares (gha, calculated as a hectare of land that can produce resources needed by humans and also can absorb human waste), each American over 7 gha—whereas each Indian needs less than 0.9. According to the Global Footprint Network, the earth can accommodate a per person consumption of 1.8 gha (i.e. if on average each person uses up to this amount, we will not overstrain the earth's capacity).

But the relatively low per capita consumption of countries like India hides another, equally important, reality. The inter-country contrast is mirrored by the inter-class contrast within such nations.

A back-of-the-envelope calculation that my co-author Aseem Shrivastava and I did for our book *Churning the Earth* (Shrivastava and Kothari 2012), indicated that per capita ecological footprint of the richest 1 per cent people in India (folks like us owning the products mentioned above) is 17 times that of the poorest 40 per cent. These folks have a footprint well above the global acceptable limit of 1.8 gha.

One factor behind these levels of consumption and impact is the enormous wealth owned or controlled by the rich; the same 1 per cent of India's population owns over 50 per cent of its private wealth, the richest 10 per cent nearly three-fourths, and in contrast the poorest 10 per cent have less than 0.1 per cent. The inequality has been steadily growing, with the richest 10 per cent increasing their share of wealth from 65 per cent in 2000 to almost 75 per cent in 2014. This mirrors a global trend. So while on one side there is shameless profligacy and waste in consumption, on the other (and partly because of), there are several billion people (worldwide) or several hundred million people (in India) who do not have enough to consume, suffering deprivations of food, energy, water, shelter, clothing, and other basic needs. This too is a reason for the rich to cut down, because only then will global ecological space be created to enable the poor to enhance their lives; else such enhancement will take us further along the path of ecological suicide and socioeconomic conflict.

Unfortunately, we live in an upside-down world in which the poor and powerless continue to face all kinds of limits to their consumption, while the rich and powerful have a virtual free-for-all. Take for instance, natural resources. In many countries, communities that live inside or adjacent to forests have quotas on the amount of timber, non-timber forest produce, fuel, and other such products they can use. If they happen to fall within a protected area (over 13% of the earth's surface is under such land use), the restrictions are even stricter, and in some cases absolute (leading to physical displacement). This is justified in the name of forest and wildlife conservation.

But is there any such limit on rich (mostly urban or semi-urban) consumers? Their distance from forests and other natural ecosystems makes their use of natural resources virtually invisible, but it is very real. So for instance there is no limit to how much electricity an urban (or rich rural) family can consume, notwithstanding that it comes from power stations or dams that have had major ecological impacts on forests, wetlands, grasslands or marine areas, and have displaced or dispossessed local communities. There is no limit on the amount or kind of minerals the rich can use, regardless of the fact that mining threatens crucial ecosystems and cultures worldwide. In India alone, over 100,000 hectares of forest land has been diverted for mining in the last 30 years, and countless rivers and lakes have been polluted beyond repair by mining run-off. There is no limit on how much vehicular fuel the rich can use, for we are collectively blind to the impact this has on areas from where fuel is extracted, or the pollution and climate change being caused by vehicular emissions. Americans and Europeans are of course past masters at this, but parts of the erstwhile poor world are also fast catching up, joining their consumerist big brothers in what can be called the 'Global North'. For instance, Greenpeace India estimates that the richest Indians are already reaching the global average of per capita carbon emissions (of about 5 tonnes per year); and that their emissions are almost double the per capita limit (2.5 tonnes) considered necessary if we want to restrict temperature increase to below 2° (Ananthapadmanabhan et al. 2007).

Perhaps amongst the few limits imposed on urban populations is landholding; in India for instance there was a ceiling on how much land a family could own. Increasingly, though, in the post-1991 economic globalisation phase, such ceilings in both cities and villages are being done away with or diluted.

The Sustainable Consumption Line

'Sustainable development' has become quite a buzzword. Virtually every agency of the United Nations (UN), every big multilateral and bilateral agency, and most big civil society organisations have bought into the Sustainable Development Goals (SDGs) agenda, which replaced the current Millennium Development Goals (MDGs) in late 2015. Sustainability is supposed to be a fulcrum of this framework. One crucial component of this is 'sustainable consumption', but unfortunately, there is very little talk of the need to drastically cut down existing consumption levels of the global North.

To make consumption truly sustainable, there is a need for a measure to determine what is sustainable, and ways to implement this measure. Several countries have measures or indicators by which they determine people eligible for social welfare schemes, e.g. in India we have a BPL (below poverty line). As a counterpart, what is needed now is a SCL (sustainable consumption line), which determines whether as an individual (or, extrapolated, a family, community or region) is living sustainably. Then those transgressing (being above) the SCL would be eligible for actions that help or force them to scale down.

Of course, both the conceptualisation of the SCL and even more, its implementation, will be highly complex. Full information on what kinds and levels of consumption are sustainable is sketchy, and global averages could be misleading. Any individual or group will have a unique mix of products and services being consumed that will make composite calculations difficult. Assessments will need to include not only how much of what is consumed, but how it was obtained, transported, processed, and so on.

This complexity should however not keep us from making a start; the SCL can be made more and more sophisticated and meaningful over time. At the beginning, some relatively simple aspects can be taken. As examples:

- *Sustainable energy consumption*: Every household of average size is to be allowed only a certain kw per month of electrical power from the grid, at subsidised rate; it can buy more at the full cost incurred to supply it, but up to a limit beyond which no-one is allowed; concomitantly, the government and other agencies commit to vigorously promote energy-saving in all devices so the family quota can go a longer way, as also to support energy self-sufficiency at household and community level using decentralised renewable sources. In calculating consumption, 'embedded' energy that goes into the making of various products and services, could also progressively be integrated.

- *Sustainable water:* Every household of average size is allowed only a certain number of litres of water use in a day. To begin with, this could be the direct water use, but eventually the 'embedded' water use (i.e. needed to produce the products and services that a household is using) can also be integrated, or dovetailed with a measure for sustainable materials consumption.
- *Sustainable transport*: Every household of average size is allowed only one private motorised vehicle, and its use too is restricted within some limits, e.g. in the form of the odd-even numbers policy of the Delhi government; concomitantly there is a commitment by governments or other public agencies to urgently improve public transport, cycle lanes and footpaths, and special facilities for the elderly and disabled, in all settlements; eventually private motorised vehicles could be phased out almost completely. Additionally, every individual is entitled to a certain maximum number of trips by air and by train in a year.
- *Sustainable shelter*: Every household of average size is allowed some maximum sq ft built up area for its dwelling; anything in excess of this already owned or used by the household will be made available for housing the homeless or those with less than average built up area. Unoccupied houses will be eligible for take-over by the homeless, as is the case in some European countries.
- *Sustainable waste:* Every household of average size can generate only a certain maximum amount of waste in a month; anything in excess has to be recycled, composted, or otherwise dealt with within its premises or the premises of the community/colony it resides in; for its part the government and businesses commit to eliminate wasteful use of materials in all products (e.g. in packaging), and facilitate

household and community-level recycling, composting, and other safe disposal of waste.

And so on, for the consumption of materials, food, and other products, and for the use of spaces and services (land, roads, other infrastructure). There would need also to be some exceptions built in, for instance in the case of travel for essential services like medical professionals, government officials on necessary duty, etc.

Setting and Implementing the Limits

How would the actual amounts in each of the above be calculated? One option is to calculate what would be a sustainable ecological footprint per person, building in the impacts of the use of various resources and services, and then working out the per capita that could be allowed if the total footprint was not to cross the relevant country's or region's ecological and social capacity. This is of course simpler said than actually worked out, but it is possible to get a rough idea, and keep refining it over the years. There is an average worked out by the Global Footprint Network, of 1.8 gha, as the per person upper limit of what the earth can provide. This does not include freshwater use, and planetary space needed for other species, so the figure is likely to be smaller. Also this would need to be further nuanced for specific ecological and cultural conditions. But it is a reasonable starting point to build on.

But if setting limits is complex, even harder will be their actual implementation. We need social, cultural and legal measures that (i) guide and facilitate the transformation towards sustainable consumption patterns, (ii) impose strong disincentives and penalties for those seriously breaching the ASCL, (iii) provide incentives for those who proactively and voluntarily comply, (iv) empower communities from whom resources are being snatched away to feed the consumerism of the rich, and (v), underlying all the above, create conditions in which psychological satisfaction and happiness is met through affective relations with nature and each other rather than through 'retail therapy'.

The last point may well be the most important. The recent refusal by 12 *gram sabhas* in Odisha to allow Vedanta corporation to mine bauxite from their hills and forest lands, and similar actions by other communities in many parts of the world, have shown the potential of local, direct democracy. Villages impacted by waste dumping from nearby cities (e.g. Devachi Urali near Pune) are also increasingly protesting such stinking imposition by their more powerful neighbours. The more such resistance takes place, and the more the victims are empowered by policies such as the requirement of free prior informed consent and the conditions of self-reliance and self-governance (*swaraj*), the more difficult it will be for the rich to extract or dump what they want wherever they want.[1] On a broader level, the extraction of labour surplus in a capitalist economy, one of the foundations of the enormous profits that some are able to make, requires resistance from the labouring classes (including women) and more democratic modes and ownership of production (on which a bit more, later in this essay).

A potentially strong measure to achieve consumption limits would be to provide upper limits to incomes and wealth. Some civil society organisations do this voluntarily. They impose both an upper limit of salary or honorarium because it is considered profligate for someone to earn more, and a minimum ratio between and maximum and minimum pay to reduce the levels of inequity. Governments too set limits, though these are based more on what is affordable rather than on considerations like personal profligacy and equity. The private sector and the world of virtual incomes have hardly any such limits, as is clear from the obscenely high incomes or returns that CEOs and investors around the world take home. A path-breaking national referendum on limiting pay in Switzerland in 2014 (with top executives not getting more than 12 times the lowest paid employee) was defeated by the private sector saying it would reduce the country's competitiveness and cut tax revenues; nevertheless the fact that a referendum was held and received considerable support (about 35% of the vote) is a hopeful sign (Hooper 2013).

Inevitably this is also linked to questioning the very fundamentals of today's model of 'development' and growth, and the political

1. For some discussion related to this, see Kothari 2014.

economy of both capitalism and state socialism as also the much older inequities of patriarchy. These are all based on ignoring the ecological limits that the earth places on us, not to mention the serious inequalities of power and wealth such models inevitably result in. And arguments that technology will provide ways out of the limits the environment places on us, have repeatedly been shown to be false. It is therefore crucial to envision fundamentally transformative pathways of well-being, on which there is considerable work already in various parts of India. But this is not the place to go further into this complex subject, it is only necessary to flag it here to put the ASCL into a macro-context.[2]

Of utmost importance is reigning in the advertising industry, and other ways that companies push their products, including the use of mass media, movies, celebrities, fashion shows, professionals, and so on. Civil society naming and shaming of companies that use unethical means of various kinds to create consumerist demand, such as for instance done by forums like Adbusters, is one method. But government regulation will also be necessary, at least till social pressure and monitoring are adequate. Prohibitive taxation on luxury and wasteful items, till such products exist, would also be required, taking care that these are not misused by the rich to avoid becoming responsible consumers. Then, as a part of the restructuring and reinvention of education and learning (towards creating responsible and self-thinking adults rather than willing cogs in the system), curricula and materials have to be made sensitive to these issues.

Should some form of 'consumption trading' be allowed, in which individuals and families can use the quota of those who voluntarily agree to use less that what they are entitled to, like carbon trading? I would not recommend this, considering the widespread and systematic abuse of the carbon trading mechanisms (or related ones like clean development mechanism). Market-based measures have a way of being hijacked and distorted by the powerful, and in any case are a bit like asking the crime mafia to regulate itself!

2. For some views on fundamental alternatives to development, see Kothari 2014, and Kothari et al 2015.

Unfair and Unfeasible?

Most readers will think that these ideas are downright unfair, and impossible to implement. There will be the inevitable outcry regarding the supposed infringement of private or personal freedoms, and the restrictions on what are claimed to be 'deserved' renumeration and compensation. But keep in mind that such freedoms cannot be a license for trashing the earth, or taking up more than one's fair share of the earth's resources thereby depriving someone (or something) else. In so far as overconsumption leaves other people impoverished, or results in ecological catastrophes that leave others homeless or dead, or snatches away the space of other species to survive, it is akin to theft or murder. Consider the movement against smoking in public, so successful in so many countries; if over-consumption of any product is socially harmful, why should it be tolerated in the name of personal freedom?

For forest-dwellers in India, it would seem equally unfair that they can take out firewood only as much as they can lift on the head, when they could be cutting much more to sell. Those of us who make environmental policy (forest-dwellers rarely do!) think it is justified to put this limit, because the forest needs to be protected from over-harvesting. But then why not the same for our consumption, which has an equally if not worse impact, albeit often in far-away ecosystems invisible to us?

As for being impossible to implement, that's a function of governance, and of convincing people that this is for their (our) own good—or at least the good of our children. Ultimately, more than laws and regulations, it will be awareness and concern about our collective future, social compacts and customs, and peer pressure, that will make the ASCL system work. A culture of 'enoughness' (*aparigraha*) rather than 'more and more', creating conditions for people to achieve happiness and satisfaction through affective relations (with the rest of nature and other humans), the celebration of voluntary simplicity (not to be equated with poverty) rather than profligacy, a respect for other humans and the rest of nature such that we continuously, almost subconsciously assess the impacts of our actions on them, creating awareness that it is not the earth's resources and material goods that are in unlimited abundance (the supermarket syndrome) but rather the human potential in intellectual, cultural, and social development which do not require us to trash the earth ... these and other aspects need to be the basis of a powerful culture and psyche underlying our lives and lifestyles.[3] Then, we will be looking at our neighbour with envy if they are BSCL (yes, you guessed it, Below Sustainable Consumption Line) while we are still that little bit profligate.

Will the Middle Classes Adopt a SCL?

To any observer, it is obvious that a SCL like measure will not go down well with the rich in India, and perhaps especially the middle classes as they aspire to move even further up the economic and social ladder. But the middle classes are internally diverse, and there are many sources of hope, and avenues of influence, that could be used for making the SCL more palatable and implementable.

Firstly, there appears to be a growing ecological awareness and concomitant concern in the middle classes. An explosion in information and news regarding the environment, the inclusion of environmental issues in school and college curricula, and other factors have contributed to this. A substantial section of the civil society active on environmental issues is from the middle classes. By no means are all environmental CSOs (civil society organisation) sensitive to the complex issues of social injustice and inequalities; many are abysmally ignorant of the condition of marginalised people like Dalits, many even advocate policies that cause further marginalisation such as exclusionary wildlife conservation. By the same token, many such CSOs do not strive for fundamental structural changes in society (or even having an understanding of these as driving forces of ecological destruction), with many restricting themselves to reformist and often superficial solutions. But there are indeed sections of environmental CSOs that do confront the

3. I am aware these are complex issues and need more detailed treatment, but am leaving that for another occasion; for the moment I would point to the following sources for thoughtful commentaries: Cox 2013, Sterling 2016 (and accompanying comments), Alexander and McLeod 2014.

system or ally with peoples' movements who do, and that argue for an environmentalism inclusive of the rights of the marginalised. One can, of course, question whether the radical elements within civil society can still be called a part of the middle classes, but that depends on one's conception of what constitutes a class, and I won't get into that complex issue here.

An issue raised in some circles is whether a Green Party can be successful in India, as it has (partially) been in some countries of Europe. Lahiri (2015) argues that some parties may become green as middle class attitudes towards the environment get stronger, but that they will be more reformist than radical, which I agree with. I am not sure, however, how this squares with his view that middle classes have a "strong commitment to ... social justice, grass roots democracy, non-violence, and respect for diversity"; if indeed they did (especially to justice and grass roots democracy), they would be much more open to radical ecological ideas, for in a country like India where the majority of people have day-to-day and survival dependence on the natural environment, there is no way to separate political, economic, social, and ecological issues. I doubt that the majority of the middle classes are today, or will be in the near future, ready for a system in which community consent is needed for all development projects (which would surely be an essential tenet of 'grass roots democracy').

Nevertheless, I believe there is a fringe but strong (and widening) part of the middle classes that are willing to be radical. An example of this reality or potential is the continuing support that Greenpeace India is receiving, despite a head-on attack by the government that has dubbed it 'anti-national' and 'anti-development' and tried shutting it down in recent times. Rather than get scared by such tactics, over 60,000 people have continued to provide the organisation their financial support, and many more their support in campaigns. It is also indicated by the outbreak of support (notably from many middle class youth) for students and others persecuted by the state when they have tried to raise critical political voices (e.g. the ongoing issue, even as I write this in early 2016, of the JNU students charged with sedition). Not all these people will come out on the streets for open protests, nor would all be aware of or empathetic to environment-rights-justice links and the plight of marginalised populations. But arguably, many of them are or would be open to supporting such radical agendas.

At both individual and collective level, parts of the middle classes are also challenging and asking for changes in consumerist patterns. This includes simple personal actions such as seeking out organic food (outlets for which have sprung up in many cities), or switching to ecologically sensitive household products (increasingly being produced by many collectives), or doing rooftop gardening (Bangalore has 10,000 households doing this), or composting one's wet waste. It also includes more collective actions such as neighbourhood water recycling and renewable energy production (Rainbow Drive in Bangalore is a good example), helping communities to make producer companies or consumer-producer-investor links to promote sustainable agriculture and other livelihoods (e.g. the individuals who catalysed Just Change in the Nilgiris, and Timbaktu Collective in Andhra Pradesh), and helping marginalised sections to mobilise for more equitable distribution of resources and greater local community controls (such as civil society organisations facilitating community claims under the Forest Rights Act). It could also be doing research on how to cut down consumption demand through technological or policy innovations, such as less energy-guzzling appliances and more ecofriendly architecture, and advocating relevant policies and programmes; a recent Indo-German collaborative report identifies several such topics for further work (Lehman and Chella Rajan 2015). And it needs to transform the consumer movement (if it can be called such) in India from one focusing on prices and quality to one that also demands fairness, ecological principles, and justice to be embedded in products and services that are accessed by consumers.

There is of course a danger that some of these actions become a substitute for the fundamental structural changes required to make society more ecologically sustainable and socially just, or at times even make it worse by allowing the rich to live healthier lifestyles while the poor are condemned to degrading ones (the poor in cities are forced to eat junk food which ironically is cheaper than organic food!). It is important that they be located within movements of fundamental transformation towards radical democracy, economic localisation and community/public control over means of production, cultural diversity, knowledge commons and other actions leading to a future of eco-swaraj or radical ecological democracy (Shrivastava and Kothari 2012, Kothari 2014). One of the earliest reports to focus on consumption in the Asian region also stressed the need for "a more holistic approach towards sustainable consumption ... (which) rejects the notion that eco-innovation or greening the consumer should be the main focus of sustainable consumption in Asia, and essentially proposes that the primary goal of sustainable consumption should be to assure quality of life for all. It suggests that sustainable consumption planning should target to enable well-being and ensure happiness for all people ... (and) argues that sustainable consumption needs to be discussed in the interest of half of the world's population that are in poverty, while addressing the over consumption issues of the developed countries" (de Zoysa 2007, bracketed text added).

But can the middle classes be part of a transformation that would mean the erasure of the middle classes themselves (if a classless society is part of the end-goal), or at the least a considerable reduction in inequities which could include restrictions on the wealth of the rich? This is a question I am unable to answer, except to say that I do believe sections of the middle classes could and indeed have to be part of this transformation.

A crucial component of the above is greater awareness of the impacts of the lifestyles of the rich, and greater dialogue and engagement of the middle classes with marginalised sections of society. Several organisations are attempting such processes, including amongst the youth of cities and villages. One of the platforms of dialogue that promotes sharing and collaboration around alternatives in a range of fields is Vikalp Sangam, initiated by several civil society organisations.[4] Such processes hope to not only point to the problems and crises we face, but also to alternatives, both practical for individuals and collectives, as also conceptual and

4. *http://www.kalpavriksh.org/index.php/alternatives/alternatives-knowledge-center/353-vikalp-sangam-coverage*

visionary leading to structural transformations in economic, political and social spheres.

References

Alexander, S. and A. McLeod (2014). *Simple Living in History: Pioneers of the Deep Future.* Melbourne: Simplicity Institute Publishing.

Ananthapadmanabhan, G., K. Srinivas and V. Gopal (2007). *Hiding Behind the Poor: A Report by Greenpeace on Climate Injustice.* Bangalore: Greenpeace India.

Cox, S. (2013). *Any Way You Slice It: The Past, Present and Future of Rationing.* New York: The New Press.

de Zoysa, U. (2007). *Sustainable Consumption: An Asian Review.* Colombo: Centre for Environment and Development.

Hooper, J. (2013). "Switzerland Votes against Cap on Executive Pay", *The Guardian*, 24 November. *http://www.theguardian.com/world/2013/nov/24/switzerland-votes-against-cap-executive-pay*

Kothari, A. (2014). "Radical Ecological Democracy: A Path Forward for India and Beyond", *Development* 57(1): 36-45. *http://www.palgrave-journals.com/development/journal/v57/n1/full/dev201443a.html*

Kothari, A., F. Demaria and A. Acosta (2015). "Buen Vivir, Degrowth and Ecological Swaraj: Alternatives to Sustainable Development and the Green Economy", *Development* 57(3-4): 362-75. *http://www.palgrave-journals.com/development/journal/v57/n3-4/full/dev201524a.html*

Lahiri, A.K. (2015). "Green Politics and the Indian Middle Class", *Economic and Political Weekly* 1(43): 35-42, 24 October.

Lehman, H. and S. Chella Rajan (2015). *Sustainable Lifestyles: Pathways and Choices for India and Germany*. Berlin: Indo-German Expert Group on Green and Inclusive Economy, GIZ.

Shrivastava, A. and A. Kothari (2012). *Churning the Earth: The Making of Global India.* Delhi: Viking/Penguin India.

Sterling, P. (2016). *Why we Consume: Neural Design and Sustainability.* Great Transition Initiative. *http://www.greattransition.org/publication/why-we-consume*

Others:

Global Footprint Network. *http://www.footprintnetwork.org/*

Vikalp Sangam. Alternatives India. *http://www.vikalpsangam.org/*

12

ASHOK K. LAHIRI

Green Politics and the Indian Middle Class[1]

In India, Mahatma Gandhi, the father of the nation, was a practitioner of 'green politics' far ahead of his times in the first half of the last century. He embraced all the six principles of green politics, namely social justice, ecological wisdom, grass roots democracy, nonviolence, ecological wisdom and sustainability, adopted in 2001 at the first Global Greens Conference at Canberra, Australia.

Despite Gandhi's green politics, no established political party in India can claim to be a 'green party' in the accepted sense of the term. Perhaps, a vibrant middle class of reasonable size, necessary to support such a green party did not exist so far. It has emerged or is emerging in India only in the last couple of decades.

On the background of the emergence of BRICS—the association of five major emerging economies, namely Brazil, Russia, India, China and South Africa—in the last decade, it is instructive to also compare the perspective of green politics of the middle class in Brazil and India. Brazil has had Partido Verde (PV) or the Green Party since 1986. Though not a major political force in Brazil, PV has a presence in both the Chamber of Deputies and the Senate at the national level. Furthermore, in the 2010 presidential election, its candidate Marina Silva got 19.3 per cent of the votes in the first round and forced a second round of run-off election. Future president Dilma Rouseff won an absolute majority only in the second round. India has no equivalent of the Brazilian PV in its political firmament.

---

1. Much of this paper is based on an earlier publication "Green Politics and the Indian Middle Class', *Economic and Political Weekly* L(43): 35-42, 24 October 2015.

In this context, three questions of interest are: Why has a green party not occupied more political space in India for so long?[2] How green is the politics of the Indian middle class? And, what are the differences in green politics of the middle class in Brazil and India?

This paper is an attempt at answering these questions. It is not about the right approach to the environment and associated lifestyle, including such important issues as consumerism, large-scale industrialisation and urbanisation. It is a simple attempt at examining whether, with the emerging Indian middle class, a conventional political party contesting elections is likely to champion environmental issues in the same way as green parties do in the developed north.

The plan of the paper is as follows. First, there is a categorisation of people in terms of their approach to the environment. Second, there is a short description of the essence of green parties. Third, a brief discussion about the rapid growth of the Indian middle class in the post-liberalisation period follows. Thereafter, the three questions are taken up in sequence.

Environment and Categories of People: Missing Middle

Mahatma Gandhi had a significant impact on the new social movements in Europe and America, whose participants were middle class people concerned about nature (Björk and Ulvila 2008). In India also, the environmental groups, for example, Chipko (embrace) movement and Narmada Bachao Andolan (NBA), have adopted Gandhi's methods of protests such as demonstrations and hunger-strike. But the protesters have been generally the people at the margin–peasants, tribal communities, fishermen and other underprivileged people–'empty-belly' environmentalists in Ramachandra Guha's spectacular words, very different from the 'full-stomach' environmentalists in the North (Guha and Martinez-Alier 1997).

2. See for example, Narain (2009).

After the pursuit of five decades of development policies, from the ecological point of view, Gadgil and Guha (1995) categorised people in India into three categories, differentiated according to their relationship to, and use of, natural resources: the 'omnivores', the 'ecological refugees', and the 'ecosystem people'. Omnivores, typically the landowners, industrialists, and urban elite, devour resources and are the real beneficiaries of development that inefficiently uses and exhausts resources. Ecological refugees are the peasants and tribal people who lose their livelihood as a result of projects, for example, a hydroelectric or multipurpose dam that submerge their land. The ecosystem people are the majority of rural people who depend for their livelihood on nature, for example, on fuel wood or dung for cooking, and bamboo for building homes.

The classification of people into 'full stomach' and 'empty-belly' environmentalists or, alternatively, as omnivores, ecological refugees and ecosystem people perhaps does not deal adequately with the emerging middle class in India in the context of green politics. The Indian middle class is neither rich nor poor, nor ecological refugees, nor ecosystem people. With their education and access to the media, they have some awareness of the ecological issues. At the receiving end of many environmental problems, day to day, they suffer problems of unsafe and inadequate water supply, poor air quality and sewerage. Furthermore, ecological wisdom and sustainability are albeit two critical, but only two of the six pillars of green politics. The Indian middle class has a strong commitment to the other four pillars, namely social justice, grass roots democracy, nonviolence, and respect for diversity.

Essence of Green Parties

Before taking up the two questions under discussion, it is useful to recall that the term 'green' of green parties comes from a heightened concern for the environment and its sustainability. 'Greenpeace—the well-known organisation that carries out nonviolent campaigns and creative confrontations to expose global environmental problems—has 'green' in its name. Established in 1971 to protest against United States (US) underground nuclear testing at Amchitka, the ship MV

Phyllis Cormack chartered for the voyage to the tiny island off the West Coast of Alaska. The ship was renamed Greenpeace for the protest.[3]

The term 'green' also became popular worldwide with the 'green bans' movement in Australia in the early 1970s. Workers under the New South Wales Builders Labourers' Federation (NSWBLF), on a large scale, refused to work on ecologically unsound projects. It came to be known as the 'green bans' movement after the term was used by the Australian trade union leader and environmentalist, Jack Mundey in May 1973. Soon the term 'greenies' designated not only supporters of the NSWBLF 'green bans' but also environmentally concerned people in general (Burgmann 2008: 69).

Single issue parties find it difficult to mobilise popular support. Thus, given the reach of politics beyond just the environment, green parties slowly came to embrace a few more fundamental agendas. Environmentalists and peace activists in erstwhile West Germany came together to form the political party 'The Greens' on 13 January 1980 and adopt the 'Four Pillars of Green Politics'—social justice, ecological wisdom, grass roots democracy, and nonviolence. Soon, these became the four accepted pillars of green politics. The four pillars got expanded to six principles in 2001 at the first Global Greens Conference at Canberra. The additional two principles were sustainability and respect for diversity.

The emergence of the six principles is partly explained by the roots of the green parties. These parties were established in countries across Western Europe in the 1980s and arose from four different social movements—the environmental movement, the labour movement, the civil rights movement, and the peace movement. The philosophy of the four movements got enshrined in the six principles. There is widespread popular support in India across classes for four of the six pillars of green politics, namely social justice, grass roots democracy, nonviolence and respect for diversity,

3. Bill Darnell, the Canadian environmentalist, is reported to have coined the name in February 1970, when someone flashed him a peace sign and Darnell said "let's make that a green peace!"

and these are endorsed by almost all political parties in India.[4] Thus, in what follows, the discussion on green politics in India focuses on the residual two environmental pillars, namely ecological wisdom and sustainability.

Emergence of the Indian Middle Class

Green parties are a characteristic of Western Europe, Australia, New Zealand, and of some Latin American and East Asian countries. All of them have a sizable middle class. A post-materialist philosophy is congenial for the growth of a green party. The appeal of such a philosophy gained in popularity with humanity's demand on nature exceeding, for over 4 decades, what nature can replenish. The danger from the regenerative capacity of 1.5 Earths required to supply the ecological goods and services that mankind needs every year has more resonance in the middle class placed comfortably far beyond the poverty line. Poverty is not conducive for such a world view. That brings us to the important development: the recent emergence of the Indian middle class.

The median, a technical term in statistics, refers to the entity that separates the lower half of a sample or population from the upper half. The celebrated 'median voter rule' states that, in a majoritarian democracy, political parties and leaders will select the policy or outcome most preferred by the median voter. Thus, the middle class, separating the poor from the rich, often play a critical role in many countries in determining not only who wins the election but also the nature of policies promised by political parties in manifestoes and even the nature of political parties. What is important to note, however, is that the median voter will not be from the middle class unless the class is reasonably large. With say more than a half the population in poverty, it will be a poor at the median separating the even poorer from the richer in two equal halves. This brings us to the problem of defining the middle class itself.[5]

---

4. The clause 'almost all' refers to some parties in the fringe with low commitment (at least in practice) to non-violence and respect for diversity.
5. Much of the discussion that follows about the definition of the Indian middle class is from Lahiri (2014).

The limited definition of the middle class in terms of income or consumption has come to be questioned because of the wider expectation that the middle class will play the role of protagonists of social change and be more caring about sustainable development, which may not have happened in all countries, for example, Brazil.[6] Furthermore, Marilene de Paula (2015b) argues that Brazil's NMC (new middle class) is barely educated, earns low salaries, has little or no savings and is surviving on a day-day basis; also, 'they are more gender and racially diverse as a group' and are very different from the traditional middle class. The traditional middle class is 'largely educated, are financially stable and have savings and investments.' She suggests that the NMC should be defined as the new working class.

How about self-categorisation? Surely, people themselves will know whether they belong to the middle-class or not. But as Harris (2007) reported, curiously, in response to a survey question in the poorest parts of Bengaluru, the great majority of the respondents categorised themselves to be 'middle class'. Thus, self-categorisation is not very useful for defining the Indian middle class. However, there are some, e.g. Kapur et al. (2015), who suggests self-categorisation rather than ascription as the classification criterion. According to a survey across 24 states in India, they found that people self-categorising themselves as middle class had the common trait of being optimistic about different aspects such as future of children, social status improvement across generations, and economic improvement in household.

In common parlance, the middle-class means beyond the poverty line, but not rich. But defining the poverty line itself and who is rich is a contentious matter. The Asian Development Bank (ADB 2010), in 2010, defined the middle class as \$2-\$20 per person per day in 2005 PPP\$. But, this definition is not universal. The Economist (2009) defines it as people with roughly a third of their income left

6. For example, Grzybowski (2015) argues that classes emerge through a political process, whereby they forge a collective identity, values and views of society. This process, which takes place in social struggle, may lead to political autonomy or subordination to another class or class fraction.

for discretionary spending after paying for basic food and shelter. In 2011, in India, this would have left out the poorest with income below ₹27.2 per person per day and ₹33.3 per person per day in rural and urban areas, respectively from the middle class. So it would 'the aspirers' just above the poverty line, who typically were small shopkeepers, farmers with their own modest landholdings or semi-skilled industrial and service workers. They had enough food to eat and might have owned items such as a small television, a propane stove and an electric rod for heating water, but may not have had a third of their income for discretionary purposes to be counted as middle class. Of course, the middle class has been defined in many more ways than these two.

The size of the middle class changes with its definition. For example, Meyer and Birdsall (2012), using 2005 PPP minimum and maximum thresholds of $10 and $50, and National Sample Survey 2009-10 data, estimate the Indian middle class in 2009-10 at less than 6 per cent of the population or just under 70 million people, which is less than half of what National Council of Applied Economic Research estimates for 2004-05. There appears to be consensus that no matter how it is defined, the middle class in India is growing with the pace of change also dependent on the definition. However, it is also true that no matter how it is defined, the median voter in India is not from the middle class as yet.

Why No Green Party for So Long?

The Gandhian Tradition

Mahatma Gandhi, right from 1909, when he wrote his book '*Hind Swaraj*', had a vision of idyllic, simple and unchanging rural life. In *Hind Swaraj*, he wrote against over-consumption:

> We notice that the mind is a restless bird; the more it gets the more it wants, and still remains unsatisfied. The more we indulge our passions the more unbridled they become. Our ancestors, therefore, set a limit to our indulgences. They saw that happiness was largely a mental condition. A man is not necessarily happy because he is rich, or unhappy because he is poor...Observing all this, our ancestors dissuaded us from luxuries and pleasures.

Gandhi had written against mechanisation and urbanisation in this book in 1909 (68-69):

> It was not that we did not know how to invent machinery, but our forefathers knew that, if we set our hearts after such things, we would become slaves and lose our moral fiber. They therefore, after due deliberation, decided that we should only do what we could with our hands and feet... They further reasoned that large cities were a snare and a useless encumbrance and that people would not be happy in them, that there would be gangs of thieves and robbers, prostitution and vice flourishing in them and that poor men would be robbed by rich men. They were, therefore, satisfied with small villages.

Between 1909 and independence in 1947, he did modify his views somewhat.[7] But the strain of the nostalgic vision of idyllic, simple and unchanging rural life continued. Gandhi believed in decentralised and *panchayat*-or village-based democracy. And, of course, he believed in *ahimsa* and nonviolent struggle.

Many of the green movements or 'new popular movements' in Europe, for example, 'The Operation Gandhi 1952' in London and the peace movement in the 1960s in which philosopher Bertrand Russell participated, were inspired by Gandhi (Björk and Ulvila 2008). Yet in India, although there were movements such as Sunderlal Bahuguna's 'Chipko' movement in Garhwal and 'NBA' led by Medha Patkar and Baba Amte, there are no 'green parties' in the conventional political arena. Four principles of green politics, namely social justice, grass roots democracy, non-violence and respect for diversity have become integral part of the avowed goals of every major Indian political party. But, commitment to the two others of the six principles, namely,

7. As the Mahatma himself said in the *Harijan* on 29 April 1933: 'In my search after Truth I have discarded many ideas and learnt many new things. Old as I am in age, I have no feeling that I have ceased to grow inwardly or that my growth will stop at the dissolution of the flesh. What I am concerned, with is my readiness to obey the call of Truth, my God, from moment to moment, and, therefore, when anybody finds any inconsistency between any two writings of mine, if he has still faith in my sanity, lie would do well to choose the later of the two on the same subject.' Furthermore, he recognised that even his *charkha* (spinning wheel) was a machine, and clarified that he was against machines substituting humans in production activity and in favour of labour-intensive technologies.

ecological wisdom, and sustainability, appears weak.[8] While Gandhi in loin-cloth with his simple lifestyle may be worshipped as the Father of the Nation, Babasaheb Ambedkar in a suit also continues to be the role model of many middle-class people.

Ecological Thinking in India

The lack of a green party in India is in spite of a wide variety of ecological wisdom in the country. Indeed, given the vibrant intellectual atmosphere in India, there are quite a few studies about the environmental issues in India. First, is the measurement of 'ecological footprint', which is an integrated measure of the habitat or space (for example, crop land, pasture, aquatic area, forests) required continuously for biophysical services to support people's lifestyle. The measure converts goods and services demanded into area required to supply the renewable resources (e.g. food, fuel or fibre) and to absorb the waste (e.g. energy lands or forests required for carbon absorption).

The Confederation of Indian Industry (CII) and Global Footprint Network did a collaborative study in 2008 entitled 'India's Ecological Footprint: A Business Perspective'. It found that India has the third largest ecological footprint after US and China, and the footprint was increasing with economic growth. However, much of this was also because of India's large population. The report noted that 'India represents approximately 6 per cent of the world's Ecological Footprint, 4 per cent of the world's biocapacity, and 17 per cent of the world's population. Focusing on individual consumption, India's Ecological Footprint in 2003 was 0.8 gha (global hectares) per person, significantly lower than the world average of 2.2 gha, and ranking India 125th among 152 countries. At the same time, because of population growth, India's total national footprint has doubled

---

8. Even on nonviolence, particularly nuclear non-proliferation, the political commitment is ambiguous at best. In April 1954, Indian Prime Minister Pundit Nehru was in the lead of non-aligned countries to criticise US hydrogen bomb tests in the Pacific (see *http://www.san.beck.org/GPJ29-AntiNuclearProtests.html*). Over time, India's position on nuclear armament has changed and India itself has become a nuclear power. The geopolitics of the region may explain the lack of enthusiasm for unilateral disarmament or anything beyond a pledge of no first use of nuclear weapons.

since 1961, contributing to the degradation of its natural capital.' The Living Planet Report 2014 also found that in 2010, India continued to be the 3rd largest in terms of total ecological footprint, and in per capita terms, it ranked 136th among 152 countries.

Second, there are studies recommending solutions for reducing the ecological problems in India. Some are in the Gandhian tradition. For example, Bhaduri and Patkar (2009) argue against corporate-led large-scale industrialisation and urbanisation because it requires land acquisition and displacement of farmers, and such industrialisation cannot absorb the surplus labour from agriculture fast enough. Benefits come unacceptably slowly to the poor. Instead, they recommend setting up small-scale village-based industry on waste and vacant land. They also note:

> The composition of output, produced in this manner at the local level would require less energy; no big dam would be needed to provide electricity nor would expensive and dangerous nuclear power be required; production in general would become much less intensive in its use of natural resources like land, water, forest and mineral products.

Kothari (2009) argues from 'a more fundamentally ethical perspective that respects all life forms' against consumerism and the pursuit of growth in general and even the use of waste and non-cultivated land for industry in particular. He reminds the reader how with human encroachment on nature, '10 to 30 per cent of mammal, amphibian and bird species were threatened with extinction'.

Third are studies on the appropriate approach to wildlife conservation. Saberwal et al. (2001), for example, argue against exclusionary wildlife conservation and separation of humans from nature. They recommend giving a greater stake to local communities in conservation, including joint management, limited harvesting of forest products and better incentives through a share of tourism revenue.

Modernisation and Industrialisation

Notwithstanding these studies and advocacy, the support-base for pro-environment conventional politics has been limited right from the time of independence. Mahatma Gandhi's vision of idyllic, simple and unchanging rural life was overtaken by the model of socialist planning and modernisation. As I.G. Patel (2002: 2) observes about his growing years just before independence,

> Our heads then were full of dreams of a strong India—India strong industrially, if not militarily (we did not see the connection then), able to stand with its head high among the nations of the world, India reversing the humiliation of the past two hundred years by making up for lost time.

After independence, there was a headlong modernisation drive through large-scale industry such as steel plants, cities and dams. After Lahore, the capital of undivided Punjab went to Pakistan, the first planned city of independent India, Chandigarh, was built to house the capital of Indian Punjab. Steel cities of Durgapur, Rourkela, and Bokaro, Ranchi around HEC (heavy engineering corporation), and capital cities of Bhubaneswar and Gandhinagar followed.

For irrigation and water supply, flood control, and hydroelectric power generation, India started to build dams at a rapid pace, and by 2000, it ranked 3rd among all countries of the world (of course, not adjusted by area or population), after China and the USA (World Commission on Dams 2000: 9). Environmentalists now allege that all third-world leaders such as Nasser, Nkrumah, and Nehru, striving to give material solidity to a newly acquired state of independence, were seduced by the symbolism of epic dams. But, these leaders had a different view when these dams were being built. After inaugurating the Bhakra Canal System the previous day, Prime Minister Nehru delivered a speech on 8 July 1954 entitled 'Temples of the New Age.'[9]

India after independence sought science and technology to ameliorate the burden of poverty rapidly. In Guha and Martinez Alier's (1997: xiv) words "... fertilizer, pesticides, and fungicides

---

9. Immerwahr (2015) states that, "It does not appear that Nehru actually uttered the phrase 'dams are the temples of modern India' which is often attributed to him. But he did give a speech in 1954 on dams that has been given the title (perhaps by Nehru perhaps not) 'Temples of the New Age', in which he described the dam as 'the biggest temple and mosque and gurdwara' of the day." See also *http://www.nehruinternationalconference2014.com/nehru_speech4.aspx*

and not organic farming' were seen as the solution to the food problem. The environmental issues connected with industrialisation, urbanisation and hydroelectric or multipurpose dams had not come to the forefront in the first two and a half decades after independence. Indeed, there were problems of resettlement and rehabilitation connected with projects such as Bhakra-Nangal, but these were seen as issues waiting for appropriate administrative solutions.[10] Over time, since the 1970s, environmental issues attracted greater attention. Of these, Chipko movement in the Himalayan state of today's Uttarakhand already alluded to and the Silent Valley Movement in Kerala down south are the most notable.

Environmental Protest

A major environmental movement in post-independence India was 'Chipko' action launched in Mandal village in Garhwal against the allotment of a forest plot to a sports good company in 1973. Similarly, a dam for a hydroelectric project proposed at Sairandhri on the Kunthipuzha River in the Silent Valley in Kerala stirred a major controversy from 1973 because of concern about the endangered lion-tailed macaque. With participation by poet activist Sugathakumari and Kerala Sasthra Sahithya Parishad (KSSP), ornithologist Salim Ali, and many others, the movement mobilised a large support base. Though the legal challenges to the project were overcome, the debate, also known as 'man versus monkey' debate, ended at least temporarily when the Government of Kerala stopped work on the project in 1980 at the request of Prime Minister Indira Gandhi. In December 1980, Government of Kerala declared the Silent Valley, excluding the hydroelectric project area, as a National Park. The two movements culminated in the promulgation of the Forest Conservation Act, 1980 by Parliament mandating, among other things, that 'No part of a reserved forest land can be used for non-forest purpose by the state government without prior approval from the central government.' It came into force from 25 October 1980.

---

10. As early as 8 November 1953, the Bhakra Dam Sufferers Association presented a memorandum addressed to Prime Minister Nehru outlining their demands. See Modi (2009: 137).

In spite of these movements, significant green parties in India continued to be conspicuous by their absence. The Indian National Green Party (INGP) was registered with the Election Commission of India on 7 January 1999.[11] INGP forfeited its deposits in all the 4 assembly constituencies of Bikram, Gaighat, Motihari and Pipra in Bihar where it contested in 2010. The IPGP, established in Jaipur in 2011, contested in 27 assembly constituencies in the 2013 Rajasthan Vidhan Sabha polls and lost its deposit in all 27. In the 2014 Lok Sabha election, IPGP, the only party with 'green' in its name, contested in 3 constituencies in Rajasthan and forfeited its deposit in all 3.[12] Green Party of India,. a non-profit organisation on a predominantly environmental platform, was founded by a self-proclaimed group of young nature lovers in India on January 2010. It was led by environmental activist Subhas Dutta, famous for his public interest litigations in West Bengal for permanently removing Kolkata's most toxic vehicles, those more than 15 years old, from the roads, and for relocating Kolkata's annual book fair from the '*maidan*', the largest of Kolkata's few green spaces. Though the founding of the Green Party received quite a bit of media coverage, particularly internationally, nothing much has been heard about it since.[13]

There was a 'green party' ring about the spectacular rapid rise of the Aam Admi Party (AAP) since 26 November 2012. In February 2015, the AAP won a landslide victory in the Vidhan Sabha election in Delhi, the nation's capital, bagging 67 of the 70 seats. AAP is an offshoot of the IAC (India against corruption) mass-agitation led by Anna Hazare, described by some as 'Second Gandhi'.[14] Its supporters

11. Led by Prof Priya Ranjan Trivedi, described as 'the only person of his type having excelled in the new and emerging area of neology and neocracy for his passion for evolving new doctrines for solving different problems of the world in general and of India in particular,' it did not gain any traction in the polls.

12. In April 2014, Election Commission sought withdrawal of tax exemption benefit from IPGP from Central Board of Direct Taxes because of the party's failure to file their mandatory expenditure contribution reports on time to the poll body. See Press Trust of India (2014).

13. See, for example, Bhaumik (2009) and Ahmed (2009).

14. Anna, however, has modestly stated: "I am not Gandhi, I don't consider myself anywhere close to him in stature. ... I would like to appeal to the people not to compare me with him—that is not right. It doesn't do justice to his greatness." See Byatnal (2011).

were mainly from the middle class.[15] The birth of AAP from a popular protest movement, its decision on removing government encroachment from Yamuna, opposition to the nuclear power plant in Kundalkunam and support to Narmada Bachao Andolan (NBA) had unleashed expectations about AAP transforming itself into India's new green party (Shrivastava 2014). However, even the AAP has never laid a claim to be a 'green party.'

Green Politics Internationally

One of the critical characteristics of a green party is its spontaneous emergence from popular agitations. The agitations in Europe were often against nuclear power generation and deployment of nuclear weapons. After the oil price shock of 1973, there was a move in favour of nuclear power in West Germany. In the mid-1970s, large demonstrations prevented the construction of a nuclear plant at Wyhl, in south-west part of erstwhile West Germany. In 1976 and 1977, mass anti-nuclear demonstrations took place at Kalkar, the site of Germany's first fast breeder reactor, and at Brokdorf, north of Hamburg. Several local green political groups came together in March 1979 in Frankfurt to form the Alternative Political Union, the Greens (Sonstige Politische Vereinigung, Die Grünen) and get the first green representative elected to the state parliament of Bremen.[16]

Like in Germany, some of the green parties in other countries in Europe also arose from agitations about other environmental issues. Koijärvi, a small lake in the Häme province in northern Finland, was an important breeding place for many birds (Paastela 2008: 63). It used to flood the surrounding farms, and the local farmers wanted to drain the lake to prevent the flooding and extend their farm land. The farmers obtained a legal right to drain the lake. Outraged local

15. See Mishra (2012): "Led by Anna Hazare ... the movement was presented by sections of the media in both India and the West as a long overdue political awakening of the middle class, even as India's 'second freedom struggle." See also Ganguly (2011).

16. The Three Mile Island accident in the US in 1979 bolstered the anti-nuclear mood and the peace movement in Germany against the US deployment of Pershing II and cruise missiles in Western Europe mobilised support for the Greens in West Germany. The Chernobyl disaster in 1986 reinforced the anti-nuclear sentiments, and after unification, between 1998 and 2005, the Greens were minor partners in the coalition government ruling Germany.

ornithologists organised people to gather and stop the digging. The agitation by environmentalists in 1979-80 failed to stop the draining of Koijärvi, but according to some commentators, the Finnish Greens started with the agitation about the drainage project.

Similarly, the four-nation Scandinavian Link or Scanlink attracted protests from environmentalists in Sweden in the 1980s.[17] The mobilisation culminated in October 1987 when activists climbed trees that were to be cut down to make way for the construction of the road on the west coast. Arrest and conviction of activists attracted a lot of attention and contributed to a strong emergence of the Green Party in Sweden.[18] Though the Green Party in Sweden was founded much earlier in 1981, its political breakthrough came in the 1988 general election when they won seats in the Swedish Riksdag for the first time, capturing 5.5 per cent of the vote, and becoming the first new party to enter parliament in 70 years.

At about the time when the AAP was born in India, there were popular protest movements in many Arab countries. Christened the 'Arab Spring', it destabilised regimes in Tunisia, Egypt, Libya, and Yemen; and unfolded as civil uprisings in various other countries in the Middle East. The Snow Revolution in Russia, which was against the allegedly flawed 2011 legislative election, and Occupy Wall Street movement in the US against social and economic inequality, greed, corruption and corporate capture of government, also coincided with IAC in India. Many of these movements turned out to be symbolic citizenship movements without converting themselves into political parties, leave alone green parties. Being born out of a popular movement is not a sufficient condition for becoming a green party.

---

17. Scanlink, a railway, highway, bridge and tunnel network, starts in Oslo, goes down the west of Sweden, hops over the Danish islands of Zealand and Funen to the Danish mainland and then moves to the Autobahns and rail systems of West Germany near Hamburg. It involved a bridge between Malm and Copenhagen, and the building of highways along the west coast of Sweden. A particular part of the road, between Uddevalla and Stora Höga was planned to run straight through a town called Ljungskile, spurred a resistance among citizens, environmental justice organisations and youth organisations which was called the largest case of civil disobedience in Swedish history.

18. *http://ejatlas.org/conflict/highway-part-of-scan-link-ljungskile-sweden*

A sizable middle class is a necessary but not a sufficient condition for a green party. Most notably, prosperous Japan and the US, with thriving middle classes, do not have any green party comparable to what exists in Western European countries.[19] Also, the Indian middle class is not sizable enough as yet to provide the requisite political support-base for a green party. The 'median voter' in India is still not from a middle-class background.

Importantly, the Indian middle class wants the country to harness science and technology to eliminate poverty and usher in growth. Many of its members view the Western environmentalists advocating against dams, large industry and urbanisation as compromised idealists who are not willing to repudiate their technological heritage and the benefits of their 'progress' in their own countries. As Guha and Martinez Alier (1997) describe, 'Greenness is the ultimate luxury of the consumer society,' and India is not yet such a society. Environmentalism in a poor country such as India, to many, appears as 'antihuman' environmentalism. Perhaps, there is little popular support for environmentalists whom Gadgil and Guha (1995) describe as the wilderness enthusiast, crusading Gandhians or ecological Marxists.[20] To the environmentalists, they attribute pessimism about human agency, technology, and its effect on nature. The middle class is aspirational and does not share this pessimism.

How Green is the Politics of Indian Middle Class?

It is not only the size of the Indian middle class that has changed, but also its attitude towards environmental issues. In the initial years after independence, the attitude was, like in many other countries of the world, perhaps close to apathy or even denial. Over time, the middle class appears to be more engaged with environmental issues. These issues can be classified into three categories or a combination thereof—those with an impact on the local, state or national

19. See Naoto et al (2010) and Ask (2014).

20. Gadgil and Guha (1995) categorise nine strands of environmentalists, the six other categoriess are guardians of the sacred, community managers, technocratic conservationists, appropriate technologists, technocrat planners, and judicial activists.

environment, those with an impact on resource distribution, and those with a broader global impact, such as carbon emission.

Local Environmental Issues

The local 'in my backyard' environmental issues, particularly better civic amenities as roads, public transportation, air quality, water supply, parks and recreational areas, appear to be generating informed support among the Indian middle class. In Bengaluru, residents of upscale Richmond Town and Shanthinagar, otherwise known for their gentle behaviour, took to the streets on the morning of Saturday, 11 April 2015, staging a silent protest march against bad roads, shortage of water and mishandling of garbage by the Bruhat Bangalore Mahanagar Palike (BBMP) (Bangalore Mirror 2015). On 7 March 2015, the office and plant of a chemical factory was attacked in Kohlapur, Maharashtra because people claimed that the tar pitch emanating from the factory was a health hazard (Times of India 2015a). On 6 April 2012, there was a 24-hour agitation to mount pressure on management to improve civic amenities in slums in the steel city of Jamshedpur (The Telegraph 2012). A study of willingness to pay—a good measure of demand—for safe drinking water in Kolkata found that qualitative risk perception and the awareness level increases with education. The middle class, who were already spending money on purifiers for drinking water, were willing to pay for quality water supply (Roy et al. 2004). Various NGOs and nature lovers gathered at Aarey Colony, Mumbai on the morning of Sunday, 15 February 2015 to protest against the Mumbai Metropolitan Region Development Authority's (MMRDA) proposal to remove 2,298 trees to set up the proposed Metro III car shed.[21]

Some of the 'local' environmental issues go beyond just purely local and embrace a larger area across the country. An obvious case is Ganga Action Plan and Namami Gange launched in 1986 and 2014, respectively to clean the river Ganga. The river, an embodiment of sacredness to the Hindus, flows through about 2,300 kms in India

21. Times of India (2015b). The protest was in spite of the fact that 254 trees would be cut down and 2,044 would be transplanted.

before entering Bangladesh. Covering one of the most densely populated areas of the world and traversing major cities such as Allahabad, Kanpur, Patna and Varanasi, it was identified as one of the ten most endangered rivers in the world in 2007.[22] The Ganga Action Plan, launched in 1986, has been the subject of considerable research. One key question asked by researchers, for example Alley (1994), is how to reconcile sacred purity with the concept of 'secular' pollution. Many subscribers of the 'purity' school used to believe that "Ganga is like a mother, ... who cleans up the messes her children makes ... It keeps carrying away *gandagi* (waste) into the ocean." It may be argued that with the march of the Indian middle class and the spread of education, the reconciliation has become easier.

There is no denial of the pollution problem of the Ganga anymore. With participation of people like Swami Gyan Swaroop Sanand and Veer Bhadra Mishra in the cleaning of Ganga debate, there has been a major change in the level and quality of the discourse. The Swamiji, before his *sanyas* (renunciation of worldly things) in 2011, was G.D. Agrawal, an alumnus of IIT Roorkee and University of California at Berkeley, who had headed the Civil Engineering department at IIT Kanpur. Hydraulic engineer Veer Bhadra Mishra, the founding president of the Sankat Mochan Foundation, was not only a former Head of the Civil Engineering Department at the Indian Institute of Technology (BHU) Varanasi but also the *Mahant* (High Priest) of the Sankat Mochan Hanuman temple, Varanasi founded by poet-saint Goswami Tulsidas.

Even the conservation of wildlife is attracting more support from the people, including the middle-class. A reflection of this support was the introduction in 1976 of Article 51A(g), under Fundamental Duties, which enjoins the citizens 'to protect and improve the natural environment including forests, lakes, rivers and wildlife, and to have compassion for living creatures.'[23] Wildlife tourism has been growing

---

22. "Focusing analysis on watersheds with high ecological importance and those affecting large human populations, with a view to continental representation, the ten most endangered rivers emerge as: the Salween, La Plata, Danube, Rio Grande, Ganges, Murray-Darling, Indus, Nile, Yangtze and Mekong." WWF (2007: 4).

23. The Constitution (Forty-second Amendment) Act, 1976, s.11 (w.e.f. 3-1-1977).

at an average over 15 per cent per year and visitors were well-educated spending over $600 for the visit (Karanth 2012). The wildlife is seen as a national resource, and sympathy appears to favour wildlife more than human settlements within protected areas.

Impact on Resource Distribution

The Indian middle class appears sensitive to the resource distribution issue involved in large projects with environmental impact. The Chipko movement and NBA may not have been able to mobilise middle class support against projects aimed at harnessing nature for the benefit of the people, but what they have done is to bring to the fore the fundamental questions of proper resettlement and rehabilitation of the displaced people.

There is an increasing recognition that many of the protests, stemming from what Guha calls 'empty-belly' environmentalism of the poor, are inseparable from distributive justice. The genesis of Chipko action lay not in saving the trees in the hills but in a fight between local hill-people and the state over the right to trees growing in the hills in April 1973. According to TERI (n.d.):

> The first Chipko action took place spontaneously in April 1973 in the village of Mandal in the upper Alakananda valley and over the next five years spread to many districts of the Himalayas in Uttar Pradesh. It was sparked off by the government's decision to allot a plot of forest area in the Alakananda valley to a sports goods company. This angered the villagers because their similar demand to use wood for making agricultural tools had been earlier denied. With encouragement from a local NGO, Dasoli Gram Swarajya Sangh (DGSS), the women of the area, under the leadership of an activist, Chandi Prasad Bhatt, went into the forest and formed a circle around the trees preventing the men from cutting them down.

Similarly, the NBA started not as a movement against the Sardar Sarovar Dam itself but as a protest by affected people against forced displacement and for proper resettlement and rehabilitation. The dramatic showdown between pro- and anti-dam protestors starting from 2 January 1991 at the dam site at Ferkuwa village in Gujarat on the Madhya Pradesh border demonstrated the complexity of the issues. The pro-dam Narmada Age Badhao Shanti Yatra or Move Narmada Forward Peace March was determined to stop the NBA's Sangharsh Yatra or Agitation Rally led by Medha Patkar and Baba Amte from entering Gujarat. There were many people who supported the dam because of its development impact, they described the Narmada project as 'lifeline of Gujarat'. Many saw the problem as one of not being able to compensate the losers by a proper R&R (resettlement and rehabilitation) programme. In the end, perhaps the pro-development sympathy of the people was reflected in the project being completed by democratically elected governments in spite of the World Bank and other international funding agencies withdrawing support.

The natural resources such as coal necessary for sustaining growth are located in forest areas inhabited by tribal people. There is an increasing recognition that the tribal people not only have strong beliefs about their forests, land and water, but, for their survival, are also heavily dependent on the natural resources of the forests. The sympathy of the middle class appears to be in favour of a win-win solution—developing the projects after formulating a proper R&R programme expeditiously.

Global Environment: Carbon Emissions

The attitude of the Indian middle class towards global environmental public goods such as carbon emission is starkly different from its attitude towards local or national environmental issues. Its position appears aligned with that of its government.

India is often reminded of its global responsibility regarding the control of carbon emission. In Lima, at the Climate Change Conference in December 2014, after the US and China struck a deal on carbon dioxide emission, there was a lot of pressure on India to commit itself internationally to reducing such emission by 2030 (Koch 2014). India is often reminded that it is the third largest emitter of carbon in the world and its emission is increasing faster than in China or the US. India resisted the pressure and underlined the fact that India is a poor country and, in per capita terms, India's carbon emission at 1.9 tonnes is far less than China's 7.2 and US's

16.4. India insisted on the principle of 'common but differentiated responsibility.'

India is well on its way toward meeting its 2009 Copenhagen UN Climate Talk pledge of reducing its carbon emission intensity (that is amount of emission per rupee of output) 20 to 25 per cent over 2005 levels by 2020. The US pledged to cut its emissions by 26 to 28 per cent below 2005 levels by 2025.

There appears to be a lot of sympathy among the middle class for the government position and support for former Prime Minister Manmohan Singh's pledge at the G8 + 5 Summit in Heiligendamm, Germany, in 2007. Dr Singh pledged that India's per capita emissions would never exceed those of the developed world. Given India's low per capita emissions, meeting this pledge does not require any emissions reductions compared to the current policy projections up to 2030.

Green Politics of the Middle Class: Comparing Brazil with India

Brazil's middle class, termed as 'C' class, is defined at per capita monthly income of between R$320 (US$144) and R$1,120 (US$503) (Alves 2014), which roughly corresponds to the definition of the Indian middle class by some researchers. The National Council of Applied Economic Research (NCAER) (2005), for example, defines the middle class as comprising of households with annual income between ₹2 lakh and ₹10 lakh at 2001/02 prices, which translates to approximately an individual monthly income between ₹7,400 (US$136) and ₹37,317 (US$686) at 2012-13 prices.[24]

Brazil has had PV or the Green Party ever since the almost 21 year-long military dictatorship ended on 15 March 1985. Brazil has a large reserve of uranium, and building an enriched uranium nuclear power plant in Angra Dos Reis was part of the government's strategy from the 1950s. When the plant was being built, in 1982, a group of

24. See Lahiri (2014). The figures have been converted to monthly individual income at 2012-13 prices, by using a household size of 5, inflating the figures by the inflation in consumer price index for agricultural labourers and industrial workers and taking the average, and the average exchange rate of ₹54.4091 per US dollar.

antinuclear activists started to organise protests under the banner 'Hiroshima, nunca mais' (Hiroshima, never again) (Hochstetler and Keck (2007: 85). Anti-nuclear protests against Angra raised the profile of the activists in Rio de Janeiro, and after the military dictatorship ended, they went on to form the PV or Green Party.

In India also, green activism may be described to have started in the early 1980s with many civil society organisations protesting against the Sardar Sarovar Project or Narmada Valley Project in general and forcible evictions, inadequate compensation to project affected people or even large hydroelectric dams, in particular.[25] These finally coalesced together to form the NBA in 1989. It did not, however, go on to give birth to a green political party. It is a hazardous exercise to speculate about why green politics had such a different trajectory in Brazil and India. While answering such a question requires careful research to avoid myriad pitfalls, some tentative answers are suggested here.

First, though both Brazil and India are in the BRICS grouping, Brazil has been and continues to be a far more advanced country in terms of GDP (gross domestic product) than India. In 1985, for example, Brazil's per capita GDP at US$1,629 was almost 5½ times India's US$303. Even in 2014, India's per capita GDP at US$1,596 was not only a 7th of Brazil's US$11,385, but had not even caught up with Brazil's per capita GDP in 1985. Relative to its population, the middle class in Brazil was far more advanced in the mid-1980s than that in India. By 1990, the first year for which the relevant data is available from the World Bank, Brazil's GNI (gross national income) per capita in PPP dollars per day was 17.7, far above the figure of 10 relevant in this context for a discussion of the middle class. Of course, with high inequality of income distribution, in spite of the high average GNI, a lot of the population was not in the middle class. But, nevertheless the proportion of the population in the middle class in Brazil was higher than in India not only in the mid-1980s but even in 2014, when the corresponding per capita GNI per day was PPP$4.3 in India.

25. For a history of protests against the Sardar Sarovar or Narmada Valley Projects, see Jayal (1999), Chapter 4.

Second, in the mid-1980s, Brazil was coming out of a more than 2-decade long military dictatorship. With democratic institutions yet to stabilise, the role of civil society and the leadership of the middle class in participatory democracy were far higher in Brazil than in India where parliamentary democracy was firmly established. A temporary threat to such democracy in India in 1975 was resolutely defeated after a gap of 21 months. The democratic credentials of the government in India were hard to contest.

Third, in Brazil, green politics was a fight against nuclear power plant and/or environmental degradation through the destruction of the Amazon forest and disruption of life and livelihood of the indigenous people. The opposition was the 'government' or establishment. In India, on the other hand, as already discussed, the NBA had to fight against pro-dam groups such as Narmada Age Badhao Shanti Yatra. There are allegations though that the pro-dam groups were a part of the 'political mobilisations sponsored by the Government of Gujarat' (Jayal 1999: 180).

Fourth, while Brazil is far advanced compared to India in terms of the relative strength of its middle class, an important difference between Brazil and India is in the rates of growth of this middle class. Brazil with its higher level of prosperity for a longer time may have fostered a post-materialist philosophy among some members of this middle class, which is congenial for the growth of a green party. However, with average annual inflation in consumer prices between 148 per cent and 4,116 per cent during 1985-1995, there was a sense of insecurity of slipping back into poverty among the lower strata of the Brazilian middle class for a prolonged period, and hence greater political cohesion. This sense of insecurity apparently has resurfaced in recent times with rising inflation (Alves 2014). Some even go to the extent of calling some members of the NMC in Brazil as the new working class. In contrast, with sustained growth, there is anecdotal evidence of optimism among the Indian middle classes. The Indian middle class is busy saving and preparing for the future, wants to undo the centuries of deprivation by a better standard of living and has little time for post-materialist philosophy. Even in Brazil, a largely Catholic country, there has been the rise of the Neo

Pentecostal Church, whose followers believe in prosperity theology, that better life means better material life, including health.[26] It seems most of the Indian middle class are followers of this prosperity theology in practice.

Last but not the least is the fractured nature of the Indian middle class. Indeed it is true that there is stratification by income, education and location even in the Brazilian middle class, but the segmentation of its counterpart in India appears to be far higher. Apart from income, education and location, the additional identities of the Indian middle class are religion and caste. Thus, as Jodhka (2015) points out, caste is a prohibited subject for discussion among the Indian middle class. But, caste continues to be a critical axis for electoral mobilisation by political parties, and continues to inhibit the consolidation of middle class politics, including green politics.

Conclusion

Four pillars of green politics, namely social justice, grass roots democracy, nonviolence, and respect for diversity, have become more or less established accepted principles of political parties in India. The integration of the environmental dimension of green politics, consisting of the twin pillars of ecological wisdom and sustainability, is in an evolutionary phase. It is likely that increasingly this integration will reflect the views of the growing Indian middle class. The middle class, with a reasonable level of education, information base and income level, has views on environmental issues. These views may be different from those of ecological refugees or empty-belly environmentalists, but may have an edge over other views because of the opinion-maker role that the middle-class plays. Parties will get feedback on their environmental policies from the electoral battlegrounds and adapt them suitably.

The Right to Fair Compensation and Transparency in Land Acquisition, Rehabilitation and Resettlement Act, 2013 (LARR 2013), enacted 6 months before the 16th Lok Sabha elections in 2014, provides a good illustration of this adaptive process. Around the same

26. *Marilene de Paula*, Communication in Delhi, April 2015.

time as the AAP was born, the grand old party of India, namely the Congress started to demonstrate some pronounced greenish hues under the leadership of Sonia Gandhi, supported by the erstwhile environment minister Jairam Ramesh. It got focused on 'Three R's'—'Relief, Rehabilitation and Resettlement'—associated with land acquisition for infrastructure, urbanisation and industry, and culminated in the now controversial LARR 2013. A major emphasis of LARR 2013 was on the ecological refugees. Opposition in Parliament at the time of its passing was muted at best. The LARR Bill was passed by the Lok Sabha on 29 August 2013 with 216 votes against 19, and by the Rajya Sabha on 4 September 2013 with 131 votes against 10. Electoral outcomes are the resultant of many factors. Through LARR 2013, the Congress was perhaps trying to transform itself into a green reformist party without rejecting free economic enterprise and the social welfare state. It appears that the electoral dividend from LARR 2013 for the Congress was poor and there are moves afoot to amend the Act. Amendment debate on LARR 2013 is still on in Parliament.[27]

The future of any political party is difficult to predict in a vibrant democracy such as India. But, going by the views of the Indian middle class, some parties are likely to gravitate towards becoming reformist green parties. No party is likely to follow Alvares's (1992) prescription for pursuing alternatives to development and an assertion of peoples' right to 'pursue one's way of life, irrespective of nuclear plants, dams, thermal plants, or big industries; the right to refuse to be developed according to whims and fancies of outsiders who think they know best.'[28] With the maturing of Indian democracy, the electoral prospect

27. After the 2014 election, 'The Right to Fair Compensation and Transparency in Land Acquisition, Rehabilitation and Resettlement (Amendment) Ordinance' was promulgated on 31 December 2014. LARR Amendment Bill to replace the Ordinance, introduced on 24 February 2015, was passed by the Lok Sabha on 10 March 2015. Pending its passage by the Rajya Sabha, the Amendment Ordinance was repromulgated with nine amendments on 3 April 2015.

28. According to Alvares (1992), "development' is a label for plunder and violence, a mechanism of triage.... The logic of industrialisation demands ample space, geographical space, colonies. The industrialisation effort of the South had to interiorise the concept of the colonies-colonising its own hinterlands, mostly settled with subsistent and ecologically harmonious communities, and subordinating these to the requirements of the industrialisation programme."

of a green radical party—as against a green reformist party—seeking fundamental changes in social and political institutions and following a new radical democratic paradigm appears dim. Parties will try to harmonise development policies with environmental policies, and instead of opposing industrialisation, markets and globalisation, emphasise national and local environmental issues such as water supply, sewerage and air quality.

Elected representatives and electoral candidates receive and have to respond to the general views and concerns of those who they represent. And these views, in a poor country such as India, have not transformed from materialistic to post-materialistic as yet. The Indian middle class is still too poor to be environmentalists in the western sense of the term. They seem to have more sympathy for transforming nature than just preserving it. They seem to agree with the proposition that 'All human activity alters the composition of the natural world which in itself is never static. A critique which regards all change as decay begs the very legitimacy of human survival.'[29] They see the current development process flawed by governance failures but basically positive and inevitable. They are likely to welcome a green party that addresses these governance failures, e.g. in resettlement and rehabilitation, without militating against progress, modernity and emancipation from poverty.

References

Ahmed, Anisha (2009). "Environmentalist Who Wants to Unite India's Greens to Meet UK Counterparts", *The Guardian*, 20 September. *http://www.theguardian.com/world/2009/sep/20/india-activist-environment-green-party*

Alley, Kelly D. (1994). "Ganga and Gandagi: Interpretations of Pollution and Waste in Benaras", *Ethnology* 33(2) (Spring): 127-45.

Alvares, Claude (1992). *Science, Development and Violence: The Revolt Against Modernity*. Delhi: Oxford University Press.

Alves, Lise (2014). "Brazil's Middle Class Going Back to Essentials", *Rio Times*, 27 May. *http://riotimesonline.com/brazil-news/rio-business/brazils-middle-class-going-back-to-essentials/#sthash.RbMNIFVd.dpuf*

Asian Development Bank (2010). "The Rise of the Asian Middle Class", Special Chapter in *Key Indicators of the Asia and the Pacific: 2010.* Manila. Available at: *http://www.adb.org/sites/default/files/KI/2010/KI2010-Special-Chapter.pdf*

29. William Beinart and Peter Coates, quoted in Nixon (2011: 255).

Ask, Vegard (2014). *No Country for Green Men? A Case Study of the Green Party of the United States.* Master's thesis. Institute for Comparative Politics, University of Bergen. May. Available at: *https://bora.uib.no/handle/1956/8288*

Bangalore Mirror (2015). "Goons Thwart Silent Protest", *Bangalore Mirror*, 1 February.

Bhaduri, Amit and Medha Patkar (2009). "Industrialisation for the People, by the People, of the People", *Economic and Political Weekly*, 3 January.

Bhaumik, Subir (2009). "India Crusader Plans Green Party", *BBC News*, Calcutta, 26 August. Available at, *http://news.bbc.co.uk/2/hi/south_asia/8221698.stm*

Björk, Tord and Marko Ulvila (2008). *Gandhi and the New Popular Movements in Europe.* 15 April. Available at: *http://www.demokratiafoorumi.fi/Bjork_Ulvila_Gandhi_article_080415.pdf*

Burgmann, Verity (2008). "The Green Bans Movement: Workers' Power and Ecological Radicalism in Australia in the 1970s", *Journal for the Study of Radicalism* 2(1) (Spring): 63-89.

Byatnal, Amruta (2011). "I am not Gandhi: Anna Hazare", *The Hindu*, 17 September. Available at: *http://www.thehindu.com/news/national/i-am-not-gandhi-anna-hazare/article2462369.ece*

Confederation of Indian Industry and Global Footprint Network (2008). *India's Ecological Footprint: A Business Perspective*. Available at *http://portalsostenibilidad.upc.edu/archivos/fichas/informes/india_report_2008.pdf*

The Economist (2009). "Burgeoning Bourgeoisie", *The Economist*, 12 February. Available at: *http://www.economist.com/node/13063298.*

Gadgil, Madhav and Ramachandra Guha (1995): *Ecology and Equity: The Use and Abuse of Nature in Contemporary India.* Routledge, New York and London.

Gandhi, M.K. (1909). "Hind Swaraj", in Anthony J. Pavel (ed): *Gandhi: Hind Swaraj and Other Writings (Cambridge Texts in Modern Politics).* Cambridge University Press.

Gandhi, M.K. (1933). *Ramanama*. Ahmedabad: Navajivan Publishing House (1949). Available at: *http://www.mkgandhi.org/ebks/ramanama.pdf*

Ganguly, Swagato (2011). "It's the Middle Class, Stupid", *Times of India*, 19 August. Available at: *http://timesofindia.indiatimes.com/edit-page/Its-the-middle-class-stupid/articleshow/9651012.cms*

Grzybowski, Cândido (2015). "Are We Seeing New Collective Subjects?", Conference on *Green Perspective of NMC*, organised by Henrich Böll Stiftung-India and Development Alternatives, New Delhi, 13-14 April.

Guha, Ramachandra and Juan Martinez-Alier (1997). *Varieties of Environmentalism: Essays North and South.* Abingdon, Oxon, UK: Earthscan.

Harris, John (2007). "The Onward March of the New 'Great Indian Middle Class'", *The Hindu*, 15 August. Available at *http://www.hindu.com/af/india60/stories/2007081550681800.htm*

Hochstetler, Kathryn and E. Keck Margaret (2007). *Greening Brazil: Environmental Activism in State and Society.* Duke University Press. p.85.

Immerwahr, Daniel (2015). *Thinking Small: The United States and the Lure of Community Development.* Harvard University Pres.

Jayal, Niraja Gopal (1999). *Democracy and the State: Welfare, Secularism and Development in Contemporary India.* Delhi: Oxford University Press.

Jodhka, Surinder (2015). "Caste, Privilege, Power and Citizenship: A Biography of the Indian Middle Class", Paper presented at the Conference on *Green Perspectives of NMC*, organised by Development Alternatives and Henrich Boll Stiftung-India, Delhi, 13-14 April.

Kapur, Devesh, Neelanjan Sircar and Vaishnav Milan (2015). "Being Middle Class in India", Paper presented at the Conference on *Green Perspectives of NMC*, organised by Development Alternatives and Henrich Boll Stiftung-India, Delhi, 13-14 April.

Karanth, Krithi K. (2012). *Wildlife Tourism–New Study, New Revelations.* Conservation India. 29 April. Available at: *http://www.conservationindia.org/articles/wildlife-tourism-%E2%80%93-new-study-new-revelations*

Koch, Wendy (2014). "In Climate Talks, Spotlight Turns to India", *National Geographic*, 27 November.

Kothari, Ashish (2009). "A Sympathetic Critique of the Bhaduri-Patkar Model", *Economic and Political Weekly* XLIV(12), 21 March.

Lahiri, Ashok K. (2014): "The Middle Class and Economic Reforms,' *Economic and Political Weekly* XLIX(11): 37-44, 15 March.

Meyer, Christian, and Nancy Birdsall (2012). *New Estimates of Indian Middle Class: A Technical Note.* Centre for Global Development. November. Available at: *http://www.cgdev.org/doc/2013_MiddleClassIndia_TechnicalNote_CGDNote.pdf.*

Mishra, Pankaj (2012). "Indians Against Democracy", *The New York Review of Books*, 24 January. Available at: *http://www.nybooks.com/blogs/nyrblog/2012/jan/24/indians-against-democracy/*

Modi, Renu (ed.) (2009). *Beyond Relocation: The Imperative of Sustainable Resettlement.* Sage Publication.

Naoto, Higuchi, Ito Midori, Tanabe Shunsuke and Matsutani Mitsuru (2010). "Explaining Japan's Lack of Green Parties: A Social-Milieu Approach", *Social Sciences Research* 23, February. University of Tokushima. Available at: *http://web.ias.tokushima-u.ac.jp/bulletin/soc/soc23-4.pdf*

Narain, Sunita (2009). "Where is the Green Party?", *Down to Earth*, 30 April.

National Council of Applied Economic Research (2005). *The Great Indian Market.* 9 August. Available at: *http://www.ncaer.org/downloads/PPT/thegreatindianmarket.pdf*

Nixon, Rob (2011). *Slow Violence and the Environmentalism of the Poor.* Harvard University Press.

Paastela, Jukka (2008). "The Finnish Greens: From 'Alternative' Grassroots Movement(s) to a Governmental Party", in E.Gene Frankland, Paul Lucardie and Benoît Rihoux (eds.), *Green Parties in Transition: The End of Grasroots Democracy?* England: Ashgate Publishing Limited. Available at *https://books.google.co.in/books?id=BJmqUTBiZ3EC&pg=PA63&lpg=PA63&dq=Green+party+and+Draining+a+lake+in+Finland&source=bl&ots=kKM_dwRJYX&sig=9MTYMk0tT-kbghGc_H1FRZPbfO0&hl=en&sa=X&ei=LHIRVaesPJOiugTzjIHwCQ&ved=0CB0Q6AEwAA#v=onepage&q=Green%20party%20and%20Draining%20a%20lake%20in%20Finland&f=false*

Patel, I.G.(2002). *Glimpses of Indian Economic Policy: An Insider's View.* Oxford University Press, India.

Paula, Marilene de (2015a). "Culture of New Brazilian Middle Class", Conference on *Green Perspective of NMC*, organised by Henrich Böll Stiftung-India and Development Alternatives. New Delhi, 13-14 April.

———. (2015b). "Debates in Brazil: NMC or the New Working Class?", Conference on *Green Perspective of NMC*, organised by Henrich Böll Stiftung-India and Development Alternatives. New Delhi, 13-14 April.

Press Trust of India (2014). "EC Seeks Cancellation of Tax Benefits to 10 Political Parties", *Business Standard*, 21 April. Available at: *http://www.business-standard.com/article/elections-2014/ec-seeks-cancellation-of-tax-benefits-to-10-political-parties-114042000064_1.html*

Roy, Joyashree, Subhorup Chattopadhyay, Sabyasachi Mukherjee, Manikarnika Kanjilal, Sreejata Samajpati and Sanghamitra Roy (2004). "An Economic Analysis of Demand for Water Quality: Case of Kolkata", *Economic and Political Weekly* 39(2): 186-92, 10-16 January.

Saberwal, Vasant, Mahesh Rangarajan and Ashish Kothari (2001). *People, Parks and Wildlife: Towards Coexistence.* New Delhi: Orient Longman.

Shrivasta, Sanskar (2014). "AAP: India's Own Green Party", *The World Reporter*, 21 January. Available at: *http://www.theworldreporter.com/2014/01/aap-indias-green-party.html*

TERI (n.d.). "The Chipko Movement", *http://edugreen.teri.res.in/explore/forestry/chipko.htm*

The Telegraph (2012). "JVM Steps up Amenity Protest", *The Telegraph*, 7 April.

Times of India (2015a). "Villagers Attack Maha Chemical Plant", *Times of India*, 8 March.

———. (2015b). "500 Greens Gather at Aarey Against Metro Car Shed Plan", *Times of India,* 16 February.

World Commission on Dams (2000). *Dams and Development: A New Framework for Decision Making.* London and Sterling, UK: Earthscan. *http://www.internationalrivers.org/files/attached-files/world_commission_on_dams_final_report.pdf*

World-Wide Fund for Nature (WWF) (2007). *World's Top Ten Rivers at Risk.* 20 March. Available at: *http://wwf.panda.org/?97680/Worlds-Top-10-Rivers-at-Risk*

World-Wide Fund for Nature (WWF), Global Footprint Network, Water Footprint Network, and Zoological Society of London (2014). *Living Planet Report, 2014: Species and Spaces, People and Places.* Available at: *http://assets.worldwildlife.org/publications/723/files/original/WWF-LPR2014-low_res.pdf?1413912230&_ga=1.167913314.214306443.1428947898*